D1547666

Waking to Wonder

Man has to awaken to wonder—and so perhaps do peoples.
Science is a way of sending him to sleep again.

Zum Staunen muss der Mensch—und vielleicht Völker—
aufwachen. Die Wissenschaft ist ein Mittel um ihn wieder
einzuschläfern.

—Wittgenstein, 1930, *Culture and Value*

SUNY Series in Philosophy
George R. Lucas, Editor

Waking to Wonder

Wittgenstein's Existential Investigations

Gordon C. F. Bearn

STATE UNIVERSITY OF NEW YORK PRESS

Published by
State University of New York Press, Albany

©1997 State University of New York

For information, address State University of New York Press,
State University Plaza, Albany, NY 12246

Production by Dana Foote
Marketing by Bernadette LaManna

Library of Congress Cataloging-in-Publication Data

Bearn, Gordon C. F., 1955–
    Waking to wonder : Wittgenstein's existential investigations /
Gordon C. F. Bearn.
        p.   cm. — (SUNY series in philosophy)
    Includes bibliographical references and index.
    ISBN 0-7914-3029-4 (alk. paper). — ISBN 0-7914-3030-8 (pbk.   :
alk. paper)
    1. Wittgenstein, Ludwig, 1889–1951.   2. Nietzsche, Friedrich
Wilhelm, 1844–1900. Geburt der Tragodie.   I. Title.   II. Series.
B3376.W564B42   1997
192—dc20   96-28483
                                                                              CIP

10 9 8 7 6 5 4 3 2 1

Coast of Trees

The reality is, though susceptible
to versions, without denomination:
when the fences foregather
the reality they shut in is cast out:
if the name nearest the name
names least or names
only a verge before the void takes naming in,
how are we to find holiness,
our engines of declaration put aside,
helplessness our first offer and sacrifice,
except that having given up all mechanisms of
approach, having accepted a shambles of
non-enterprise, we know a unity
approach divided, a composure past
sight: then, with nothing, we turn
to the cleared particular, not more
nor less than itself, and we realize
that whatever it is it is in the Way and
the Way in it, as in us, emptied full.

A. R. Ammons, *A Coast of Trees*

Contents

Preface

Relativism, Skepticism, and the Meaning of Life

This book was imagined differently at different times, and it may help to place the final result if I recount some of the stages of its development. In 1985, I completed the first large writing project I had ever undertaken: a dissertation defending epistemological relativism from a variety of realisms variously defined by Dummett and Putnam.[1] And this book first began as a presentation of the results of that work. I thought of my dissertation as in the "results" business because logic produces "results," and the central problem that any defense of relativism must address is the logical problem—as old as the *Theaetetus*—of relativism's self-refutation. My trick was to use Wittgenstein's Tractarian distinction between what can be said and what can only be shown to circumvent the problem of self-refutation. What the relativist means, I wanted to be able to say, is quite correct; only it cannot be said, it makes itself manifest.[2]

Conceding to relativism's opponents that any attempt to present a full-fledged Relativistic Theory of Knowledge would refute itself, I suggested that the truth in relativism could be made manifest otherwise. The truth in relativism, so I argued, is manifest in the fact that sometimes we find others—other people, cultures, historical periods, and so on—beyond understanding. Beyond understanding in the specific sense that while we seem to understand the words we hear or read, we cannot understand how anyone could seriously mean these words. We understand the words but not the people speaking, much as we understand the words a parrot squawks, but not the parrot squawking. This approach to the tangled problem of relativism had the double virtue of explaining both why it has always seemed easy to refute and why, in spite of this, relativism has always refused to retire.

This book was originally going to deploy the results of that dissertation. But I grew to think that the shadow of relativism—even if inevitable—owes its existence to what Wittgenstein's last notes called the "groundlessness of our believing."[3] I take this expression to indicate that there is no more secure foundation to our epistemic practices than the fact that we find *this* to be a good reason for *that*. Relativism is a live possibility, because, as a matter of fact, all people do not share all judgments about what is relevant to what. On this account relativism is a consequence of something deeper, the groundlessness of epistemic practices. So I began to think that what truth there was in relativism was a consequence of what truth there was in skepticism.

In the spring of 1989, I found myself writing the second incarnation of this book. This time I was going to do for relativism one of the things that Cavell had done for skepticism. According to Cavell, what philosophy knows as skepticism, literature knows as tragedy. And I asked: If tragedy is what literature knows skepticism as, what does literature know relativism as? Comedy. Skepticism and tragedy, so it first seemed, confront their readers with brute nothingness, the abyss. I was encouraged in this thought by the fact that it projected a possible reading of Oedipus's enveloping darkness in Sophocles' *Oedipus Rex*. Relativism and comedy, on the other hand, confront their readers with the brute absurdity of the difference between two somethings, not, as in tragedy, between something and nothing. The doubleness of relativism and that of comedy seemed made for each other. I was reminded of the laughter that shattered Foucault when he confronted the stark impossibility of thinking in accord with a bizarre classification scheme he discovered in Borges.[4] And I found myself thinking about Abbott and Costello, unable to get straight whether "who" is a proper name or an interrogative pronoun, and of Groucho shooting an elephant in his pajamas, only to wonder how the elephant had managed to fit.[5]

But this simple division between tragedy and comedy didn't hold. For there are tragedies whose motor is the conflict between two different attitudes. Sophocles' own *Antigone* is a famous example of one of these, and, in fact, Hegel's interpretation of that play focuses precisely on the conflict between Creon and Antigone. Realizing that tragedy could house the doubleness I had been saving for comedy, I gave up the simple pairing of skepticism with tragedy, and relativism with comedy. In any case, progress on the second plan of this book would have required saying something short and true about the essence of tragedy and comedy, a task I cannot now imagine taking up. But, for all that, I still remain attracted to the thought that relativism shows itself in that kind of communicative failure which, when disjoined from weighty matters, incites laughter.

During the summer of 1992, at an NEH seminar conducted by Michael Williams, I devoted my energies to working out what I thought of Cavell's interpretation of the sources of philosophical skepticism. In *The Claim of Reason*, Cavell's "major claim" about the origin of skepticism is that the philosopher's skeptical problem owes its existence to an experience Cavell has some difficulty conveying:

> My major claim about the philosopher's originating question—e.g., "(How) do (can) we know anything about the world?" or "What is knowledge; what does my knowledge of the world consist in?"—is that it (in one or another of its versions) is a response to, or expression of, a real experience which takes hold of human beings. . . . It is, as I might put it, a response which expresses a natural experience of a creature complicated enough to possess language at all.[6]

On this account the intellectual problem of skepticism is itself an expression of the existential condition of a creature "complicated enough to possess a language at all." This is a puzzling claim, puzzling especially if you think of skepticism, for example skepticism about the external world, as a matter of how you get from here to there: a matter of validating claims about material objects on the basis of knowledge of our sense experiences.[7] It is easy to wonder how this intellectual puzzle could possibly be illuminated by reference to anything as difficult to understand as the existential condition of language animals.

In other places, Cavell elaborates his vision of what that existential condition might be. In an essay devoted, among other things, to the use of J. L. Austin by literary theorists, Cavell speaks of

> the intuition I had taken away from my first useful encounter with the *Philosophical Investigations* that the repudiation of the world is as internal to what ordinary language is as its revelation of the world; or put otherwise, that skepticism would not be possible unless ordinary language is such that it can, sometimes must, repudiate itself, put its own naturalness into question.[8]

Again, while writing about Coleridge, Cavell describes the "pervasive thought" of *The Claim of Reason* as being that one

> mark of the natural in natural language is its capacity to repudiate itself, to find arbitrary or merely conventional, the lines laid down for

> its words by our agreement in criteria, our attunement with one
> another (which is to say, in my lingo, that the threat of skepticism is
> a natural or inevitable presentiment of the human mind).[9]

Cavell roots the philosopher's skeptical puzzles in the groundlessness of our linguistic practices. Our possible alienation from the language we speak is one of the characteristic marks of a natural (and, even more, of an artificial) language.[10] If we become alienated from the language we speak, we will also be alienated from what we need language to understand: the self we understand ourselves to be, the life we take ourselves to live, the emotions we take ourselves to suffer or to enjoy. In short, there is no part of our lives that can remain unaffected by the alienation from language which—according to Cavell—is an inevitable presence on the horizon of creatures complicated enough to possess language at all.

This feature of language incites an experience that provides the originating energy of philosophical skepticism. It is an experience Cavell describes as "terrifying":

> We learn and teach words in certain contexts, and then we are
> expected, and expect others, to be able to project them into further
> contexts. Nothing insures that this projection will take place (in par-
> ticular, not the grasping of universals nor the grasping of books of
> rules), just as nothing insures that we will make, and understand, the
> same projections. That on the whole we do is a matter of our sharing
> routes of interest and feeling, modes of response, senses of humor
> and of significance and of fulfillment, of what is outrageous, of what
> is similar to what else, what a rebuke, what forgiveness, of when an
> utterance is an assertion, when an appeal, when an explanation—all
> the whirl of organism Wittgenstein calls "forms of life." Human
> speech and activity, sanity and community, rest upon nothing more,
> but nothing less, than this. It is a vision as simple as it is difficult, and
> as difficult as it is (and because it is) terrifying.[11]
>
> We begin to feel, or ought to, terrified that maybe language (and
> understanding, and knowledge) rests upon very shaky foundations—
> a thin net over an abyss.[12]

The experience that—according to Cavell—originates philosophical skepticism is one of terror: the terror that follows the thought that we can no longer word the world.

The terror Cavell locates as the source of philosophical skepticism is cousin to the black picture of human existence described by Schopenhauer. According to Schopenhauer, when you consider life as a whole you will reach the conclusion that nothing is worth saying or doing, that "nothing whatever is worth our exertions, our efforts, and our struggles, that all good things are empty and fleeting, that the world on all sides is bankrupt, and that life is a business that does not cover its costs."[13] In *The Birth of Tragedy*, Nietzsche ascribes this nihilistic attitude to Dionysus's teacher, Silenus: "What would be best for you is quite beyond your reach: not to have been born, not to *be*, to be *nothing*. But the second best is to die soon."[14] The terror that Cavell points to is the terror attendant on a complete loss of confidence in whether anything means what we think it means, whether there is any meaning at all in the world or in language. According to Cavell this is the existential source of what philosophers know as the "problem of the external world."

Cavell's account of the sources of skepticism helps to explain one feature of philosophical discussions of skepticism that Hume may have been the first to emphasize: skeptical and antiskeptical considerations do not produce stable results.[15] In some moods—perhaps we are alone, snowed in, by a fire, in a house not our own—skeptical arguments can convince us that we do not know what we thought we knew. In other moods—perhaps we are dining with friends, laughing, playing games—skeptical arguments can appear ridiculous. But circumstances can change, and the force of this antiskeptical mood can alter: the conclusions of skeptical arguments are unstable. Cavell's account of this instability is simple. If the philosopher's "problem of the external world" is an intellectual expression of an existential anxiety, then it is only to be expected that intellectual resolutions of the intellectual problem, which leave the existential sources of that problem untouched, would be found disappointingly unstable. A better strategy would be to address the existential sources as directly as possible.

From relativism I was led to skepticism, and from skepticism I was led to the existential problem of the value of existence, the meaning of life. I had been relying on Wittgenstein to bear the weight of many of the central arguments of my discussion of relativism and of skepticism, and Cavell's writings had promised a Wittgensteinian route to a resolution of the existential terror at the heart of skepticism. So it was natural for me to turn to Wittgenstein to help address this existential problem as directly as possible. But Wittgenstein is not widely taken as the author of existential investigations, so I thought to introduce my reading of Wittgenstein with a glance at Nietzsche's engagement with the problem of the value of existence. That was when I made the discovery that produced the third, and final, incarnation of the plan for this book. The plan I proceeded to follow was to present Wittgenstein in Nietzschean perspective. What I have done is to read Wittgenstein's investigations in the light of a reading of the development of Nietzsche's existential investigations. For what I discovered was that Nietzsche's development, his turn from the position articulated in *The Birth of Tragedy* (1872), provides a fine model of Wittgenstein's development, his turn from the position articulated in the *Tractatus Logico-Philosophicus* (c. 1918). Mine is a Nietzschean reading of Wittgenstein.

My introduction to the *Tractatus* was contemporary with browsing my way through the Radcliffe Camera until I happily ran across Erich Heller's essay "Wittgenstein and Nietzsche," published in *Encounter* in 1959.[16] So it is a pleasure to observe that Heller had already announced this connection between Nietzsche and Wittgenstein in that essay. He wrote:

> The break between the *Tractatus* and the *Philosophical Investigations* is of the same kind as that between Nietzsche's *The Birth of Tragedy* (1872) and his *Human, All-Too-Human* (1879). In both cases it was brought about by the abnegation of metaphysics, the loss of faith in any preestablished correspondence between, on the one hand, the logic of our thought and language, and, on the other hand, the "logic" of Reality.[17]

I did not understand the connection when I first read this. In fact, all I really remember from that first reading is the good feeling Heller's essay gave me and its promise that my previous work on Nietzsche would help me in coming to grips with the *Tractatus.* By the time I ran across Heller's essay for the second time, I had already rediscovered the connection between Nietzsche and Wittgenstein. The second time round I realized that Heller and I look at this congruence of two philosophies from rather different directions. Heller finds in the later Wittgenstein the same disastrous turn from "metaphysics" that the mature Nietzsche also manifests. According to Heller, if "European thought and history continue" it will be due to some "miracle."[18] And he insinuates that this miracle is simply the miracle that the influence of Nietzsche and Wittgenstein would disappear. The black closing words of Heller's article as much as charge Wittgenstein with the same nihilistic turn from the value of Truth that Heller finds in Nietzsche:

> In *Philosophical Investigations* Wittgenstein said: "What is your aim in philosophy?—To show the fly the way out of the fly-bottle." [*PI* par. 309] But who asks? Who answers? And who is the fly? It is an unholy trinity; the three are one. This way lies no way out. This way lie only fly-bottles, and more fly-bottles.[19]

According to Heller, Wittgenstein and Nietzsche are indeed linked philosophers: they share credit for starting the dry rot of contemporary thought and culture.

Although I agree with Heller that Nietzsche's and Wittgenstein's philosophical developments trace the same arc, I do not see these two as exacerbating the nihilism of contemporary culture. Quite the reverse. I read them as providing a rest for that nihilistic anxiety described by Schopenhauer and indicated by Cavell. They aim to ease our existential cares, waking us to the wonder of existence, the wonder of human communication, the wonder of human satisfaction. Nietzsche and Wittgenstein point the way to a precarious peace, an earthly peace. This, in any case, is where I will argue Nietzsche and Wittgenstein end up. I will also argue that it is not where they began. This book defends Heller's thesis that Wittgenstein's turn is helpfully understood in terms of Nietzsche's turn. But unlike Heller's, this defense is thorough; and unlike Heller's, this defense is sympathetic to the movement of Wittgenstein's and Nietzsche's writing.

In chapter 1, I use a reading of Nietzsche's *Birth of Tragedy* (1872) to lay the groundwork for the extended reading of the *Tractatus* and the *Investigations* that occupies the rest of this book. The *Birth* is widely recognized as being committed to just the distinction between the apparent world and the true world that Nietzsche came to reject. The first person to make this observation in print was Nietzsche himself in the "Attempt at a Self-Criticism," which he prefaced to his republication of the *Birth* in 1886. If Nietzsche found so much in his first book to detest, why would he bother republishing it? (He did not, after all, republish everything he wrote.) In chapter 1, my answer is that Niezsche's "Attempt at a Self-Criticism" provides the motivation and the equipment for a rereading, indeed a rewriting, of *The Birth of Tragedy*. This unwritten 1886 revision of the original 1872 edition presents the mature

Nietzsche's answer to the problem of nihilism, his mature attempt to remove the big question mark concerning the value of existence. Chapter 1 interprets both of these versions of *The Birth of Tragedy*: the written version of 1872 and the unwritten version of 1886. In the rest of the book, I use these two approaches to the riddle of existence to orient my readings of Wittgenstein's *Tractatus* and *Investigations*.

The difference between *The Birth of Tragedy* of 1872 and that of 1886 is the difference between the *deep* and the *superficial*. Suppose the problem of existence is, in terms I recite from Schopenhauer, that "nothing whatever is worth our exertions, our efforts, and our struggles, that all good things are empty and fleeting, that the world on all sides is bankrupt, and that life is a business that does not cover its costs."[20] Nietzsche's 1872 answer to this problem involves discovering, deep beneath the superficial variety of our cares, the one primordial unity of the world. This primordial unity, the substance of all things, defies linguistic depiction. To the extent that it can be represented at all it is made manifest in music. Life is a despairing sight so long as we think of the failures of our lives as real. But when we recognize that the woes of life are not real, but merely superficial, when we realize that deep beneath the surfaces of our lives, we are one with the primordial power of the world, then we can return to our lives, accepting them as meaningful, significant, valuable.

This is the answer to the problem of existence offered by the 1872 *Birth of Tragedy*. But there is another *Birth of Tragedy*, the one indicated by the 1886 "Attempt at a Self-Criticism" and, indeed, by the whole series of prefaces Nietzsche wrote in 1886 for the republication of a number of his books. The trick to finding the focus of this unwritten book is to subtract from the 1872 *Birth* those elements which come in for the most criticism in the "Attempt at a Self-Criticism." Central among these despised ingredients was the reliance on the primordial unity itself. The prefaces of 1886 imagine a way of overcoming nihilism which can accept the absence of any metaphysical support for our lives and for the world. This can seem an impossible task. Wasn't the problem of nihilism precisely the absence of such a ground? How could nihilism be overcome while conceding the sources of nihilism?

In 1886, Nietzsche's astonishing answer is that the value of existence can be found without metaphysical support if we simply accept the superficial features of our lives. Quite unexpectedly, by rejecting the metaphysical support of the primordial unity, the existential terror described by Cavell and Schopenhauer can be overcome. The very groundlessness of the things nearest to us renders them wonderful, fills them with a bloom and magic we had thought lost forever. The wonder of the world is not diminished, but preserved by the brute groundlessness of our judgments that *this* is what I love, *this* is what I care about. A fragile, precarious peace can still be ours, not thanks to the metaphysical substance of the world, but thanks to nothing. Thanks only to our acceptance of the things nearest, with all their bloom and magic; so thanks only to our thankfulness. The passage that describes this strategy most neatly comes from one of the 1886 prefaces:

> Oh, those Greeks! They knew how to live. What is required for that is to stop courageously at the surface, the fold, the skin, to adore appearance, to believe in forms, tones, words, the whole Olympus of appearance. Those Greeks were superficial—*out of profundity*. And is not this precisely what we are again coming back to, we daredevils of the spirit who have climbed the highest and most dangerous peak of present thought and looked around from up there—we who have looked *down* from there? Are we not, precisely in this respect, Greeks? Adorers of forms, of tones, of words? And therefore—*artists?* [21]

Realizing the groundlessness of our linguistic life, yet managing nevertheless to accept the language we speak, the life we lead. To say: Yes. This is what I do. This is what I care about. This rediscovery of wonder is the key to Nietzsche's mature solution to the value of existence.

In 1872, Nietzsche had turned from the surfaces of language and life to the deeper unity of all things, a unity deceptively clothed in the language of our everyday concerns. In 1886, Nietzsche returns to the surface. He had awoken to the wonder of our lives, a wonder whose preciousness is made possible, but also precarious, by the groundlessness of what we care about, of life itself. [22] In chapter 2, I argue that the concluding pages of Wittgenstein's *Tractatus* develop an answer to the riddle of existence congruent with that in the 1872 *Birth of Tragedy*. In chapters 3, 4, and 5, I rely on the unwritten 1886 *Birth* to outline my reading of the mature Wittgenstein's answer to the big question mark concerning the value of existence. The *Tractatus* is a logico-philosophical treatise with an existential coda, but the *Philosophical Investigations* has no such coda. In chapter 5, I will be using an unwritten version of Nietzsche's first book to guide my interpretation of the unwritten existential coda of the *Investigations*. By the conclusion of that chapter my defense of Heller's thesis will be complete: the break between the *Tractatus* and the *Investigations* is of the same sort as the break between the 1872 edition of *The Birth of Tragedy* and the 1886 revision of that work projected by the prefaces of 1886.

In this incarnation, the completed plan of this book, the epistemologists' concerns with relativism and skepticism appear only to be set aside. I still believe that what truth there is in relativism is manifest in a certain failure to understand others. I still believe that what truth there is in relativism depends on what truth there is in skepticism. And I still believe that what truth there is in skepticism is made manifest in the terror described by Cavell and named by Nietzsche nihilism. But this means that any successful quieting of skeptical doubt, of relativistic confusion, will require the quieting of this existential unease. That is the goal of Wittgenstein's existential investigations: peace. On my interpretation the peace for which he yearned will be ours when we give up the search for metaphysical comfort, when we give up the thirst for explanation, when we awaken to wonder. The happy surprise—our good fortune—is that the absence of what we thought essential to our satisfaction can itself satisfy. Coming face to face with the dumb fact that some things do and some things do not make sense can incite the feeling that one is, in Wittgenstein's words, "walking on a mountain of wonders."[23]

Acknowledgments

I would not read Wittgenstein the way I do, nor would I approach philosophy in the terms I do, had I not looked a second time into Stanley Cavell's *The Claim of Reason* (New York: Oxford University Press, 1979). My first reading of sections of that book left me rather uneager to give it the energy that reading it required. It was a second attempt, helped along by regular conversations with Louis Goldring and attendance at a seminar on the *Investigations* led by Norton Batkin, which convinced me that Cavell had something important to teach. Although I have not, here, provided a stand-alone interpretation of Cavell's work, I hope the references to Cavell that pepper my notes indicate the importance of Cavell's writing in orienting my approach to Wittgenstein and to philosophy.

But without the support of friends, I would never have found the courage to write a book that takes the problem of existential meaning seriously. Philosophical conversations can be miserable things. Terrified of the false, we pinch and poke a delicate new idea to death, leaving one of us hollow and the other proud, but leaving us both empty handed. Fortunately philosophical conversations don't have to be miserable, they can be thrilling afternoons of joyful discovery, together. I have been very lucky to find philosophical friendship among the colleagues and students I have met at Lehigh.

Since I arrived at Lehigh in the fall of 1986, I have enjoyed the best kind of philosophical conversation with Joseph Volpe, in Bethlehem where we once worked together, in Evanston where we were once NEH seminarians, and throughout it all at the Burger King thirty minutes from each of our homes. Joe is the person who told me to look at the 1886 preface to the first volume of *Human, All-Too-Human*. And thinking through Nussbaum's *Fragility of Goodness*, Joe helped me to find the insight of the later Nietzsche and the later Wittgenstein; namely, that the groundlessness of our footing in the world is not in conflict with the world's wonder. It is a necessary condition of that very wonder. Beyond particular tips about Nietzsche, conversation with Joe helped me to sort out how I wanted to settle the anxieties at the heart of epistemological skepticism, and often recalled me to the fact that the importance of philosophical investigation reaches beyond the confines of the philosophical profession.

Conversation with Norman Melchert, more often than not over a pair of gyros, helped me at two critical moments. An early version of the Nietzsche chapter focused—like Nussbaum—on value, not wonder. It was under pressure from Norm that I realized that what I really wanted to be talking about was not value, in general, but wonder. So Norm titled the book. Again when I was trying to draw the book to a close, Norm's reading of chapter 5 gave me the courage to stop.

At various times when I was not writing, I have been helped by conversation in corridors or under the sky with Melissa Baker, Robert Barnes, Mark Bickhard, Evan Conyers, Michelle DeMooy, Robin Dillon, John Hare, Patrick Kilgarriff, Ruth Lorand, Elizabeth Olsen, Michael Raposa, Melissa Rowell, Donna Wagner, and Roslyn Weiss. Marianne Napravnik helped me assemble the first complete version of these chapters and kept me sane as I simultaneously packed to leave for Scotland.

Mark Taylor played a significant role in launching this project. By completing it, I am at last keeping a promise made some time ago to him.

For a number of years Russel Wiebe has been the second reader of almost everything I have written, including these chapters as they were completed. His careful reading of a late version of the entire typescript helped me immeasurably both in detail and by validating my sense that what I had here was indeed a book. John Madritch's sensitive reading of the penultimate draft of the book gave me confidence in its content, and also, to a certain extent, in its tone. A final, Fife reading of the typescript by A. Norman Jeffares reminded me that every good sentence deserves a verb.

It has taken longer to call this book finished than I ever anticipated. The occasional references to Cary and Alice, now nine and six, provide datable moments, and indicate the heart of all this intellectual effort. However much I have been helped by the friends I have just mentioned, this book was written in the shelter of my family: Ellen, and our two girls. As Cary and Alice grow up, cutting teeth, losing teeth, figuring out the tooth fairy, I realize that the passage of time is one side of the precarious wonder of those nearest, their preciousness. But nearer still, least precarious and therefore most magical, whatever I have known of wonder at all, I owe to my life with Ellen.

Crail, Fife
May 29, 1995

Abbreviations

The Works of Nietzsche

The following abbreviations will be used when referring to the writings of Nietzsche. References will be to section and paragraph number; page references, if any, will be to the English translations except in the case of *KSA*.*

A	*The Antichrist* (1888), W. Kaufmann, trans., in *The Portable Nietzsche*; see *TI* below.
BGE	*Beyond Good and Evil* (1886), W. Kaufmann, trans. (New York: Vintage Books, 1966).
BGE P	Preface to *BGE*.
BT	*The Birth of Tragedy* (1872), W. Kaufmann, trans. (New York: Vintage Books, 1967).
BT SC	"Attempt at a Self-Criticism," in 1886 edition of *BT*.
D	*Daybreak* (1881), R. J. Hollingdale, trans. (Cambridge: Cambridge University Press, 1982).
D P	Preface (1886) to *D*.
EH	*Ecce Homo*, in *On the Genealogy of Morals and Ecce Homo*, W. Kaufmann, trans. (New York: Vintage, 1967).
GS	*The Gay Science* (1882, enlarged 1886), W. Kaufmann, trans. (New York: Vintage Books, 1974).
GS P	Preface (1886) to *GS*.
HH	*Human, All-Too-Human*, R. J. Hollingdale, trans. (Cambridge: Cambridge University Press, 1986). This is a translation of the two-volume 1886 edition.

---

*Whenever I have altered the standard translation I cite the German, but I usually cite the German for informational purposes alone. In such cases the German text has come from F. Nietzsche, *Sämtliche Werke: Kritische Studienausgabe in 15 Bänden*, G. Colli and M. Montinari, eds. (de Gruyter: Deuter Taschenbuch, 1980). I will refer to this as *KSA*. *KSA* is a reprinting of selected passages from the much more complete *Kritische Gesamtausgabe*, and *KSA* v. 15 includes a concordance of these two editions.

HH I, P	Preface (1886) to the first volume of *HH*.
HH II, P	Preface (1886) to the second volume of *HH*.
HH II AO	*HH*, volume 2, part 1: "Assorted Opinions and Maxims" (1879).
HH II WS	*HH*, volume 2, part 2: "The Wanderer and His Shadow" (1880).
KSA	See footnote, p. xxi.
NCW	*Nietzsche Contra Wagner* (1888), W. Kaufmann trans., in *The Portable Nietzsche*; see *TI* below.
P	"The Philosopher" (1872), D. Breazeale, trans., in *Philosophy and Truth* (Atlantic Highlands, N.J.: Humanities Press International, 1979, 1990).
TI	*Twilight of the Idols* (1888), W. Kaufmann, trans., in *The Portable Nietzsche* (New York: Viking, 1954, 1974).
WP	*The Will to Power*, W. Kaufmann and R. J. Hollingdale, trans. (New York: Vintage, 1967, 1968). I indicate approximate date at which each note cited was written.

The Works of Wittgenstein

I use the following abbreviations to refer to the works of Wittgenstein. References will be either to paragraph number (par. 34) or to page number (p. 34). Except in the case of Wittgenstein's lectures and letters, these are all available in bilingual editions. A comprehensive description of Wittgenstein's writings is accessible in Georg H. von Wright, "The Wittgenstein Papers," in *Wittgenstein* (Minneapolis: University of Minnesota Press, 1982).

B.n	The nth letter, in L. Wittgenstein, *Briefe*, B. F. McGuinness and G. H. von Wright, eds. (Frankfurt am Main: Surkamp Verlag, 1980). This volume reprints (in chronological order) letters to Russell, Moore, Keynes, Ramsey, Eccles, Engelmann, and von Ficker. Since 1980, more letters have been published.
BigT	The so-called Big Typescript. This is typescript no. 213 in von Wright's catalog; see "The Wittgenstein Papers" (1981), in *Wittgenstein* (Minneapolis: University of Minnesota Press, n.d. [1982]). The "Big Typescript" was dictated to a typist in 1933 from manuscript volumes

written between July 1930 and July 1932. The chapter on
philosophy has been published in German with English
translation on facing pages in L. Wittgenstein,
Philosophical Occasions: 1912–1951 (Indianapolis:
Hackett, 1993), pp. 160–99.

BlB   L. Wittgenstein, "The Blue Book," in *The Blue and Brown
Books* (New York: Harper Torchbooks, 1965). Notes
dictated to students in Cambridge, 1933–34.

BrB   L. Wittgenstein, "The Brown Book," in *The Blue and
Brown Books* (New York: Harper Torchbooks, 1965).
Notes dictated to students in Cambridge, 1934–35.

CV   L. Wittgenstein, *Culture and Value*, G. H. von Wright, ed.,
P. Winch, trans. (Chicago: University of Chicago Press,
1990). References will include date of writing.

E.n   The nth letter to Engelmann, in Paul Engelmann, *Letters
from Ludwig Wittgenstein with a Memoir* (Oxford:
Blackwell, 1967).

F.n   The nth letter to Ludwig von Ficker, in L. Wittgenstein,
"Letters to Ludwig von Ficker," B. Gillette trans., in C. G.
Luckhardt, *Wittgenstein: Sources and Perspectives*
(Hassocks, Sussex: Harvester Press, 1979).

GM.n   The nth letter from L. Wittgenstein to G. E. Moore, in L.
Wittgenstein, *Letters to Russell, Keynes and Moore* (Oxford:
Blackwell, 1974).

L   L. Wittgenstein, *Letters to Russell, Keynes, and Moore*
(Oxford: Blackwell, 1974).

LCA   L. Wittgenstein, *Lectures & Conversations on Aesthetics,
etc.*, Cyril Barrett, ed. (Berkeley: University of California
Press, n.d.).

"LE"   L. Wittgenstein, "Lecture on Ethics" (c. 1929–30), in *The
Philosophical Review* (January 1965): 3–12.

LFM   Cora Diamond, ed., *Wittgenstein's Lectures on the
Foundations of Mathematics, Cambridge 1939* (Ithaca,
N.Y.: Cornell University Press, 1976).

L R.n   The nth letter to Russell in *L.*

NB   L. Wittgenstein, *Notebooks 1914–1916*, G. E. M.
Anscombe, trans. (New York: Harper Torchbooks, 1961).
A second edition with an index (of the first edition) and a
new version of Wittgenstein's "Notes on Logic: 1913" was

	published by the University of Chicago Press in 1979. The pagination up to p. 91 is the same.
NM.n	The nth letter from Norman Malcolm to L. Wittgenstein, in Malcolm's *Ludwig Wittgenstein: A Memoir*, 2d ed. (Oxford: Oxford University Press, 1984).
OC	L. Wittgenstein, *On Certainty* (New York: Harper Torchbooks, 1969). Notes from 1950–51.
PI	L. Wittgenstein, *Philosophical Investigations*, 3d ed., 1967, G. E. M. Anscombe, trans. (Oxford: Blackwell, 1976).
RFM3	L. Wittgenstein, *Remarks on the Foundations of Mathematics*, 3d ed. (Oxford: Blackwell, 1978). References will give approximate date of composition.
RPP I	L. Wittgenstein, *Remarks on the Philosophy of Psychology*, vol. I (Chicago: University of Chicago Press, 1980). *RPP* I was dictated to a typist in 1947; *PI* Part II is a 1949 dictation from the same series.
RPP II	L. Wittgenstein, *Remarks on the Philosophy of Psychology*, vol. II (Chicago: University of Chicago Press, 1980). *RPP* II was dictated to a typist in 1948; *PI* Part II is a 1949 dictation from the same series.
TLP	L. Wittgenstein, *Tractatus Logico-Philosophicus*, D. F. Pears and B. F. McGuinness, trans. (London: Routledge & Kegan Paul, 1961, 1977).
WVC	F. Waismann, *Wittgenstein and the Vienna Circle* (New York: Barnes and Noble Books, 1979).
Z	L. Wittgenstein, *Zettel* (Berkeley: University of California Press, 1967).

Wittgenstein Commentaries

These paragraph-by-paragraph commentaries on the *Philosophical Investigations* (*PI*) are already becoming canonical. They will be referred to by the following abbreviations:

Baker and Hacker, *Volume I*

G. P. Baker and P. M. S. Hacker, *An Analytical Commentary on the* Philosophical Investigations *Volume 1* (Chicago: University of Chicago Press, 1980).

Baker and Hacker, *Volume II*

> G. P. Baker and P. M. S. Hacker, *An Analytical Commentary on the* Philosophical Investigations *Volume 2* (Oxford: Blackwell, 1985).

Hacker, *Volume III*

> P. M. S. Hacker, *An Analytical Commentary on the* Philosophical Investigations *Volume 3* (Oxford: Blackwell, 1990).

Chapter 1

Superficial—Out of Profundity: Nietzsche's Unwritten Birth of Tragedy

> Here is the Preface for the new edition of *The Birth of Tragedy*. Given this very meaty Preface which provides so much orientation, you can launch this book once more—it even seems very important to me that this should be done.
>
> —Nietzsche to Fritzsch, August 29, 1886[1]

> Oh, those Greeks! They knew how to live. What is required for that is to stop courageously at the surface, the fold, the skin, to adore appearance, to believe in forms, tones, words, the whole Olympus of appearance. Those Greeks were superficial—*out of profundity.* And is not this precisely what we are again coming back to?
>
> —Nietzsche, "Preface for the second edition
> [of *The Gay Science*]," Fall 1886

Nietzsche never completely disowned the discoveries announced in his first book, *The Birth of Tragedy* (1872). More than fifteen years later, during Nietzsche's last year of literary activity, *Twilight of the Idols* invokes and recommends the portrait of Socrates presented in *The Birth of Tragedy* (*TI* ii, par. 2) and concludes on this note:

> And herewith I again touch that point from which I once went forth: *The Birth of Tragedy* was my first revaluation of all values. Herewith I again stand on the soil out of which my intention, my *ability* grows— I, the last disciple of the philosopher Dionysus—I, the teacher of the eternal recurrence. (*TI* x, par. 5)[2]

This continuing respect for his first scholarly production is surprising because, as Nehamas observes, *The Birth of Tragedy* seems committed to

1

"the very contrast between things-in-themselves and appearance" that the mature Nietzsche attacked.[3]

Recent discussion of *The Birth of Tragedy* is no longer dominated by questions of whether Nietzsche's account of the birth of tragedy is historically and philologically correct.[4] Discussion now centers on whether this early work speaks with the voice of metaphysics—by and large Schopenhauer's voice—or whether in spite of this being his first book Nietzsche had already moved beyond metaphysics. As I read it, Nietzsche's text faces both directions. Let Nehamas represent those interpreters who emphasize passages in *The Birth of Tragedy* that seem to identify one of the art deities of tragedy, Dionysus, with the world as it is in itself, the true world behind the apparent world (e.g., *BT* par. 1, p. 37; par. 6, p. 55; par. 8, p. 61; par. 16, p. 100). This is the group who read *The Birth of Tragedy* as a work of traditional metaphysics.[5] Members of the second, antimetaphysical group emphasize those parts of *The Birth of Tragedy* that insist that tragedy cannot reveal the in-itself of the world, but is—like every art—a form of "illusion" (e.g., *BT* par. 18, p. 110; par. 19, p. 118; par. 21, p. 129; par. 25, p. 143). Let deMan represent this group of interpreters. They do not understand *The Birth of Tragedy* to privilege Dionysus and music as against Apollo and language; sometimes they even discover in this early work the first moves of a general overcoming or deconstruction of metaphysics.[6] My own view is that the original 1872 *Birth of Tragedy* invites the kind of interpretation I have associated with Nehamas, but that there is another antimetaphysical version of *The Birth of Tragedy*, an unwritten 1886 edition.

Curiously, Nietzsche's prefatory "Attempt at a Self-Criticism," which was published with the second edition of *The Birth of Tragedy* (1886), anticipates both the metaphysical and the antimetaphysical interpretations of that book. This "Self-Criticism" describes and unequivocally denounces the metaphysical elements of his first literary project.[7] So Nietzsche seems to have been the first of his readers to notice that his first book could be criticized from the antimetaphysical standpoint of the author of his later works. Nevertheless, in 1885, at just about the time of these self-critical remarks, that same more mature author could write: "Thinking out the principal problems . . . always brings me back . . . to the same conclusions: they are already there, as veiled and obscure as possible in my *Birth of Tragedy*, and everything I have since learned has become an ingrown part of them."[8] Nietzsche can help us understand our own divided reflections on his first book, for we can think of his later work as suggesting a strategy for reading that book against the grain of its sometimes traditional metaphysical vocabulary: a strategy for reading an unwritten book.

The Birth of Tragedy argues that tragedy, and hence tragic knowledge, should be construed as the offspring of the "fraternal union" (*BT* par. 24) of the two art deities: Apollo and Dionysus. Although this book often associates Apollo with appearance and Dionysus with the truth behind the veil of appearance, the mature Nietzsche praised a *Birth of Tragedy* which was not, in this way, metaphysically mired. In this unwritten book, Dionysus anticipates the figure of the death of God, and Apollo anticipates what Nietzsche was to call the great health or the love of fate, *amor fati*. The mature Nietzsche thought of tragedy and tragic knowledge as a way of moving beyond nihilism, of discovering the precious value of what is near (*HH* preface, par. 5), the value of "little things" that had once seemed of no consequence:

> My formula for greatness in a human being is *amor fati*: that one wants nothing to be different, not forward, not backward, not in all eternity. Not merely bear what is necessary, still less conceal it . . . but *love* it. (*EH* ii, par. 10; see *WP* par. 1016 [1888])[9]

Nietzsche's philosophy, no less than Wittgenstein's, "leaves everything as it is."[10] The semipopular view that Nietzsche aims to transcend the ordinary is a mistake.[11]

(1) Nietzsche's *Seven Prefaces* (1886)

Toward the end of 1885, having finished *Thus Spoke Zarathustra* and while working on *Beyond Good and Evil*, Nietzsche began to imagine the publication of his collected works (*KSA* 11.669). Dissatisfied with the reception his work had received, and blaming his publisher Schmeitzner, he planned to republish all his books with a new publisher, Fritzsch.[12] Thus he produced, mostly in 1886, a number of prefaces to help orient readers to his work. At times, he even imagined collecting them into a book to be called simply *Seven Prefaces* (*KSA* 12.123–24, 231–32). In the end, Nietzsche published five new prefaces, not as one book but as prefaces to new editions of his early works.[13] Had they been collected they would have amounted to Nietzsche's own "point of view for my work as an author." That he considered them in this light is apparent from a letter to Fritzsch.

> Perhaps it would be equally useful to issue now, immediately, also the new edition of *The Birth* (with the "Attempt at a Self-Criticism"). This "Attempt," together with the "Preface to *Human, All-Too-Human*," provides genuine enlightenment about me—the very best preparation for my audacious son, Zarathustra.[14]

He described these prefaces as the "new 'wings'" for the second flight of his literary production, and I will rely on them to frame my reading of the unwritten *Birth of Tragedy*.[15]

The five published prefaces persistently use imagery of sickness and health. Nietzsche describes his writings as the history of a sickness and convalescence [Genesung] (*HH* II, P par. 6). *The Gay Science* itself is called the "gratitude of a convalescent" [Dankbarkeit eines Gene-senden], and this seems to refer to another moving "song of thanks of a convalescent" [Dankgesang eines Genesenen], that one by Beethoven, String Quartet Op. 132 (*GS* P par. 1).[16] The most detailed description of Nietzsche's sickness and recovery appears in the first preface he wrote in 1886, the preface to the first volume of *Human, All-Too-Human*, whose subtitle tells us it is "A Book for Free Spirits." The anatomy of convalescence is presented as a genealogy of the free spirit in four stages, which I have named "hearth health," "sickness," "convalescence," and finally, "the great health of the free spirit."[17]

(i) Hearth Health

Those who will become free spirits do not begin by being sick, but by being healthy. Although they feel healthy, they are in fact bound by "what fetters fastest": by their dutiful reverence for their elders, their country, their teachers, and for "the holy place where they learned to worship" (*HH* I, P par. 3). They are fettered by all those ideals that warm one on the family hearth. These ideals are normally taken to be of the highest value, and so Nietzsche can write of those who will be free spirits that "their highest moments themselves will fetter them the fastest, lay upon them the most enduring obligations" (*HH* I, P par. 3).

Nietzsche would have associated these fetters with what some philosophers have called metaphysics, with deflating the value of this earthly world and inflating the value of another, heavenly world. Moreover, as he saw it, there was not much difference between Christian and Platonist forms of the will to the otherworldly, so he announced that "Christianity is Platonism for 'the people'" (*BGE* P). *Beyond Good and Evil*, published in 1886—the same year Nietzsche was writing this new preface—italicizes what Nietzsche called the "fundamental faith of metaphysicians . . . *the faith in opposite values*" (*BGE* par. 2). This approach to metaphysics elaborates the hearth health from which future free spirits set out.

Metaphysicians want to understand the origins or essences of things, that is, what makes anything the kind of thing that it is: what makes stones stones, illusions illusions, the good good, and the nasty nasty. As Nietzsche sees it, metaphysicians think they know where the nasty comes from; it originates in our embarrassingly human urges. But then where can the true, the good, and the beautiful come from? Not from this (nasty, illusory, changing) human world. Hence, the metaphysician's quest for what makes the good good faces a decision: *either* there is no metaphysical accounting for the goodness of the good *or* we will find ourselves inventing a second world, a world designed to possess just those features that we require of metaphysical explanations.[18] Nietzsche puts the following words in the mouth of a metaphysician:

> The things of the highest value must have another, *peculiar* [*eigenen*] origin—they cannot be derived from this transitory, seductive, deceptive, paltry world, from this turmoil of delusion and lust. Rather from the lap of Being, the intransitory, the hidden god, the "thing-in-itself"—there must be their basis, and nowhere else. (*BGE* par. 2)

The good is wholly different from the evil, and the origin of evil is in this world; so the origin of good must be in another world, in the other-worldly. Hegel presented a perfect example of the metaphysician's faith in opposite values when he wrote: "the means should correspond to the dignity of the end, and [hence] not appearance and deception but only the truth can create the truth."[19] The fundamental faith of the metaphysician is that opposite values must have opposite genealogies. The value of the true, the good, and the beautiful must therefore be grounded not on the details of this world but on those of another world, revealed to us in our "highest moments" (*HH* I, P par. 3). And the obligations revealed to us in these moments fetter us fastest.

I have called this stage "hearth health" to indicate that the warmth of this health derives from the artificial heat of the family's fireplace. It will contrast with the natural warmth of the great health.

(ii) Sickness

Nietzsche refers to the stage of sickness as the "great liberation," and the German expression (die grosse Loslösung) has some of the force of the great separation (*HH* I, P par. 3). This great liberation comes "suddenly" and tears us away—with nearly suicidal consequences—from the hearth virtues that had been granted the highest value. "'Better to die than to go on living *here*'—thus responds the imperious voice and temptation: and this 'here,' this 'at home' is everything it had hitherto loved" (*HH* I, P par. 3). This is a "sickness that can destroy the man who has it" (*HH* I, P par. 3). The symptoms of this sickness include a suspicion and contempt of all that once was loved, a "hatred of love" itself, and a "wicked laugh" that accompanies the demonstration that the things of highest value are of no value (*HH* I, P par. 3).

Nietzsche reports that persons suffering from this sickness may praise those things that were formerly considered evil, but he cautions that this simple inversion[20] of received values manifests a lack of courage for "the question mark of a more perilous curiosity":

> Can *all* values not be turned round? and is good perhaps evil? and God only an invention and finesse of the Devil? Is everything perhaps in the last resort false? And if we are deceived, are we not for that very reason also deceivers? *must* we not be deceivers? (*HH* I, P par. 3)

The more perilous thought is that nothing is of any value at all, not what was formerly considered good, but neither what was formerly considered evil. Is everything perhaps in the last resort false? This skeptical thought is the one Nietzsche came to call nihilism: "that there is no truth, that there is no absolute nature of things nor a 'thing-in-itself.' This, too, is merely nihilism—even the most extreme nihilism" (*WP* par. 13: 1887). Nietzsche understood the genesis of nihilism in terms of the first two stages of the genealogy of the free spirit: "one interpretation has collapsed; but because it was considered *the* interpretation it now seems as if there were no meaning at all in existence, as if everything were in vain" (*WP* par. 55: 1887).

If we think of this one interpretation as theocentric—God, too, nothing—then this skeptical nihilism recalls one place were Nietzsche speaks of God's death:

> Whither are we moving? Away from all suns? Are we not plunging continually? Backward, sideward, forward, in all directions? Is there

still any up or down? Are we not straying as through an infinite nothing? Do we not feel the breath of empty space? Has it not become
colder? Is not night continually closing in on us? Do we hear nothing
as yet of the grave diggers who are burying God? . . . God is dead. God
remains dead. (*GS* par. 125: 1882)

The thought that God is dead, that we are wandering through an infinite
nothing, neatly fits the potentially fatal sickness that Nietzsche describes
in this preface: Nietzsche's sickness unto death (*HH* II, P par. 3).

(iii) Convalescence, in Two Phases

Nietzsche notes that between the sickness and the great health there is
what he calls a "midway condition," "long years of convalescence"
[Genesung] (*HH* I, P par. 4). I follow Nietzsche in distinguishing two
phases of this convalescence, one colder and one warmer: two phases in
the coming to health of those suffering from skepticism, from nihilism.

The first, colder phase of convalescence. The sickness, itself, was
characterized by a hatred of what was formerly loved, including love
itself. During this first phase of convalescence, "one lives no longer in the
fetters of love and hatred, without yes, without no" (*HH* I, P par. 4). In
this phase one neither hates nor loves, but looks on all values with a
certain coolness and a certain distance. The great liberation proceeds
further. One is so disengaged from what one formerly loved that it can
be viewed without hatred, contempt, and suspicion. Or the contempt is
tempered. It becomes tender (*HH* I, P par. 4). Nietzsche tells us that this
phase of convalescence has three elements, that it

> is characterized by [1] a pale, subtle happiness of light and sunshine,
> [2] a feeling of bird-like freedom, bird-like altitude [Vogel-Umblick],
> bird-like exuberance, and a third thing in which curiosity is united
> with a tender contempt. (*HH* I, P par. 4)

Like a bird, this convalescent can soar high above what was troubling the
sick spirit. Nothing that seemed valuable on the family hearth seems so
now. But this is no longer the source of a feverish hatred. What others
trouble [bekümmern] themselves about is no longer of any concern to
the colder convalescent (*HH* I, P par. 4). Like a bird, the colder convalescent has "seen a tremendous number of things *beneath* him" (*HH* I,
P par. 4). The convalescent looks down on what others worry about,

with tender contempt, with cosmic irony. The convalescent is just as confident as the feverish had been that everything is in the last resort false, but the convalescent is no longer frightened by that thought. The convalescent smiles gently at what others take so seriously.

At this height, everything is far away. Everything is small.[21] Everything is flat. Nothing matters. This is the mood equally of a scientist sure that ours is a world of valueless facts and of those literary characters who float through a world from which they have been estranged and which they look on with a species of tender contempt.[22]

The second, warmer phase of convalescence. Although enjoying a sunny happiness [Sonnenglück], the temperature of the first phase of convalescence is not quite warming; it is "cool" (*HH* I, P, par. 4). This is the paradoxically cool sunshine of the higher altitudes. The second phase of convalescence brings the patient back to the earth[23] where the sun warms.

> It again grows warmer around him, yellower, as it were; feeling and feeling for others acquire depth, warm breezes of all kinds blow across him. It seems to him as if his eyes are only now open to what is *near* [*Nahe*]. He is astonished [verwundert] and sits silent: where *had* he been? These near and nearest [nahe und nächsten] things: how changed they seem! what bloom and magic [Flaum und Zauber] they have acquired! (*HH* I, P par. 5)

Where *had* he been? He had never seen these near, nearest things. He hadn't seen them in the colder phase of convalescence when he had looked down on all things from his birdlike altitude that shrinks everything, so that nothing is worthy either of love or hate. Certainly he had overlooked them when—in his sickness—he had steamed with a feverish hatred of the theological values and the metaphysics of the family hearth.

But it is essential to an understanding of Nietzsche that these nearest things were also veiled from him before his sickness, and by the very things that, in his sickness, he had reacted so contemptuously *against*. On the family hearth, before his sickness, he had absorbed the fundamental faith of metaphysicians in opposite values, and there is no need to infer *from* this hearth health *to* the veiling of the things that are nearest. To open one's eyes to the heavenly metaphysical world just *is* to close one's eyes to things that are nearest. Only in the warmer phase of convalescence are the near, nearest things disclosed at all. Here they are disclosed for the first time, but they are disclosed as having been there from the very beginning.

The metaphors work well enough. Convalescents are to come down from the height of cosmic distance, cosmic irony, from which bird's-eye view [Vogel-Umblick] all earthly things must seem tiny and of no importance. On the surface of earth the world is not flat; it has a terrain. Here the sunlight the convalescents had begun to enjoy in the cold, thin, upper atmosphere can finally warm them. And for short spells this winter sun gives them an occasional taste of what Nietzsche calls "health": the magical delicacy of the near, nearest (*HH* I, P par. 5). The metaphors work well enough, but how are we to understand what Nietzsche calls the bloom and magic of the things that are near(*HH* I, P par. 5)?

I suggested we construe the sickness from which these convalescents are recovering as the sickness of nihilism, so we might try to discover the meaning of this bloom and magic by looking at Nietzsche's discussion of how to overcome nihilism.[24] Nihilism is a "transitional stage," because the nihilist is incompletely liberated from the hearth side values of the Platonic or Christian tradition (*WP* par. 13: 1887).

> Briefly: the categories "aim," "unity," "being," with which we have injected some value into the world—we *pull out* again; so the world looks *valueless.* . . .We have to ask about the sources of our faith in these three categories. Let us try if it is not possible to give up our faith in them. Once we have devalued these three categories, the demonstration that they cannot be applied to the universe is no longer any reason for devaluing the universe.
>
> Conclusion: The faith in the categories of reason is the cause of nihilism. We have measured the value of the world according to categories *that refer to a purely fictitious world.* (*WP* par. 12: 1887–88)

This passage can help elaborate the two phases of convalescence. The death of God can only seem to deprive the earth of its significance if we persist in assuming that there can be no value except theological value. Sacrilege delivers its familiar frisson, but only for those who still believe. So enjoying the shiver of sacrilege is a sign rather of faith than of its overcoming.[25] In terms of Nietzsche's genealogy of the free spirit: even the cool birdlike detachment that flattens the earth can only flatten the earth because of its height.[26]

The most concise (and least figurative) presentation of this defusing of nihilism apears in this section from Nietzsche's published account of how the so-called true world became a fable.

> The true world—we have abolished. What world has remained? The apparent perhaps? But no! *With the true world we have also abolished the apparent one.* (*TI* iv, par. 6)

What *Human, All-Too-Human* describes as a potentially fatal sickness is the abolishing of the so-called true world, that is, the metaphysical world and theological values absorbed at the family hearth. During the convalescent's colder phase, the bird's-eye view of a completely flat world is the thought that, without the true world, nothing is real: everything is merely apparent, flat. The warmer phase of convalescence arrives when the convalescent finally casts off the last hearth value: the belief that if there were anything of value at all, that value would have to be metaphysically or theologically grounded. To cast that off is to recognize that by abolishing the metaphysical world we have thereby abolished the merely apparent world. Nietzsche can still write that "the 'apparent' ['scheinbare'] world is the only one: the 'true world' ['wahre Welt'] is only added by a lie" (*TI* iii, par. 2). But Nietzsche's scare quotes show that he is talking about what the *tradition* had thought of as the true and the apparent world. The world that the tradition devalued as merely apparent is the only world there is. So it is no longer *merely* apparent.

In 1888 Nietzsche still figured this as becoming warm. The last indented quotation is immediately followed by these parenthetical images: "(Noon; moment of the briefest shadow; end of the longest error; high point of humanity; INCIPIT ZARATHUSTRA)" (*TI* iv, par. 6). What Nietzsche calls the "spots of sunlight" of the warmer phase of convalescence are the first taste of the sunshine of this health (*HH* I, P par. 5). The bloom and magic [Flaum und Zauber] of the near, nearest things comes into view in these spots of sunshine. "Flaum" has some of the force of down or fluff and can refer to the tiny, infinitely delicate hairs that grow on the stems, leaves, or seeds of plants. Things that fine can be called precious in the sense of being delicate and refined. In such a mood, it is easy to be amazed, to stare in silent wonder [er ist verwundert und sitzt stille] that such soft, slender, slight things can manage to exist at all. They seem to owe their existence to some impossible magical spell. This is the bloom and magic of the things nearest:

precisely the spirit of the line from Emerson that Nietzsche used as the motto of the 1882 *Gay Science:* "To the poet and sage, all things are friendly and hallowed, all experiences profitable, all days holy, all men divine."[27]

Nietzsche has observed that without the metaphysical grounding provided by Platonic or Christian heavens, the persistence of the things of this world will be revealed in their fragility. This is not the robust, confident pragmatic or neopragmatic world of the man of affairs, immune to doubt, invulnerable to disaster. This is a more delicate, per-haps even more feminine[28] world shadowed by the threat of insecurity, whose security comes, if at all, as a magical spell. It is for these reasons that when the things nearest come into the "spots of sunlight," they are cherished (*HH* P par. 5). We care for them.

Of course fragility of every sort is not wonderful, for we cannot, normally, increase our wonder at the delicacy of a chair by cracking it. But speaking roughly, when the healthy state of a natural object[29] is to be fragile, or scarce, or delicate, then that very fragility will contribute to our wonder. The delicacy of the things nearest is of precisely that sort. They are not wonderful *in spite of* lacking metaphysical grounding; their value is constituted by their lack of such grounding. Their wonder *is* their fragility.[30]

The character Nietzsche calls the wanderer's shadow[31] says to the wanderer: "Of all that you have said nothing has pleased me *more* than a promise you have made: you want again to become a good neighbor to the nearest things" [gute Nachbarn der nächsten Dinge] (*HH* II, WS last dialogue, p. 394).[32] The spots of sunlight that warm this second phase of convalescence are the first signs that the convalescent has also made this promise. Moreover the only difference between the warmer phase of convalescence and the great health is that what comes in "small doses" during recovery is always at hand when the spirits of the convalescents are finally free (*HH* I, P par. 5). The warmer convales-cents were "half turned toward life"; the free spirits are fully turned toward life (*HH* I, P par. 5).

(iv) The Great Health of the Free Spirit

Free spirits will have discovered the answer to the riddle of the great liberation. They will have discovered why their cure had to be so long and so lonely (*HH* I, P par. 6). The answer is that the future free spirits had to learn that all value judgments manifest the perspective of the person judging, and in order to become free, these spirits would have to learn to judge in accord with their own "higher goals," not the artificial warmth of the hearth, but the great health: the warm sunshine that lights up the value, the significance, the meaning of the earth (*HH* I, P par. 6).[33] So the free spirits learn that their problem is "*the problem of order of rank*" (*HH* I, P par. 7). They learn to "transfer seriousness" (*WP* par. 1016: 1888) from the things heretofore considered of highest value to those "little things" (*EH* II par. 10), the things nearest to us (*HH* I, P par. 5) that were formerly considered of no value at all.

The telos of convalescence is a "tremendous overflowing security [Sicherheit] and health . . . *great* health" (*HH* I, P par. 4). Note that Nietzsche uses Sicherheit/security rather than Gewissheit/certainty to describe the feeling of great health. In chapter 5, relying on Wittgenstein, I will discuss the different dimensions of these two concepts. At this stage I will simply assert that certainty suggests being certain that X is a Q because of the presence of criteria for being a Q. Certainty is a matter of evidence supporting a conclusion, silencing doubt, delivering knowledge: Gewissheit delivering Wissen. Security is rather a lack of care, safety; it is less a matter of evidence than an affair of the heart (see *A* par. 34). Closer to faith than to knowledge (see *D* P par. 3–4). Not too distant from the magic [Zauber] of a spell, a safety, beyond reason's power to comprehend: beyond grounding's grasp.

In the second edition of *The Gay Science*, Nietzsche scorns the positivistic "demand for certainty" [Gewissheit] (*GS* par. 347: 1887), but he honors the security of priestly men of faith.

> The common people [Das Volk] attribute *wisdom* [*weise*] to such serious men of "faith" ["Glaubens"] who have become quiet, meaning that they have acquired knowledge and are "secure" ["sichere"] compared to one's own insecurity [Unsicherheit]. Who would want to deny them this word [i.e., wisdom] and this reverence. (*GS* par. 351: 1887)

What Nietzsche does want to deny is that knowledge and wisdom can be nonprecariously acquired. The overflowing security (*HH* I, P par. 4) that characterizes Nietzsche's "great health" cannot, on this account, be freed from the risk of sickness. Discovering the precious bloom of what

is normally overlooked remains a task. The great health, which is astonished and wonders at what is precious, is itself fundamentally fragile.

The solution to the problem of an order of rank will involve the discovery of our *own* virtues, those settled dispositions conducive to the
great health. But, Nietzsche observes,

> Doesn't this almost mean: *believing* in one's own virtues [an seine
> eigene Tugend *glauben*]? But this "believing in one's virtues"—isn't
> this at bottom the same thing that was formerly called one's "good
> conscience," that venerable long pigtail of a concept [Begriffs-Zopf]
> which our grandfathers fastened . . . often enough . . . behind their
> understanding [hinter ihren Verstand]. . . . In one respect we are nev-
> ertheless worthy grandsons of these grandfathers, we last Europeans
> with a good conscience: we, too, still wear their pigtail. (*BGE* par. 214)

This pigtail, this believing, trusting, or having faith in one's own virtues remains for Nietzsche beyond proof. The title page of the second
(1887) edition of *The Gay Science* replaces the quote from Emerson
with Nietzsche's own rewriting of a famous line from Emerson's "Self-
Reliance" (1841) that emphasizes just this lack of proof. Emerson was
voicing his view that "nothing is at last sacred but the integrity of your
own mind," and recalled being asked "when quite young" how he
could be sure that the impulses he followed came from above and not
from below.[34] As part of his reply he exclaimed, "I would write on the
lintels of the door post, *Whim*. I hope it is somewhat better than
whim at last, but I cannot spend the day in explanation."[35] Just as in
Kant, there cannot be an explanation of autonomy.[36] Emerson draws
the conclusion that whim is what one's acceptance of one's own virtues must look like: to others, but also to oneself.[37] Nietzsche rewrote
this passage about self-reliance, and when he brought out a second
edition of *The Gay Science*, he used it instead of the straight Emerson
that had been on the title page of the first edition. Nietzsche's rewrit-
ten version is:

> I live in my own place,
> have never copied nobody even half,
> and at any master who lacks the grace
> to laugh at himself—I laugh.
>
>   OVER THE DOOR TO MY HOUSE (*GS* title page: 1887)

Nietzsche's laugh underlines the whimsy in whim, and acknowledges that we cannot prove, or make certain, that our own virtues are either *ours* or *virtuous*. At best we can trust them without care, with security, with that "overflowing security" [Sicherheit] of the great health (*HH* I, P par. 4).

Without the weight of metaphysics, all the anchors of our lives can drift. And while that can indeed seem a sickness, nihilism, Nietzsche saw further.

> The trust in life is gone: life itself has become a *problem*. Yet one should not jump to the conclusion that this necessarily makes one gloomy. Even love of life is still possible, only one loves differently. It is the love for a woman that causes doubts in us. The attraction of everything problematic, the delight in an x ... flares up again and again like a bright blaze ... over all the danger of insecurity [Unsicherheit], and even over the jealousy of the lover. We know a new happiness. (*GS* P par. 3)

There is a love of life that requires complete freedom from all risk of disaster, a comfortable happiness resting on certain knowledge of what is right and wrong. On Nietzsche's account this is inaccessible. The different kind of love, producing a new happiness, is a love of what is precisely not immune to disaster, of what is delicate. This happiness, this great health, is a security within the shadow of risk, of fragility. It is the overflowing security with which we greet the downy magic of what is nearest with gratitude (*HH* I P par. 4 and 5).

The *Seven Prefaces* of 1886 display the genealogy of the free spirit. (i) The artificial metaphysical comfort of the family hearth succumbs to (ii) the sickness of nihilism, the hateful assault on everything that had seemed so comforting. (iii) Convalescence proceeds in two phases: a first cooler phase in which the convalescent lives without any love of metaphysical comforts but also without any hatred. The cooler convalescent—neither alive nor dead—floats above the earth. The second warmer phase of convalescence discovers the natural warmth of the spots of sunlight on the wall, the bloom and magic of things that are nearest. And (iv), the final phase of great health lives these moments of natural warmth as a way of life. This spirit freed from the tradition that seeks metaphysical comforts is surprised by a new happiness and a new love for all that is delicate. The great health is a life attuned to what is near.

(2) Dionysian Terror and Dionysian Ecstasy

The title *Seven Prefaces* would not have been precisely correct. Four of the published prefaces were indeed prefaces [Vorrede], but one of them was an attempt [Versuch], an "Attempt at a Self-Criticism." *The Birth of Tragedy* was republished in 1886 with only two significant changes: the first was the "Attempt at a Self-Criticism" and the second was its new subtitle.[38] The 1872 edition wasn't exactly subtitled, it simply had a long title: "The Birth of Tragedy out of the Spirit of Music." The 1886 edition wasn't exactly subtitled either; it was doubly titled: "The Birth of Tragedy. Or: Hellenism and Pessimism." By drawing attention to pessimism Nietzsche would have been drawing attention to Schopenhauer.

According to Schopenhauer, "*all life is suffering.*"[39] He described tragedy as the "summit of poetic art" because it made the "terrible side of life" so wholly unavoidable.[40] On his account, tragic drama tears aside the veil of illusion, "the veil of Maya," revealing that the principle of individuation is merely apparent.[41] The deep truth is that there are no individuals and every individual person or thing we have ever cared for is only apparent. According to Schopenhauer, tragedy

> sees through the form of the phenomenon, the *principium individua-tionis;* the egoism resting on this expires with it. The *motives* that were previously so powerful now lose their force, and instead of them, the complete knowledge of the real nature of the world, acting as a *quieter* of the will [als *Quietiv* des Willens], produces resignation, the giving up not merely of life, but of the whole will-to-live itself. Thus we see in tragedy the noblest men, after a long conflict and suffering, finally renounce for ever all the pleasures of life and the aims till then pursued so keenly, or cheerfully and willingly give up life itself.[42]

The 1886 prefaces were eager to distance themselves from this Schopenhauerian position. In the preface to the second volume of *Human, All-Too-Human,* Nietzsche brags about how early he had separated himself from Schopenhauer (*HH* II, par. 1), and it starts its final paragraph with this thought:

> Finally, to reduce my opposition to *romantic pessimism,* that is to say to the pessimism of the renunciators, the failed and defeated, to a formula: there is a will to the tragic and to pessimism that is as much a sign of severity and strength of intellect (taste, feeling, conscience).

> With this will [to the tragic] in one's heart one has no fear of the fear-
> ful and questionable that characterizes all existence; one even seeks it
> out. . . . This has been *my* pessimistic perspective from the begin-
> ning—a novel perspective, is it not? (*HH* II par. 7)

The Birth of Tragedy's "Self-Criticism" drew a related distinction between:
a (Schopenhauerian) pessimism of weakness that craves the beautiful
and would rather die than face the terrible, the ugly; and a (Nietzschean)
pessimism of strength that craves the ugly and would rather risk death
than turn away from the terrible (*BT* SC par. 1, par. 4).[43]

There are reasons for thinking that the Schopenhauerian strands of
The Birth of Tragedy were unduly emphasized because of Nietzsche's
friendship and admiration for Wagner,[44] but conversely these 1886 prefaces probably exaggerate his distance from Schopenhauer.[45] Still, I am
not concerned with how far Nietzsche misread his own past. My concern
is not with whether it is a misreading, but with the misreading itself.

The 1886 "Self-Criticism" insists that *The Birth of Tragedy* is about
how to make life worth living:

> You will guess where the big question mark[46] concerning the *value of
> existence* had thus been raised. (*BT* SC par. 1; my emphasis)

Given the role that Nietzsche's 1886 genealogy of the free spirit gave to
the sickness unto death of nihilism, this is just the emphasis we would
have expected. Yet many of the antimetaphysical interpreters of
Nietzsche, here represented by de Man, sneer at what de Man calls "the
entire semipopular 'existential' reading of Nietzsche."[47] De Man would
focus rather on Nietzsche's deconstruction of metaphysics than on the
existential dimension of Nietzsche's concern with sickness and convalescence. But de Man needlessly opposed the deconstructive side of
Nietzsche to the side displayed in Nietzsche's genealogy of the free spirit.
That genealogy shows that Nietzsche's antimetaphysical stance, not
only issues in nihilism, but also that it can defuse that very nihilism, the
existential sickness, which de Man refuses to see. *The Birth of Tragedy* is
soaked in what an early letter to Rhode calls "the true and highest problems of life."[48]

In 1872 the association of Dionysus and the sickness that can make
us want to die, nihilism, is quite explicitly made in a passage presenting
"Greek folk wisdom" addressing "the big question mark concerning the
value of existence" (*BT* par. 3, p. 42; *BT* SC par. 1, p. 17).

There is an ancient story that King Midas hunted in the forest a long time for the wise Silenus, the companion of Dionysus, without capturing him. When Silenus at last fell into his hands, the king asked what was the best and most desirable of all things for man. Fixed and immovable, the demigod said not a word, till at last, urged by the king, he gave a shrill laugh and broke out in these words: "Oh, wretched ephemeral race, children of chance and misery, why do you compel me to tell you what it would be most expedient for you not to hear? What is best of all is utterly beyond your reach: not to be born, not to *be*, to be *nothing* [nicht zu *sein, nicht* zu sein]. But the second best for you is—to die soon." (*BT* par. 3, p. 42)[49]

Silenus reveals to Midas that there is no reason for living, that existence has no value; so it would be better to be dead: "Better to die than to go on living *here*" (*HH* P par. 3).

Opposed to Apollo, who is associated with "*measure*" [das *Maas*], is Silenus's friend Dionysus, who is associated with "*excess*" [das *Übermaas*] (*BT* par. 4, p. 46).[50] Explicitly referring to Schopenhauer, Nietzsche notes that Dionysian excess is the source both of tremendous terror [Grausen] and blissful ecstasy [Verzückung] (*BT* par. 1, p. 36). Nietzsche uses various words for this terror and for this ecstasy, but it remains clear that there are two sides to the Dionysian experience: (1) one which is confrontation with something that is terrifying, horrifying, dreadful, or fearful [e.g., Grausen, Entsetzliche, Schrecken][51] and (2) one which is ecstatic union with what transcends the individual [e.g., Verzückung, Entzückung].[52] Nietzsche structures his discussion of these emotions so that terror is caused by a lapse in the "principle of sufficient reason," and ecstasy by a lapse in the principle of individuation (*BT* par. 1, p. 36). *The Birth of Tragedy* links Dionysus with both terror and ecstasy; the author of the "Self-Criticism" uncouples Dionysus from ecstasy. That uncoupling is the center of Nietzsche's mature misreading of his earliest literary project. His mature interpretation of tragedy is simply his earlier interpretation *minus* the Dionysian ecstasy: the ecstatic union with the metaphysical heart of the world.

Dionysian terror. Silenus's statements are so grim that we should understand them as inspired not by Dionysian ecstasy but by Dionysian terror. But why would the appearance that the principle of sufficient reason had suffered an "exception" cause terror (*BT* par. 1, p. 36)? The principle of sufficient reason is that nothing happens without reason, that there is a reason for everything; nothing is beyond reason's reach. Nietzsche declares that when we suspect that this principle has suffered exception we will feel tremendously terrified. But why? Contrast this homely example. Suppose we endorse the principle that car mufflers wear out in seven years. We can discover a functioning eight-year-old muffler without threatening our general belief. Why must matters be different with the principle of sufficient reason?

Our belief about mufflers can be protected from falsification because each exception to our belief will have its own particular reason. The exceptions can be corralled. Apparent exceptions to the principle of sufficient reason cannot be similarly corralled. When the principle of sufficient reason suffers exception this cannot be for a reason, for in that case it would not have suffered exception in the first place. So giving up the principle and discovering an exception to the principle are the same thing. When the principle suffers exception the game of reason is over.[53] The end of the principle of sufficient reason, the revelation of the absurdity of the world, comes all at once. It has the same tempo as the loss of the world in skepticism: *Presto.*

Suddenly all that we thought reasonable and justified takes on the appearance of being simply due to brute, unintelligible contingency. The light of reason becomes blind fate. *The Birth of Tragedy* assumes that confrontation with this absence of sense is terrifying, and this reaction is preserved as the "sickness that can destroy the man who has it" in the 1886 genealogy of the free spirit. But Nietzsche's first book associates Dionysus not only with this particular form of terror, but also with ecstasy.

Dionysian ecstasy. Whereas terror is induced by the appearance that the principle of sufficient reason has suffered exception, ecstasy is induced by the appearance that the principle of individuation has suffered exception. This is the experience that Nietzsche describes as feeling joined to the primordial unity [Ur-Eine] of the world, uniting all humanity and all of nature in one primordial unity:

> Now, with the gospel of universal harmony, each one feels himself not only united, reconciled, and fused with his neighbor, but as one with him, as if the veil of *maya* had been torn aside and were now merely fluttering in tatters before the mysterious primordial unity [Ur-Eine].
> (*BT* par. 1, p. 37)

Nietzsche's praise of Wagnerian music in this book rests on the thought that Wagner's music overpowers the individuality of the listener, uniting the listener with the primordial unity [Ur-eine].

> To these genuine musicians I direct the question whether they can imagine a human being who would be able to perceive the third act of *Tristan und Isolde*, without any aid of word and image, purely as a tremendous symphonic movement, without expiring in a spasmodic unharnessing of the wings of the world? Suppose a human being has thus put his ear, as it were, to the heart chamber of the world will and felt the roaring desire for existence pouring from there into all the veins of the world, as a thundering current or as the gentlest brook, dissolving into the mist—how could he fail to break suddenly? (*BT* par. 21, 126–27)

This is not death through suicide as intimated by Silenus, this is death through ecstatic union with the heart chamber of the world will. It is such passages that rely most heavily on Schopenhauer's view that music represents "*what is metaphysical*, the thing in itself" normally veiled by the principle of individuation (*BT* par. 16, p. 100).

The mature Nietzsche uncoupled Dionysian ecstasy from Dionysian terror and discarded the ecstasy.[54] Ecstasy can be understood as our acquaintance with that which "explains" the lapse in the principle of sufficient reason: the principle suffers exception because the *world in itself* is ultimately contingent, inexplicable, beyond reason's reach. Moreover this paradoxical explanation of the inexplicable can only be revealed by music:

> Language can never adequately render the cosmic symbolism of music, because music stands in a symbolic relation to the primordial contradiction and primordial pain at the heart of the primordial unity [den Urwiderspruch und Urschmerz im Herzen des Ur-Eine], and therefore symbolizes a sphere which is beyond and prior to all phenomena [über alle Erscheinung und vor aller Erscheinung]. (*BT* par. 6, p. 55)

Thus granting priority to contradiction and pain is an instance of the weakness that Nietzsche speaks about in 1886: the weakness of hiding from one's sickness by taking what was formerly considered bad, evil, apparent, and making it over into the good and the true (*HH* I P par. 3). The author of these prefaces is up to a "more perilous curiosity" than the author of the 1872 *Birth of Tragedy*: Dionysian terror without Dionysian ecstasy (*HH* I, P par. 3).

In 1886 Nietzsche set himself against "romantic pessimism" and against the romantic music of Wagner, a composer he had come to think of as a "decaying, despairing romantic" (*HH* II P par. 7, par. 3). Whereas Wagner's music had been the young Nietzsche's access to an ecstatic union with the "innermost abyss of things" (*BT* par. 21, p. 126), the author of the seven prefaces thought of this union simply as the "greedy, spongy desire" of a typical romantic.

> I began by *forbidding* myself, totally and on principle, all romantic music, that ambiguous, inflated, oppressive art that deprives the spirit of its severity and cheerfulness and lets rampant every kind of vague longing and greedy, spongy desire. (*HH* II P par. 3)

In the 1886 "Self-Criticism," *The Birth of Tragedy* is itself described as romantic: "the typical creed of the romantic of 1830, masked by the pessimism of 1850. . . . Even the usual romantic finale is sounded—break, breakdown, return and collapse before an old faith, before *the* old God" (*BT* SC par. 7). What Nietzsche is here associating with the comforting God is immediately linked to the metaphysical Ur-Eine of the world heard behind the veil of *maya* (*BT* SC par. 7). The "Self-Criticism" thus purges the Dionysian of the ecstatic union with the Ur-Eine, and restricts it to the terror of discovering an exception to the principle of sufficient reason.

This interpretation of *The Birth of Tragedy* is not shared by Henry Staten. He cites Nietzsche's description of how a purely musical *Tristan* could overpower the principle of individuation and unite us with the Ur-Eine (*BT* par. 21, 126–27), and he explicitly asserts that this very passage represents beliefs Nietzsche retained throughout his life.[55] And Staten does indeed cite descriptions of similar psychological experiences from Nietzsche's later writings (e.g., *GS* par. 337: 1882). But Nietzsche has revalued what he still calls rapture or ecstasy [Entzücken] (*GS* par. 338: 1882). The loss of one's self—a lapse in the principle of individuation—is no longer seen as our longing for unification with the Ur-Eine. It is seen as a danger and threat to Nietzsche's own virtues. So *The Gay Science* (1882) rejects precisely what *The Birth of Tragedy* (1872) yearns for, and maintains:

> I do not want to remain silent about my morality which says to me: Live in seclusion so that you can live for yourself. Live in *ignorance*

about what seems most important to your age. Between yourself and today lay the skin of at least three centuries. And the clamor of today, the noise of wars and revolutions would be a mere murmur for you. You will also wish to help—but only those whose distress you *understand* entirely because they share with you one suffering and one hope—your friends. (*GS* par. 338: 1882)[56]

Staten correctly observes that Nietzsche's work continues to stand in relation to these ecstatic experiences, and so he is correct to observe that this relation remains "proper to Nietzsche's own economy." But the mature Nietzsche has nevertheless effected a strategic reversal within that economy.

What the author of the "Attempt at a Self-Criticism" would like to do away with is, in one word, "metaphysics" (*BT* SC par. 7). This means that in the unwritten 1886 version of *The Birth* the figure of Dionysus must lose its association with ecstasy, with the musically mediated union of the self with the metaphysical ground of the world, the Ur-Eine. A Dionysus thus uncoupled from ecstatic union might have taught King Midas a wisdom wholly horrific.

Socrates and Science

Opposed to this Dionysian terror is not the Apollonian art deity, but Euripides and Socrates. "This is the new opposition: the Dionysian and the Socratic—the art of Greek tragedy was wrecked on this" (*BT* par. 12, pp. 82, 86).[57] To the Socratic type, Aeschylean and Sophoclean tragedies presented events in which the principle of sufficient reason *seemed* to suffer exception. Nietzsche tells us that Euripides looked carefully at the older tragedies, exercising all his powers of "critical thinking" (*BT* par. 11, p. 80). Euripides

observed something incommensurable in every feature and in every line, a certain deceptive distinctness and at the same time an enigmatic depth, indeed an infinitude, in the background. Even the clearest figure always had a comet's tail attached to it which seemed to suggest the uncertain [Ungewisse], that which could never be illuminated. (*BT* par. 11, p. 80)

Euripides observed that the older tragedies did not respect the principle of sufficient reason: this was the unilluminated, wine-dark vision of Dionysus. But to Euripides, this blunt contingency, this incommensurability, was a sign of failure: how dubious the solution of the ethical problems remained to him! . . . How unequal the distribution of good and bad fortune [Glück und Unglück]" (*BT* par. 11, p. 80).

Nietzsche also tells us what Socrates saw in the older tragedies with that "one great Cyclops eye" of his. This wholly rational eye saw

> something rather unreasonable, full of causes apparently without effects, and effects apparently without causes; the whole, moreover, so motley and manifold that it could not but be repugnant to a sober mind, and dangerous tinder for sensitive and susceptible souls. We know the only kind of poetry he comprehended: the Aesopian Fable. (*BT* par. 14, p. 89)

With sufficient critical investigations, the brute contingencies presented in these dangerous tragedies might either have been avoided altogether or at least corralled by a moral explanation, or—in Aesop's case—a moral moral.

Nietzsche calls this Socratic evasion of tragedy "aesthetic Socratism." Not Nietzsche's pessimism of strength, nor even Schopenhauer's pessimism of weakness, it is a form of "optimism" (*BT* par. 12, p. 83, par. 14, pp. 91–92).

> Consider the consequences of the Socratic maxims: "Virtue is knowledge [Wissen]; man sins only out of ignorance [Unwissenheit]; he who is virtuous is happy [Glückliche]." In these three basic forms of optimism lies the death of tragedy. (*BT* par. 14, p. 91)

This is optimistic because it implies that unhappiness might always have been avoided with a little more intellectual investigation. First, virtue is knowledge. Virtue consists in obedience to certain rules that can be discovered by persistent intellectual investigation. These are the criteria for being pious, just, courageous, and so forth. Second, only from ignorance of these criteria do people sin. People work themselves out of dilemmas incorrectly and they yield to short-term pleasures only because they do not fully understand what justice requires, what justice is. And in case this seems a dubious maxim, the third maxim asserts that if you do obey the rules, the criteria for being pious, just, and so forth, you will be completely happy.

Socratic optimism is the death of tragedy because it *fills the abyss* with reason, scientific reason.

> Now the virtuous hero must be a dialectician; now there must be a
> necessary, visible connection between virtue and knowledge, faith
> and morality; now the transcendental justice of Aeschylus is degraded
> to the superficial and insolent principle of "poetic justice" with its
> customary *deus ex machina.* (*BT* par. 14, p. 91)

In human society evil can sometimes prosper, but in fiction it is always
possible for evil to be punished, for poetic justice to triumph. Unhappiness accompanies injustice. With a sneer, Nietzsche writes: "now we
are supposed to feel elevated and inspired by the triumph of good and
noble principles, at the sacrifice of the hero in the interest of a moral
vision of the universe" (*BT* par. 22, p. 132).[58] For Socrates, contingency
and inexplicability are only illusions.

Socratic optimism appears in our own time as scientism: ". . . the
unshakable faith that thought, using the thread of causality, can penetrate the deepest abysses of being [die tiefsten Abgründe des Seins], and
that thought is capable not only of knowing being but even of *correcting*
it" (*BT* par. 15, p. 95). This faith structures "our whole modern world":

> It proposes as its ideal the theoretical man equipped with the greatest
> forces of knowledge, and laboring in the service of science. . . . All our
> educational methods originally have this ideal in view: every other
> form of existence must struggle on laboriously beside it [beside sci-
> ence], as something tolerated, but not intended. (*BT* par. 21, p. 110)

Nietzsche, like Heidegger[59] and like Wittgenstein,[60] set himself
against the Socratic optimism of the scientist. His view was that after
2,000 years the limits of Socratic optimism were being reached, and that
now the time was ripe for a rebirth of tragedy at the hands of a musical
Socrates who understood the limits of science, the limits of logos. A
musical Socrates might reflect:

> Perhaps . . . what is not intelligible to me is not necessarily unintelli-
> gent? Perhaps there is a realm of wisdom from which the logician is
> exiled? Perhaps art is even a necessary correlative of, and supplement
> for, science? (*BT* par. 14, p. 93; see par. 15, p. 98)

Nietzsche thought that the scientific culture of his day was already
reaching its limits, and this in two ways: "[a] once by fear of its own consequences which it at length begins to surmise and [b] again because it

no longer has its former naïve confidence in the eternal validity of its foundation" (*BT* par. 18, p. 113).

(a) Nietzsche discerns a "disaster slumbering in the womb" of that culture he refers to equally as Socratic, Alexandrian, Theoretical, Scientific, and Modern (*BT* par. 18, p. 112). But whereas we would likely think of military or ecological disaster, Nietzsche discerned a political disaster caused by the fact that Socratic culture "requires a slave class" (*BT* par. 18, p. 111). He does not demonstrate why a Socratic culture requires a slave class, so we are on our own. A Socratic culture will place those who have been educated, those who know, in positions of power. But the decisions of those who know will be implemented by those who do not know, but only obey. Such a culture is headed for disaster because the fact of a slave class is destined to collide with the rhetoric of the "dignity of man" (*BT* par. 18, p. 111). Nietzsche predicts that this collision may incite the slave class to conjure up a "Euripidean *deus ex machina*" (*BT* par. 18, p. 111). Possibly Nietzsche was predicting that Socratic cultures would turn to dictators promising to solve all the problems of the slave class at one stroke, with one final solution.

(b) More directly, the limits of scientific culture are being discovered by the practice of science itself.

> Great men, universally gifted, have contrived with an incredible amount of thought, to make use of the paraphernalia of science itself, to point out the limits and the relativity of knowledge generally [überhaupt]. (*BT* par. 18, p. 112)

Nietzsche acknowledges Kant's discovery that the "thread of causality"—far from penetrating the "deepest abysses of being" (*BT* par. 15, p. 95)—is only able to reveal the structure of appearance, not things as they are in themselves (*BT* par. 18, p. 112).

Consider the physiology of sensation.[61] If scientific investigations of perception reveal that the same perception might be caused by a variety of different stimulations, then we can begin to doubt our perceptions, generally [überhaupt]. But if we are doubting our perceptions for these nonlocal reasons, there will be no way to keep these doubts from infecting our understanding of perception itself and so, the very basis of science. These grounds for doubt do not concern local matters—like the bad lighting here or that I am jaundiced—they concern the general structure of our perceptual systems, so we will not be able to corral the doubt. And the doubt threatens to consume even the knowledge of our perceptual systems that was the ground of this doubt in the first place. Therewith the optimism of science disappears. Nietzsche:

> Science . . . speeds irresistibly toward its limits where its optimism, concealed in the essence of its logic, suffers shipwreck. For the periphery of the circle of science has an infinite number of points; and while there is no telling how this circle could ever be surveyed completely, noble and gifted men nevertheless reach, ere half their time and inevitably, such boundary points on the periphery from which one gazes into what defies illumination. When they see to their horror [Schrecken] how logic coils up at these boundaries [Grenzen] and finally bites its own tail—suddenly the new form of knowledge [Erkenntniss] breaks through, *tragic knowledge* which, merely to be endured, needs art as a protection and remedy. (*BT* par. 15, p. 98)

In this way, the Socratic attempt to fill in the Dionysian abyss, finally opens it up again, thus revealing Nietzsche as a "philosopher of tragic knowledge" (*P* par. 37). And with the reopening of the Dionysian abyss the terror returns, terror at the thought that the principle of sufficient reason has suffered an exception. The sickness of nihilism can be slowed by Socratic cultures, but in the end, Socratic culture serves only to increase the virulence of nihilism. In this way *The Birth of Tragedy* maps the etiology of that sickness which is one stage in the genealogy of the free spirit Nietzsche articulated in the 1886 prefaces. It also presents a form of the goal of the convalescence: the great health.

(4) Tragedy 1872 and Tragedy 1886

In one of its uses, "tragedy" names the contingency, the inexplicability, which Nietzsche associates with Dionysian terror. Tragedy, the theatrical genre, is something else. As Nietzsche conceives it, Attic tragedy is the child of the "fraternal union" [Bruderbund] of two male art deities: Apollo and Dionysus (*BT* par. 21, p. 130; par. 22, p. 132; par. 24, p. 139).[62] Dionysus has been associated with what is dreadful, deep, and wine-dark, Apollo is associated with a sunlight that redeems the nihilistic vision of existence presented by Silenus. A similar healing role was granted to sunshine in the 1886 genealogy of the free spirit, but Nietzsche figures the redemptive power of light differently in 1872:

> When after a forceful attempt to gaze on the sun we turn away blinded, we see dark<del>Copyrighted Material</del>our eyes, as a cure, as it

> were. Conversely, the bright image projections of the Sophoclean
> hero—in short, the Apollonian aspect of the mask—are necessary
> effects of a glance into the inside and terrors [Schreckliche] of nature;
> as it were, luminous spots to cure eyes damaged by the gruesome
> night. (*BT* par. 9, p. 67)

Attic tragedy—in particular its Apollonian ingredients—provided just
such a cure for the terrifying, dark wisdom proclaimed by Dionysus's
friend Silenus.

Apollo embodies the "joyous necessity [freudige Nothwendigkeit]
of the dream experience" (*BT* par. 1, p. 35). Nietzsche is thinking of
what are called lucid dreams, dreams that the dreamer realizes are
dreams, even while dreaming:

> And perhaps many will, like myself, recall how amid the dangers and
> terrors [Gefährlichkeiten und Schrecken] of dreams they have occa-
> sionally said to themselves in self-encouragement, and not without
> success: "It is a dream! I will dream on!" (*BT* par. 1, p. 35)

Apollo embodies the experience of knowing that one's experiences are
not metaphysically real, and—perhaps for that very reason—still wanting them to continue. This is one way to move beyond the cooler into
the warmer phase of convalescence: recognizing the metaphysical fragility of the things nearest and nevertheless enjoying their bloom and
magic [Flaum und Zauber] (*HH* P par. 5). As if further to cement this
connection, Nietzsche describes the Apollonian experience as one in
which "we delight in the immediate understanding of figures; all forms
speak to us; there is nothing unimportant or superfluous" (*BT* par. 1, p.
34). Precisely this is required to "make life possible and worth living"
(*BT* par. 1, p. 35).

The Birth of Tragedy describes a number of ways the "Apollonian
aspect of the mask" (*BT* par. 9, 67) can overcome the bleak "wisdom of
Silenus" (*BT* par. 24, p. 140). The Homeric epics save us from the suicide
of the nihilist because they tell the stories of Gods whose lives are as
insecure as ours, but infinitely more beautiful (*BT* par. 3, pp. 42–44). We
can continue to live because we try to imitate the beautiful lives of the
Homeric Gods. The effect of this Apollonian art is to mask the terror of
existence behind the superficial beauty of the stories. The case of Attic
tragedy is different; it is both Dionysian and Apollonian, *both profound
and superficial.*[63] Without hiding the terrifying Dionysian abyss behind

beautiful illusions, Attic tragedy nevertheless "makes life possible and worth living" (*BT* par. 1, p. 35). But there are two stories to tell about the redemptive power of tragedy. One told by the *The Birth of Tragedy* (1872) and the other told by the unwritten version of that book suggested by the "Self-Criticism" and the other writings of 1886 once intended for *Seven Prefaces*.

Tragedy 1872. The original story speaks of the "metaphysical comfort—with which . . . every true tragedy leaves us—that life is at the bottom of things, and despite the changes of appearance, indestructibly powerful and pleasurable" (*BT* par. 7, p. 59).This metaphysical comfort is the fraternal child of two art deities: it opens our ears to the wildest Dionysian ecstasy, and at the same time opens our eyes to the Apollonian joy and beauty of life itself. The fluid dynamics of the redemption of the world are these. A first phase—where we accept the principles of sufficient reason and of individuation—is disrupted by viewing the dramatic tragedy. We experience the terror, the horror and absurdity of existence (*BT* par. 3, p. 42; par. 7, p. 60). We see the tragic hero cracked open and destroyed, for no reason. This provides the terrifying recognition that the principle of sufficient reason has suffered an exception, but this despair has a surprisingly redemptive consequence. Through this crack we can hear the "innermost abyss of things": the Ur-Eine (*BT* par. 21, p. 126). This is the ecstatic recognition that the principle of individuation is merely apparent, and this will prove redemptive.

We see that the hero we had thought to be an individual is in fact the creation of something infinitely more powerful: the primordial unity. The hero is part of this profound unity [Ur-Eine]. In fact, the hero is not even the creation of the human artist except insofar as that artist is a medium of the "primordial artist of the world." (*BT* par. 5, p. 52). But since the hero was cracked open for no reason, we spectators are revealed—surprisingly enough—to have just as much connection with the power and glory of this profound unity [Ur-Eine] as does the tragic hero. We too are, as individuals, "merely images and artistic projections for the true author [i.e., the Ur-Eine], and we have our highest dignity in our significance as works of art" (*BT* par. 5, p. 52).[64]

In this way, our recognition that all individuals are merely apparent, only projections of a powerful unity we share with the tragic hero, gives us the courage and the drive to continue living. The model for redemption here seems to be the strange combination of pain and pleasure associated with enjoying sex:

> The Dionysian revelers remind us—as medicines remind us of deadly poisons—of the phenomenon that pain begets joy, that ecstasy [der Jubel der Brust] may wring sounds of agony from us. At the very climax of joy there sounds a cry of horror or a yearning lamentation for an irretrievable loss. (*BT* par. 2, p. 40)

The pain that mixes with joy is the pain that attends the loss of our individuality, the pain of unification. Later in the book, Nietzsche returns to this point:

> We are pierced by the maddening sting of these pains just when we have become, as it were, one with the infinite primordial joy in existence [Urlust am Dasein] and when we anticipate, in Dionysian ecstasy [Entzückung], the indestructibility and eternity of this joy. In spite of fear and pity, we are the happy living beings, not as individuals, but as *one* living being, with whose creative joy we are united. (*BT* par. 17, pp. 104–5)[65]

This original 1872 story gives a central role to the ecstatic union of both hero and spectator with the Ur-Eine. And by figuring this primordial unity as a creator—indeed as the "primordial artist [Urkünstler] of the world" (*BT* par. 5, p. 52)—there is every reason to agree with Nietzsche's self-criticism of 1886 that this first book—by reason of its appeal to "metaphysical comfort"—is as much Romantic as it is, perhaps because it is, Christian (*BT* SC par. 7, p. 24).

The final result is to be the realization that the world of appearance—although it is appearance—is redeemed as the artwork of the primordial unity/artist of the world. The details of appearance are revealed not to be merely contingent but to be fully necessary. In this Apollonian vision "there is nothing unimportant or superfluous" [es giebt nichts Gleichgültiges und Unnöthiges] (*BT* par. 1, p. 34).

Tragedy 1886. Nietzsche did turn away from the picture of tragedy presented in the 1872 edition of *The Birth of Tragedy*. He turned away from the use of a "primordial unity" (*BT* par. 1, 4, 6, pp. 37, 45, 55) as a "metaphysical comfort" (*BT* par. 7, 18, pp. 59, 109, 113 and *BT* SC par. 7, p. 26). He turned away from that particular solution to the existential question of how to "make life possible and worth living" (*BT* par. 1, p. 35). But there is much that he retained.

He retained his existential conception of tragedy, his thought that tragedy was an answer to an existential need: the need to make life livable, acceptable, endurable, meaningful. And he retained a conception of what the goal was. The goal is to be able to say "It is a dream! I will dream on!" (*BT* par. 1, 4, pp. 35, 44). The Apollonian goal remains to be able to conceive the world we inhabit as one in which "there is nothing unimportant or superfluous" (*BT* par. 1, p. 35). In his later writings this comes to be the doctrine of the love of fate, or in the Italian Nietzsche preferred: "*amor fati*: that one wants nothing to be different, not forward, not backward, not in all eternity. Not merely to bear what is necessary, still less to conceal it . . . but *love* it" (*EH* II.10, p. 258).

What has changed by 1886 is not the existential problem to which tragedy is an answer, nor is it the goal that tragic wisdom is to achieve. What changes is the machinery that Nietzsche calls in to explain the redemptive work of tragedy. In 1872, something (beyond reason) supports and saves us. By 1886, it is the very absence of anything supporting us that saves us; nothing itself is our salvation.

In the 1886 "Self-Criticism" Nietzsche discussed the necessity of "metaphysical comfort" (*BT* par. 7, par. 18) quite critically, and shouted:

> No! you ought to learn the art of *this-worldly* [*diesseitigen*] comfort first; you ought to learn to laugh, my young friends, if you are hell-bent on remaining pessimists. Then perhaps, as laughers, you may some day dispatch all metaphysical comforts to the devil—metaphysics in front. (*BT* SC par. 7)

The comfort is not to be metaphysical. It is not to come from the Ur-Eine. But the comfort will still be artistic. It will be an art of the things of this world, the nearest things (*HH* II WS par. 5, 6, and 51): "An anti-metaphysical view of the world—yes, but an artistic one" (*WP* par. 1048: 1885–86).

The last two sections of the 1886 preface to *The Gay Science* were important enough to be reprinted (with slight changes) as an epilogue to *Nietzsche Contra Wagner*, which Nietzsche finished in January 1889. They describe the convalescence from the sickness of nihilism, a sickness and pain that, while it doesn't make us better, does make us "more profound" [er uns *vertieft*] (*GS* P. par. 3; *NCW* X par. 1). From this

Dionysian depth one is born anew into a second childhood with a "more delicate taste for joy, with a tenderer tongue for all good things, with merrier senses" (*GS* P par. 4; *NCW* X par. 2). But still with a need for art: "If we convalescents still need art, it is an *other* art—a mocking, light, fleeting, divinely untroubled, divinely artificial art" (*GS* P par. 4; *NCW* X par. 2). This will be an art that is "too experienced, too serious, too merry, too burned, too *profound*" to live by the maxim "'truth at any price'" (*GS* P par. 4; *NCW* X par. 2).

This is what makes Nietzsche a "philosopher of tragic knowledge."[66] In notes written in 1872 for a never completed book sometimes referred to as "The Philosopher" or "The Last Philosopher," Nietzsche wrote that the (Socratic) "philosopher of *desperate knowledge* will be absorbed in blind science: knowledge at any price" (*P* par. 37; *KSA* 7.428). In contrast, the philosopher of tragic knowledge understands that "when carried to its limits the knowledge drive turns against itself in order to proceed to the *critique of knowing*" (*P* par. 37; see *BT* par. 15, p. 98, par. 18, p. 112). Nietzsche is a philosopher of tragic knowledge, because he realizes that human knowledge can have no metaphysical ground: "moira [(fate) is] enthroned inexorably over all knowledge" (*BT* par. 3, p. 42; see *P* par. 37). This is the Dionysian wisdom that Nietzsche retained into his maturity. Combined with an Apollonian acceptance of the joyous necessity of all things this becomes a new vision of tragedy, a new solution to the big question mark concerning the value of existence:

> Oh, those Greeks! They knew how to live. What is required for that is to stop courageously at the surface, the fold, the skin,[67] to adore appearance, to believe in forms, tones, words, in the whole Olympus of appearance. Those Greeks were superficial—*out of profundity*. And is not this precisely what we are again coming back to, we daredevils of the spirit who have climbed the highest and most dangerous peak of present thought and looked around from up there—we who have looked *down* from there? Are we not, precisely in this respect, Greeks? Adorers of forms, of tones, of words? And therefore—*artists*? (*GS* P par. 4)

The adorers of forms, of tones, of words[68] are neighbors to what is near; now they are cured of the sickness of nihilism. That cure manifests itself in their recognition that reason has limits, a recognition that can terrify. The profundity spoken of in this passage is the discovery of the final groundlessness of our reasonings. Those who have recovered are no longer terrified of this discovery, they have the courage to stop at the surface, to love what was formerly scorned as mere appearance. The philosopher of tragic knowledge discovers that the ground of metaphysics has been withdrawn and so he cultivates a new life, the great health of a life neighbor to the things that are nearest (*P* par. 37: 1872).

"*Superficial—out of profundity*" is the center of Nietzsche's new vision of tragedy (*GS* P, par. 4). It has the appearance of paradox, but fortunately it is a paradox we have already mastered. The magical bloom of the things that are nearest requires that we care about the little things that are nearest. This requires the Dionysian insight that these nearest things have no metaphysical support, and so become precious. The great health is superficial out of profundity; it is equally Dionysian and Apollonian. Initiated into the terrifying wisdom of Silenus that fate is installed over all knowledge, that there are no metaphysical supports for our deepest commitments, we discover that the things nearest have become more fragile, more wonderful: precious.

The great health is a manifestation of Nietzsche's most mature reflections on tragedy. Were there any doubt that those enjoying great health would be tragic artists, that doubt would be stilled by the penultimate paragraph of the new edition of *The Gay Science*. That paragraph is called "The great health," and Nietzsche completes it with these words: "the tragedy *begins*" (*GS* par. 382: 1887).[69] Free spirits enjoy the great health when they muster the courage for a tragic acceptance of the value of the delicate and precious things that are nearest. This unites the figure of great health with Sophocles' portrait of blind Oedipus wandering with Antigone, a portrait of the love of fate, great health. The wanderer says to his shadow:

> My daughter—daughter of the blind old man—
> Where, I wonder, have we come to now?
> What place is this, Antigone? What people?
> Who will be kind to Oedipus this evening
> And give the wanderer charity?
> Though he ask for little and receive still less,
> It is sufficient:
>   Suffering and time,
> Vast time, have been instructors in contentment.[70]

Nietzsche is a philosopher of tragic knowledge.

(5) Coda: A Nietzschean Wittgenstein

The Birth of Tragedy is a puzzle. It was Nietzsche's first and most meta-physically tainted production, but Nietzsche refused to let it go. This puzzle solves itself in the light of the *Seven Prefaces*. The *Seven Prefaces* of 1886 provide insight into the central problem of *The Birth of Tragedy*: the value of existence. Those prefaces describe the sickness of nihilism and its slow convalescence resting finally in the great health, the accep-tance of the value of this world, the earth, of the little things that are nearest to us. The great health is lived as a neighbor to precisely the things that the metaphysical tradition only found valuable as indicators of another metaphysical world.

The opposition to metaphysics in the 1886 prefaces is at its most insistent in the "Self-Criticism" that reintroduces *The Birth of Tragedy*. I have simply followed the natural interpretive strategy of reading the metaphysics—the metaphysical ecstasy—out of that book. This permits the discovery that the mature Nietzsche's category of the great health is a form of tragic knowledge: superficial—out of profundity. Profound: what is important to us cannot be freed from its exposure to tragedy, to disaster. Superficial: the redemptive power of tragedy is that to discover the precariousness of our caring is at the same time to discover the pre-ciousness—the paper-thin surface—of what we care about, its fragility: its wonder.

The Birth of Tragedy teaches us that what is most important resists grounding. It resists the grounding of metaphysics and—even more—the grounding of science. What we care about is beyond grounding's grasp. But this depressing discovery can be redeemed (see *TI* vi, par. 8). That is the lesson of tragic knowledge. Nietzsche's hope, the hope of all convalescents recovering from the sickness he called nihilism, is to redeem the things of this world (*BT* SC par. 7), to learn to neighbor the things that are nearest. Like Wittgenstein, he does not aspire to invent a theory. What Nietzsche and Wittgenstein both aspire to is "peace on earth."[71]

The rest of this book relies on this chapter's reading of the two Nietzsches to provide an interpretation of the two Wittgensteins. Chap-ter 2 is entirely devoted to Wittgenstein's first book, the *Tractatus*. I will argue that the existential dimensions of that book are illuminated by the existential dimensions of the 1872 *Birth*. In chapter 3, I will chart Witt-genstein's own rise to the surface from the unspeakable depths of the

Tractatus. Chapters 4 and 5 are a pair. In chapter 4, I provide an account of Wittgenstein's superficial approach to linguistic meaning and, in chapter 5, his superficial approach to existential meaning. On my account the goal of Wittgenstein's approach to both linguistic and existential meaning is to awaken us to wonder.[72]

Chapter 2

The Sublime Scaffolding of Logic and Life: Wittgenstein's Tractatus

Whenever I have time I now read James' "Varieties of religious exp[erience]." This book does me a lot of good. I don't mean to say that I will be a saint soon, but I am not sure that it does not improve me a little in a way in which I would like to improve very much: namely I think that it helps me to get rid of the Sorge (in the sense in which Goethe used the word in the 2nd part of Faust) . . .

Logic must turn out to be of a TOTALLY different kind than any other science.

—Wittgenstein to Russell, June 22, 1912; R.2

Now I am afraid you haven't really got hold of my main contention, to which the whole business of logical props is only a corollary. The main point is the theory of what can be expressed (gesagt) by props—i.e., by language—(and, which comes to the same, what can be thought) and what can not be expressed by props, but only shown (gezeigt); which, I believe, is the cardinal problem of philosophy.

—Wittgenstein to Russell, August 19, 1919; R.37

(1) Nietzsche and Wittgenstein

Nietzsche's suggestion that fate is "enthroned inexorably over all knowledge" is his way of marking the fact that our epistemic practices are not fully rational and could not even be reformed so as to have a fully rational foundation (*BT* par. 3, p. 42). The fact that our epistemic practices take the form that they do is a manifestation of brute contingency: the limits of reason. Nietzsche correctly saw this tragic conception of knowledge in opposition to the scientific conception he associated with Socrates.

The previous chapter marked a difference between the ways Nietzsche expressed the limitations of science in the first edition of *The Birth of Tragedy* (1872) and the way he recast these limitations in the *Seven Prefaces* (1886). Nietzsche's first expression of the limits of reason was in terms of the Ur-Eine, the metaphysical essence of the world. The Ur-Eine transformed the absence of rational grounding into the presence of a grounding beyond reason. The dejection that originally attends discovering the contingency of reason can then be surmounted in the ecstatic realization that we too are rooted in the power of this Ur-Eine. Nietzsche's second expression of the limits of reason was not so metaphysical. Dejection was no longer to be overcome through ecstatic union with what transcends the principle of individuation. Rather, for those with the courage to live without metaphysics, the discovery that what we care about has no rational foundation is, at the same time, the discovery that what we care about is precious, wonderful.

In the remaining chapters, I will retrace this Nietzschean development from an unthinkable metaphysical to an antimetaphysical way to peace. Although there is no question that Wittgenstein (1889–1951) read Nietzsche,[1] I will not defend the historical suggestion—almost certainly false—that the arc of Wittgenstein's philosophy is actually rooted in his reading of Nietzsche. All that I claim is that the arc of Wittgenstein's philosophy is congruent with the arc of Nietzsche's. Nor am I the first to make this connection. In 1959 Erich Heller observed, "The break between the *Tractatus* and *Philosophical Investigations* is of the same kind as that between Nietzsche's *The Birth of Tragedy* (1872) and *Human, All-Too-Human* (1879)."[2] From the same place, these two unphilosophical philosophers set out in the same direction. Both write in response to the rise of what Nietzsche called nihilism and what Wittgenstein called "the darkness of this time" (*PI* preface). Both write with the hope of finding that life has meaning, the hope of finding a way to continue with existence even after learning the dark wisdom of Silenus that the practices of reason and science have no rational or scientific basis (*TLP* 6.3's, 6.5's). Both Nietzsche and Wittgenstein speak of their goal as "peace."[3]

Wittgenstein's philosophy is frequently divided into two periods[4] that precipitated as the two books on which my own interpretation will center: *Tractatus Logico-Philosophicus* (completed 1918)[5] and *Philosophical Investigations* (completed 1945, 1949).[6] There is a world of difference between these two books, but in both of the central phases of his philosophical development, Wittgenstein's thinking traces the same Nietzschean arc—from dejection to peace. The two phases of his development follow this arc in roughly the ways represented by *The Birth of Tragedy* (1872) and the *Seven Prefaces* (1886). The *Tractatus* attained peace through the recognition that there was something beyond what could be said—not exactly the Ur-Eine, but still a nonaccidental something/nothing that exceeds rational discourse. On the other hand, the *Investigations* achieves peace, not by reaching beyond sense, but rather by accepting the groundless, accidental features of what does and does not make sense. This would be peace achieved not by opening our eyes to what is beyond but by receiving the details of what is near.

(2) Placing the *Tractatus*

Although the metaphysics of Wittgenstein's *Logisch-Philosophische Abhandlung* (1921) shows points of similarity with what others have thought, there may be no other "logico-philosophical treatise" like it. In many places it seems to be a work of what is called philosophical logic— articulating the foundations of reference, truth, meaning, and so on. But when the first translators suggested that the English translation be called "Philosophic Logic,"[7] Wittgenstein wrote back:

> "Philosophic Logic" is all wrong. In fact I don't know what it means! There is no such thing as philosophic logic. (Unless one says that as the whole book is nonsense the title might as well be nonsense too.)[8]

This book is unlike any other work of philosophical logic because its author thinks that it is nonsense. Unlike Plato's analogies and allegories, this book does not bend language to indicate ideas that language cannot house. According to this book the limits of language *are* the limits of thought, so there is no thinkable realm for poetic language to point out (see *TLP* 5.61). It is true that Wittgenstein distinguishes the propositions of logic, which are senseless (sinnlos), from what is nothing but gibberish, nonsense (Unsinn), but in fact this only makes matters worse (*TLP* 4.461–4.4611). For if I knew that the author of a book that made such a distinction believed the book to be nonsense, I would unhesitatingly predict that the book's lack of sense would be of the softer, not yet gibberish sort. Wittgenstein said his book was gibberish (unsinnig) (*TLP* 6.54).

No wonder the philosophical reception of this book has been unstable. It is not clear that there is anything at all to receive. Brand Blanshard is reported as saying that "Wittgenstein . . . has the strange distinction of having produced a work on logic beside which the *Logic* of Hegel is luminously intelligible."[9] In 1923, the logician C. I. Lewis wrote to a colleague, "Have you looked at Wittgenstein's new book yet? I am much discouraged by Russell's foolishness in writing the introduction to such nonsense. I fear it will be looked upon as what symbolic logic leads to. If so, it will be the death of the subject."[10] Even now, there is no received view of the relation between the early Wittgenstein of the *Tractatus* and the later Wittgenstein of the *Investigations*, and surely one contributing factor here is that the *Tractatus* itself declares that it has no meaningful content at all. I will begin my approach to the *Tractatus* by distinguishing four phases in the history of its philosophical reception.

Phase 1: Positivism and the Centrality of Epistemology

Wittgenstein found his first readers in the Vienna Circle, the members of which invented "Logical Positivism." Gustav Bergmann, himself a member of the Vienna Circle, was well aware of the differences that separated the members of the circle, but having forced himself to characterize four theses that all Logical Positivists would have endorsed, he notes that

> these four points[11] can all be found in the *Tractatus*; two of them . . . state, no matter how inadequately, Wittgenstein's decisive contribution, the "new turn" by which Logical Positivism distinguishes itself from the earlier empiricist philosophies.[12]

Bergmann credits Wittgenstein with inciting both the rejection of metaphysics as nonsense and with conceiving logical truths as tautologies, hence also with the solution to an old empiricist quandary: how to continue to believe that the propositions of logic were necessary without conceding that humans possess mysterious nonempirical modes of access to secret realms of necessity. The Vienna Circle read the *Tractatus* together, line by line,[13] and this gave its members the courage to distinguish the sheer senselessness (Sinnlosigkeit) of logical propositions from the impenetrable nonsense (Unsinnigkeit) of traditional metaphysics.

As it happens, another member of the Vienna Circle, Rudolf Carnap, isolated exactly the same two theses as the main contributions of the *Tractatus* to his own philosophical development.[14] But Carnap also noticed a deep divergence of philosophical attitude between the Circle and Wittgenstein. Carnap recalls:

> There was a striking difference between Wittgenstein's attitude toward philosophical problems and that of Schlick [founder of the Circle] and myself. Our attitude toward philosophical problems was not very different from that which scientists have toward their problems . . . [whereas] I sometimes had the impression that the deliberately rational and unemotional attitude of the scientist and likewise any ideas which had the flavor of "enlightenment" were repugnant to Wittgenstein. . . . Earlier, when we were reading Wittgenstein's book in the Circle . . . I had not paid sufficient attention to the statements in his book about the mystical, because his feelings and thoughts in this area were too divergent from mine. Only personal contact with him helped me to see more clearly his attitude at this point.[15]

The Circle did not share and did not respect the mystical conclusion of the *Tractatus*. Later in Wittgenstein's life, his student and future translator, G. E. M. Anscombe, reminded him that he was rumored to have a mystical streak: "'Like a yellow streak,' he replied; and [Anscombe comments] that is pretty well how the Vienna Circle felt about certain things in *Tractatus*."[16]

If Wittgenstein did not share the Circle's distaste for the mystical, neither did he share their relish for reconstructing science on sound empiricist foundations. The Vienna Circle interpreted the *Tractatus* as a work in foundational epistemology. They read it as outlining how to reconstruct science on the basis of elementary propositions that characterized the observational core of experience.[17] This was not Wittgenstein's problem.

Phase 2: Frege and the Centrality of Logic

The second phase can be dated to the late 1950s and represents the first serious study of the *Tractatus*, not for the tools it could provide for positivism, but "for its own sake."[18] Where the first phase placed the *Tractatus* in the domain of the theory of knowledge and spurned the mystical dimension of the book, the second phase placed that book in the domain of Frege's philosophical logic and acknowledged the mysticism of the *Tractatus*.

The works of Anscombe (1959)[19] and Stenius (1960)[20] launched, and those of Black (1964)[21] and others[22] continued, a new style of interpretation that did not, as they might have put it, force the *Tractatus* into an epistemological frame (*TLP* 4.1121). On this new account, the true sources of Wittgenstein's problems were not the quandaries of Hume's empiricism, but the entirely nonepistemological concerns of Frege. Anscombe explains her approach:

> I devote a good deal of space to Frege in this book for the following reason: Wittgenstein's *Tractatus* has captured the interest and excited the admiration of many, yet almost all that has been published about it has been wildly irrelevant. If this has had any one cause, that cause has been the neglect of Frege and the new direction that he gave to philosophy. . . . [E]mpiricist or idealist preconceptions, such as have been most common in philosophy for a long time, are a thorough impediment to the understanding of either Frege or the *Tractatus*.[23]

One vivid difference between the first two phases of the reception is that the elementary propositions of the *Tractatus*, which the Vienna Circle tended to think of as observation sentences, were now conceived as the fundamental logical units of sense—whether observational or not. Wittgenstein was not concerned with the specific nature of the basic units of sense, but only with the fact that there *must* be such units (see *TLP* 5.555).

In this phase, the mysticism of the *Tractatus* was recognized to be an integral part of that book. At this time, the fundamentally Kantian problematic of the *Tractatus* was recognized, and Stenius demonstrated how this Kantian problematic might make sense of some of the obscurities of Wittgenstein's mysticism.[24] This division between two phases of the reception of the *Tractatus* is not original with me.[25] Nor indeed should we be surprised that the sober historical investigation of that book arrived sometime after its initial impact.

Phase 3: The Centrality of Ethics

The distinction between the second and third phases of the reception of the *Tractatus* consists only in the degree to which the text of that book is contextualized. The second phase initiated an attempt to understand this book for its own sake, and rooted it both in the logical doctrines of Frege and also in a generic Kantianism made relevant by Wittgenstein's early fondness for Schopenhauer. The third phase situates Wittgenstein's work more robustly in the cultural and intellectual climate of turn-of-the-century Vienna. This phase was incited by the letters Wittgenstein wrote to the architect Paul Engelmann, which were published in 1967 together with Engelmann's recollection of their friendship.[26] Immediate support for Engelmann's broadly ethical interpretation of the *Tractatus* was provided by the publication in 1969 of Wittgenstein's own characterizations of the *Tractatus* in letters to Ludwig von Ficker, the publisher of the literary and cultural journal *Der Brenner*.[27] Wittgenstein was trying to get his book published in von Ficker's journal. He did not quite succeed.

This phase does not disregard the mystical vision of value in the *Tractatus* as the first readers had done, nor does it simply acknowledge its position in a book primarily inspired by the logical discoveries of Frege. In this third phase, the ethical dimension of the *Tractatus* comes to the center. Wittgenstein had indeed written to von Ficker, "the point [Sinn] of the book is ethical."[28] And he explained why he had devoted so much space to logical concerns:

> For the Ethical is delimited from within, as it were, by my book; and I'm convinced that, *strictly* speaking, it can ONLY be delimited in this way. In brief, I think: All of that which *many* are *babbling* [*schwefeln*] today, I have defined in my book by remaining silent about it [ich daruber schweige].[29]

This can be explained with an analogy between speaking about ethics and drawing a chair. Many of us feel we cannot draw the world as we see it. When we sit down to draw even an object as simple as a chair, the result appears to have come out of *The Cabinet of Dr. Caligari*. Often our drawings would come out better if we simply tried to draw the shadows cast by the chair and on the chair. Similarly, many people are unable to read poetry without putting on their this-is-oh-so-so-serious tone of voice, when it might be better if they simply read the words and let the profondeur take care of itself. By clearly marking the domains of sense, Wittgenstein had defined the limits of the inexpressible domain of the ethical. This is what he means by "delimiting the ethical from within": delimiting the inexpressible by defining the expressible.

Only at this phase in the reception of the *Tractatus* did it become clear that it tracked the same arc as Nietzsche's philosophy: from dejection to peace. Although there were anticipations of this new phase of interpretation in the late 1950s,[30] this approach was first pursued at book length in Janik and Toulmin's *Wittgenstein's Vienna* (1973).[31] This book cemented the ethical conclusion to the center of Wittgenstein's book. But in spite of its many advances, this approach to the *Tractatus* is marred by its over-marginalization of the logical themes that had been brought out in the second phase of the reception of this book.[32]

Phase 4: Ethics and Logic—The "Swansea School"

The fourth phase of the reception can be construed as unifying the second phase's focus on logic and the third phase's focus on ethics. Work on Wittgenstein conducted by von Wright, Rhees, and those of the "Swansea School" influenced by Rhees unites a respect for the ethical point [Sinn] of the *Tractatus* with a detailed knowledge of the labyrinthine logical preface to the mystical conclusion of the book.[33] This phase of the reception of Wittgenstein's first book promises not to overlook its Fregean roots, while yet admiring its ethical and existential foliage. Fogelin epitomized this phase in an aperçu: "If the task of the *Tractatus* is to reveal the foundations of the Tower of Babel, its point is to show the insignificance of that structure."[34] The point of the *Tractatus* is to escape what Wittgenstein called care, equally existential and logical care (*L* R.2).

My own approach to the *Tractatus* is in the spirit of this fourth phase of its reception, but I will emphasize a feature of that book that is not yet widely recognized: its irony. Remember, this book is convinced that its own propositions are nonsense. And if we ask how one might trope one's assertion of propositions one thought to be without meaning, the answer might easily return: ironically. In 1949 Wittgenstein accepted C. D. Broad's remark that the *Tractatus* was

> highly syncopated. Every sentence in the *Tractatus* should be seen as the heading of chapter, needing further exposition. My present style is quite different; I am trying to avoid that error.[35]

And while syncopation is not irony, they are, let us say, cousins. For where irony keeps two conflicting meanings in the air, syncopation keeps two conflicting rhythms together aloft. So there is some support for the hypothesis that Wittgenstein himself might have agreed in characterizing the predominant *Tractarian* trope as irony.

Wittgenstein's official biographer, Brian McGuinness, is almost alone in recognizing that irony is a dominant mode of address in the *Tractatus*.[36] In the first paragraph of the preface, Wittgenstein asserts of the book to follow: "It is not a textbook" (*TLP* preface). McGuinness remarks, "It is a . . . rather characteristic piece of irony that the book is in fact written and arranged like a textbook."[37] The irony has become comic by the time we read proposition 4.112 (the second comment on proposition 4.11, which is the first comment on proposition 4.1, which, in turn, is the first comment on the fourth numbered proposition of the work as a whole): "Philosophy does not result in 'philosophical propositions.'" It is ironic when such a fiendishly and hierarchically numbered book as the *Tractatus* asserts at number 5.553: "There is no preeminent number."[38] The *Tractatus* is turning ironic again when Russell and Whitehead's *Principia Mathematica* (which also proceeds by numbered propositions) is taken to task for using words—not simply logical symbols—in definitions and primitive propositions: the numbered propositions of the *Tractatus* are almost entirely written in words (*TLP* 5.452). And there could be no cleaner expression of this stylistic tendency of the *Tractatus* than the riddle in number 6.5: "*The riddle* does not exist."[39]

These are ironic, self-effacing moments, but in fact the entire book is ironic. The book presents a description of the way language is connected with the world that is carefully constructed so that we may come to see that there can be no such description of the way language is connected with the world. Hence we must be alert to the irony with which that description is presented, else—as McGuinness points out[40]—we will find the final reflections incongruous and unmotivated. The last two propositions of the *Tractatus* are these:

6.54   My Propositions serve as elucidations in the following way: anyone who understands me eventually recognizes them as nonsensical [unsinnig], when he has used them—as steps— to climb up beyond them. (He must, so to speak, throw away the ladder after he has climbed up it.)

He must transcend these propositions, and then he will see the world aright.

7   Whereof one cannot speak, thereof one must be silent.[41]

Here the *Tractatus* itself ends, evaporates, or better, *sublimes*, in the sense of the verb *to sublime*, which means to change from solid to gas—

but miraculously, uncannily—without passing through the liquid phase.

This chapter works to bring the irony of the *Tractatus* more completely into the center of the fourth phase of its reception, which is already distinctive in uniting the ethical or mystical sense of that book with the logical face that first greets its readers. G. E. Moore suggested that the translation of the *Logisch-Philosophische Abhandlung* might be titled with an eye on Spinoza's "Tractatus Theologico-Politicus."[42] My interpretation can be construed as a defense of an even more famous title of Spinoza's: "Ethica Ordine Geometrico Demonstrata." Like Wittgenstein's, Spinoza's *Ethics* "extended from the foundations of logic to the nature of the world" (*NB* p. 79) and, given Wittgenstein's proneness to naked pronouncement, this new Spinoza title is appropriately ironic. The case on behalf of the title *Ethics* is virtually sealed when we remember that Wittgenstein thought his first book nonsensically tried to say what could not be said, and join to this memory a realization that for Wittgenstein (at least on December 30, 1929) "this running up against the limits of language is *ethics*" (*WVC* p. 68).

(3) Science, Showing, and (Propositional) Sense

For the author of the *Tractatus*, the doctrine of showing was the "cardinal problem of philosophy," because unless there were things that could be shown, but not said, there would have been no philosophy at all—only science (*L* R.37). And if there were only science, so he believed, there would be no sense: no sense to sentences and no sense to our lives. Hence freedom from anxiety, from care (Sorge, *L* R.2), requires that there be something beyond science, beyond reason. In the *Tractatus*, this beyond is the substance of the world, objects (*TLP* 2.021). If there were no substance of the world, there could be no propositional sense, and if we did not recognize that the substance of our lives and the substance of the world were one, there could be no existential sense (*TLP* 5.621).

This chapter now dives into an interpretation of the *Tractatus*, but in the end I will assimilate Wittgenstein's appeal to this substance beyond science to Nietzsche's early appeal to the primordial unity beyond the principle of sufficient reason.

Before we even get to the first word of the *Tractatus* we are told that the propositions of this book will be numbered according to the following system:

> The decimal numbers assigned to the individual propositions indicate the logical importance of the propositions, the stress laid on them in my exposition. The propositions n.1, n.2, n.3, etc. are comments on proposition no. n; the propositions n.m1, n.m2 etc., are comments on proposition no. n.m; and so on. (*TLP* 1, note to the numeral "1")

It is of course normal to number the propositions of a systematic textbook, and indeed Hertz's *Principles of Mechanics* (1894)—a book that Wittgenstein knew and admired throughout his life—does number its paragraphs.[43] But Hertz's numbers are not decimals and so have none of the *Tractatus's* articulation. McGuinness observes that "the most obvious exemplar of this [Tractarian] system of numbering is *Principia Mathematica* [1910]."[44] Once pointed out, it is easy to see that Wittgenstein modelled his numbering system on that of Russell and Whitehead. They introduced theirs this way:

> Following Peano, we use numbers having a decimal as well as an integral part, in order to be able to insert new propositions between any two. A change in the integral part of the number will be used to correspond to a new chapter. Definitions will generally have numbers whose decimal part is less than .1, and will be usually put at the beginning of chapters. In references, the integral parts of the numbers of propositions will be distinguished by being preceded by a star; thus "*1.01" will mean the definition or proposition so numbered, and "*1" will mean the chapter in which propositions have numbers whose integral part is 1, i.e., the present chapter. Chapters will generally be called "numbers."[45]

But Russell and Whitehead are more complete than Wittgenstein. While they introduce a convention for introducing definitions with decimals less than .1, Wittgenstein simply uses their convention. Strictly speaking, Wittgenstein's number 2.01 should be a comment on proposition 2.0, but there is no proposition 2.0. Stenius wrestled with this problem, but it disappears when we remember the precedent of *Principia Mathematica*.[46]

The fact that the *Tractatus* is so numbered means that with some confidence we can select the depth at which we will read this book. We could reserve our attention for the seven whole-numbered propositions and study the axial nerve of the book. We might add the twenty-four propositions of the next layer, those that carry the seven main propositions out to the first decimal place. Or we could dig to varying depths depending on our interests and inclinations.[47] This (therefore) will not have been a book.[48] As the author says, it is not a textbook [Lehrbuch] (*TLP* preface). It has no teaching [Lehre] to impart. Its title announces that it is a logico-philosophical treatise [Abhandlung], but we soon learn that logical propositions "treat" nothing: "Sie 'handeln' von nichts" (*TLP* 6.124). To the extent that the *Tractatus* is about logic, it is—at one remove—about nothing.

This is a strange book. On January 16, 1914, about eight months before he completed the manuscript of the *Tractatus*, Wittgenstein wrote to Engelmann:

> If you tell me now that I have no faith, you are *perfectly right*, only I did not have it before either. It is plain, isn't it, that when a man wants, as it were, to invent a machine for becoming decent, such a man has no faith. (*E*.12)

It is not obvious whether Wittgenstein is here describing a machine he wants to invent. Even if that were clear, it would remain an open question whether the machine Wittgenstein is describing is the *life*[49] he is leading in the army or the *book* he was then completing. Later, in 1944, he wrote to Malcolm:

> What is the use of studying philosophy if all that it does for you is to enable you to talk with some plausibility about some abstruse questions of logic, etc., & if it does not improve your thinking about the important questions of everyday life. . . . You see, I know that it's difficult to think *well* about "certainty," "probability," "perception," etc. But it is, if possible, still more difficult to think, or *try* to think, really honestly about your life & other people's lives.[50]

If this were also his view in 1918, then he might easily have imagined that the *Tractatus*, itself, was a machine for becoming decent. The letter to Engelmann continues:

> But what am I to do? *I am clear about one thing:* I am far too bad to be able to theorize about myself; in fact I shall either remain a swine or else I shall improve, and that's that! Only let's cut out the transcendental twaddle [transcendentales Geschwaetz] when the whole thing is as plain as a sock on the jaw [eine Watschen]. (*E*.12)

In the last section we saw that Wittgenstein wrote to von Ficker that "All of that which *many* are *babbling* today, I have defined in my book by remaining silent about it" (F.23). The machine for becoming decent might have been a machine to incite silence, and if the *Tractatus* were such a machine, it would have no teaching of its own: "Its purpose would be achieved if it gave pleasure to one person who read it and understood it" (*TLP* preface). But this is not the naive wish it seems to be, for we are also told that "anyone who understands me eventually recognizes [my propositions] . . . as nonsensical" [unsinnig] (*TLP* 6.54). So the purpose of the book would be achieved if anyone read the book, realized that it was itself only nonsense (itself only babbling), and, returning to the concrete difficulty of becoming decent, smiled. The *Tractatus* is about nothing.

Here, without its footnote, is the first proposition of the book.

1   The world is all that is the case.
       [Die Welt ist alles, was der Fall ist.]

The comma is significant.[51] It enforces the thought that the world is all. Beside the world there is nothing. And the world is all that is the case, all that happens to be the case. Farther down this page we will be told that in logic nothing just happens, nothing is accidental [zufällig] (*TLP* 2.012). And so we seem to be told that the world, what is the case, is accidental. We seem to be told: Was der Fall ist, zufällig ist. Immediately following proposition 1, we find:

1.1   The world is the totality of facts, not of things.

The world is all that is the case and what is the case is the totality of facts, not things. So things are not part of the world. Yet the world is all. So there are no things. And that is why

1.2   The world divides [zerfällt] into facts.

The world divides into what accidentally happens. It divides into facts, not into things. Things are not part of the world.

Even in the 1's there is a sign that although the world is all that is the case, there is something that is not (merely) the case—so not part of the world. This unworldly background[62] is called logical space: the scaffolding of the world (see *TLP* 6.124, 4.023, 3.42).

1.13   The facts in logical space are the world.

This is a little puzzling. Here is something that doesn't seem to be a fact, logical space, which is apparently linked to the facts that—as a whole—constitute the world. The second time through this book, we would have recognized that the "all" in proposition 1 presupposed logical space, but the first time through "logical space" would likely be our first sign that although the world of facts is the only world, this book is also about what is beyond the world, the world's unworldly background. The 2's—still on the first page of the book—complicate matters further.

2   What is the case—a fact—is the existence of states of affairs.
      [Was der fall ist, die Tatsache, ist das Bestehen von Sach-verhalten.]

It seems that although there is no more to the world than there is to facts, we cannot understand facts without going outside the world. Facts are the existence of states of affairs, and proposition 2.01 tells us what they are.

2.01   A state of affairs (a state of things) is a combination of objects (things).
         [Der Sachverhalt is ein Verbindung von Gegenständen (Sachen, Dingen).]

This proposition identifies objects, things, and affairs. A fact [Tat-SACHE] is the existence of a state of affairs [SACH-verhalt]. A state of affairs is a combination of objects or things [SACHEN, Dingen]. But we already know that the world is the totality of facts, not things [Dinge]. So things are not part of the world and so, too, combinations of things are not part of the world. The world consists only of the totality of *existing* combinations of things. So in order for there to be a world there must be something beyond the world: combinations of things, Sachverhalten. Looking back it now seems clear that even propositions 1 and 2 require states of affairs—beyond the world—simply to account for the world:

1   The world is all that is the case.

2   What is the case—a fact—is the existence of states of affairs.

States of affairs are possible facts: possibilities that might or might not obtain. And here we can see how much work a version of the principle of excluded middle is doing. The opening of the *Tractatus* draws conclusions from the fact that there are propositions that can be either true or false: the propositions of science, contingent propositions. If what is the case might not have been, then logically prior to whatever is the case is whatever might either have been or not have been the case. (In the *Tractatus* these are states of affairs, combinations of objects.) Somewhere we *must* meet a domain of sense that is prior to the domain of fact. Why "must"? Because facts are contingent. This explains why philosophy, which studies these possibilities prior to fact, cannot be a natural science (*TLP* 4.111). If there were a science of language, call it cognitive science, it would itself presuppose that its facts might not have been the case—hence its very existence would require states of affairs outside its domain. These are considerations that drive states of affairs from the world. They are the logical background, the scaffolding of the world.

In the propositions trailing 2.01, we find out what things are.

> 2.011   It is essential to things that they should be possible constituents of states of affairs.

It could not be an *accident* that things could be possible constituents of states of affairs, for then it would be a *fact* that they could and hence they would be part of, and not beyond, the world. Suppose however that whether one thing *could* combine with another thing in a state of affairs was itself a fact. In that case this fact would require the existence of a further state of affairs, so we would be forced to greet the existence of a realm beyond the world of facts in any case.[53] The section continues:

> 2.012   In logic nothing is accidental: if a thing *can* occur in a state of affairs, the possibility of the state of affairs must be written into the thing itself.

Objects (things) are the *nonaccidental*. So they cannot be within the world, for if they were within the world they would be accidental, facts (see 6.41). What is accidentally the case, the world, depends on the nonaccidental.

> 2.013   Each thing is, as it were, in a space of possible states of affairs. This space I may imagine empty, but I cannot imagine the thing

Pretending for a moment that objects are simply normal things like oak leaves and equations, it is clear that leaves and equations are in different spaces of possibility. One leaf may weigh more or less than another leaf, but it makes no sense at all to speak of that leaf weighing more or less than Schrödinger's Wave Equation. We can imagine the space of possibility with nothing in it, but we cannot imagine an object without its space of possibility. Thus

>   2.014   Objects contain the possibility of all situations [Sachlagen].

The things that are beyond the world contain the possibility of all situations, of all facts. This was anticipated in a comment on 2.012: "If all objects are given, then at the same time all *possible* states of affairs are also given" (*TLP* 2.0124). Logical space is the nonaccidental background of the world. It is the "logical scaffolding" of the world (*TLP* 3.42, 4.023).

The objects that together articulate logical space are outside the world. They are furthermore described as simple (*TLP* 2.02). Being simple they are changeless, they have no parts to change. They could however change their relations to other objects. These relations to other objects are the states of affairs that, if they do (accidentally) exist, are facts, the totality of which constitute the world (*TLP* 1.1). So there is a sense in which the objects are the substance of the world (*TLP* 2.021). Objects constitute the nonaccidental background of what is the case. Moreover these objects determine all possible states of affairs so that anything that might possibly exist—the realm of what is possible or imaginable—is determined by these simple unchanging objects (*TLP* 2.022). The *Tractatus* introduces these thoughts thus:

>   2.02   Objects are simple
>
>>   2.021   Objects make up the substance of the world. That is why they cannot be composite.
>
>>   2.022   It is obvious that an imagined world, however different it may be from the real one, must have *something*—a form—in common with it.
>
>>   2.023   Objects are just what constitute this unalterable form.

2.024   Substance is what subsists independently of what is the case.

2.026   There must be objects if the world is to have unalterable form.

2.027   Objects, the unalterable, and the subsistent are one [sind Eins].[54]

But we will want to know why there must be unalterable objects, why the world must have a substance, at all. A clue can be gleaned from 2.0201, the off-set remark on 2.02:

2.0201 Every statement about complexes can be resolved into a statement about their constituents and into the propositions that describe the complexes completely.

There had been parenthetical references to the analysis of language in 2.0122 and 2.0131, but these had simply been analogies. This is the first time that the suggestion is made that what Wittgenstein says about the world is in fact determined by his account of language. On June 17, 1915, he wrote in his notebook:

Now, however, it seems to be a legitimate question: Are—e.g.—spatial objects composed of simple parts; in analyzing them, does one arrive at parts that cannot be further analyzed, or is this not the case?
——But what kind of question is this?——

Is it, A PRIORI, clear that in analysis we must arrive at simple components—is this, e.g., involved in the concept of analysis—, or is analysis ad infinitum possible? Or is there in the end even a third possibility? (NB p. 62)

This is the question we are asking: why must there be simple objects? He seems to have felt he answered this question in what follows these musings, for the next day he writes: "The demand for simple things is the demand for definiteness of sense" (NB p. 63; see TLP 3.23).

The demand that sense be determinate (definite) derives from Frege's discussion of definition. Frege had said that an indefinite concept is really no concept at all, and Wittgenstein appears to be reciting these thoughts at the level of the proposition as a whole. Frege's idea was that for a concept to have a definite sense it must be defined for every object in the universe. If a concept does have a determinate sense, then of every object we should be able to say either "YES it falls under the concept" or "NO it doesn't"; there is no third category: *tertium non datur*.[55] Frege:

> A definition of a concept . . . must be complete; it must unambiguously determine, as regards any object, whether or not it falls under the concept. . . . Thus there must not be any object as regards which the definition leaves any doubt whether it falls under the concept; though for us men, with our defective knowledge, the question may not be decidable.[56] We may express this metaphorically as follows: the concept must have a sharp boundary. If we represent concepts . . . by areas on a plane . . . to a concept without a sharp boundary there would correspond an area that had not a sharp boundary line all round, but in places just vaguely faded away into the background. This would not really be an area at all; and likewise a concept that is not sharply defined is wrongly termed a concept. . . . The law of excluded middle is really just another form of the requirement that the concept should have a sharp boundary. Any object . . . that you choose to take either falls under the concept . . . or does not fall under it; *tertium non datur*.[57]

In the opening lines of the *Tractatus,* the fact that propositions could be either true or false motivated the move beyond the world to logical space organized by the objects. This was the first use of the law of the excluded middle. Now we see a second. The law of excluded middle guarantees that there is one and only one complete analysis to any proposition: an analysis into names that mean [bedeutet] objects such that for every concept either the object definitely falls under it or definitely does not. The configuration of names in an elementary proposition corresponds to the configuration of objects in a situation [Sachlage] (*TLP* 3.2, 3.201, 3.202, 3.203, 3.21, 3.25). Wittgenstein writes:

> 3.23   The requirement that simple signs be possible is the requirement that sense be determinate. (see *NB* p. 62)

If there were more than one complete analysis or if analysis were interminable, then sense would not be determinate. The first case is easy to see—if the meaning of the names in a proposition could be either of two objects then the sense of the proposition would be indeterminate. But also if the analysis were interminable, it would not be possible ever to say what the meaning of a sign was, and again the sense would be indeterminate. Now why *must* sense be determinate? Because Wittgenstein acquired from Frege the belief that an indeterminate sense would not even be a sense (*TLP* 5.451), so the argument is simple: Some propositions have sense, so there are objects. Propositions with no sense are not even propositions.[58] Frege puts this with characteristic vigor:

> Without complete and final definitions, we have no firm ground under foot, we are not sure about the validity of our theorems, and we cannot confidently apply the laws of logic, which certainly presuppose that the concepts, and relations too, have sharp boundaries.[59]

That is why there must be simple objects. If sense did not have to be determinate there would not have to be simple objects. (In chap. 3, I argue that much of the *Philosophical Investigations* can be constructed by imagining the *Tractatus* without this Fregean commitment.)

I have slipped into speaking of these objects as if they were objects like quacks and quarks. But they are beyond what is the case, beyond the world. This comes out in the 3.2's too:

3.22   In a proposition a name is the representative of an object.

3.221   Objects can only be *named.* Signs are their representatives. I can only speak *about* them: I cannot *put them into words*. Propositions can only say *how* things are, not *what* they are [wie eine Ding ist, nicht was es ist].

Thus although there must be objects if we are to say how anything is, *we cannot say what objects are.* This can look like the claim—by fiat—that only propositions that are contingent can be said and since objects are the nonaccidental ground of the accidental, they cannot be said.[60] But the point can be put, and more persuasively, as the observation that we cannot say what objects are because objects are what permit us to say anything. We could not say that this object, and this, are in the world, but not that (*TLP* 5.61). The difficulty is with the "but not that." Since nothing makes sense unless, in the last analysis, it involves names of objects, we cannot sensibly say what is *not* a possible state of the world, what is not in logical space. This is a perfectly general point. It has nothing to do with the peculiar foundations of sense floated in the *Tractatus*.

It afflicts any attempt to *explain* why just this and not that makes sense. If explanations explain why this rather than that, then there can be no explanation of the limits of sense. I am inclined to think that it was for analogous reasons that Heidegger sometimes felt that there was no more to say about why the world has the noncontingent features it does than to say the "world worlds" [Welt weltet].[61]

According to the *Tractatus*, while we can define one sign in terms of others, this is impossible when we reach the level of the concatenated names that are the complete analyses of propositions (*TLP* 3.26, 3.261). We cannot define primitive signs of objects.

3.262   What signs fail to express, their application [Anwendung] shows. What signs slur over, their application says clearly.

3.263   The meanings [Bedeutungen] of primitive signs can be explained by means of elucidations [Erläuterungen]. Elucidations are propositions that contain primitive signs. So they can only be understood if the meanings of those signs are already known.

Standing in front of a painting by the Futurist Umberto Boccioni you may not be able to make anything out. It is a picture of a horse dragging heavy equipment as the city rises in the background. I may try any number of things to get you to see the horse. I might draw its outline on a sheet of paper, or say in more detail which way it is facing, where its head is, and so on. But each of these alternative representations of the horse is simply another representation of the horse. I cannot hand you the content of the picture, I can only express it in other ways. Wittgenstein speaks of *elucidations* of the meaning of primitive signs for simple objects. These elucidations are simply further *uses* of the sign; one hopes they are more perspicuous uses. There is no deeper to go. We cannot step outside of language to say what it means in some finer language. And there is no escape, as Russell thought, through hierarchy.[62] Suppose we can discuss the meanings of language L.1 only in language L.2, those of L.2 only in L.3, and so on up a majestic Russellian hierarchy, then *either* hierarchy has a topmost language and we will either not be able to understand its meanings or we will understand them as Wittgenstein (rather than Russell) does *or* the hierarchy goes up forever, which simply defers addressing the philosophical question permanently without ever addressing it.[63]

4.022   A Proposition *shows* its sense.

A Proposition *shows* how things stand *if* it is true. And it *says that* they do so stand.

We can only speak about objects; we cannot, as Russell thought,[64] put them into words. Without them we couldn't say of anything that it exists. But they are not themselves part of what is the case, they are like Plato's Idea of the Good, beyond being. McGuinness:

> Certainly, our propositions in the last analysis are not about the workings of our own minds: what Wittgenstein is trying to convey is a point of view according to which what they are about is not *in* the world any more than it is *in* thought or *in* language. Objects are the form of all these realms, and our acquaintance with objects (our contact with them, to borrow a metaphor from Aristotle) is not an experience or knowledge of something over against which we stand. Thus it is not properly experience or knowledge at all [see *TLP* 5.552]. Objects are *eti epekeina tes ousias* (beyond being), and it is therefore misleading to regard Wittgenstein as a realist in respect of them.[65]

Nor would it be any less misleading to regard Wittgenstein as an antirealist in respect of them. Objects are beyond being and nonbeing (see *PI* par. 50).

The logical scaffolding of the world shows itself in propositions on the border of sense. Remember that the 1's proceeded by drawing consequences from the fact that propositions can be either true or false. As I mentioned, this is a version of the law of the excluded middle. But it is hard to know how to understand this law. It can't be a generalization about propositions for this would make it seem a contingent fact about propositions.[66] And Wittgenstein notes:

6.111   All theories that make a proposition of logic appear to have content are false. One might think, for example, that the words *true* and *false* signified two properties among other properties, and then it would seem to be a remarkable fact that every proposition possessed one of these properties. On this theory it seems to be anything but obvious, just as, for instance the proposition, "All roses are either yellow or red," would not sound obvious even if it were true. Indeed, the logical proposition acquires all the characteristics of a proposition of natural science and this is the sure sign that it has been construed wrongly.

Wittgenstein wanted to arrive at a conception of propositions that would make them essentially true or false, *tertium non datur.* His first, pre-*Tractatus* version of this was to say that every proposition was a-p-b, where "a" and "b" stood for truth and falsity (respectively) and "p" was the proposition.[67] This way of symbolizing propositions would have made it "obvious" that all propositions could be true or false, unlike the similar proposition "all roses are red or yellow" (*TLP* 6.111). This was Wittgenstein's first attempt to try to make the symbolism of logic manifest—show—what Frege and Russell were haltingly trying to put into words: "The precedent to which we are constantly inclined to appeal must reside in the symbol itself" (*TLP* 5.525).[68]

In the *Tractatus,* the obviousness of the law of excluded middle finds its home in the symbolism now known as truth tables.

1   The world is all that is the case.

2   What is the case—a fact—is the existence of states of affairs.

4.1   Propositions represent the existence and nonexistence of states of affairs. [see 2.06]

4.2   The sense of a proposition is its agreement and disagreement with possibilities of existence and nonexistence of states of affairs.

4.1 asserts that propositions represent what, if it exists, is a fact. Propositions represent possibilities of existence. 4.2 asserts that the sense of a proposition is the way its truth or falsity is determined by the truth or falsity of all possible states of affairs. 4.3 and 4.4 take this analysis into the realm of elementary propositions, propositions that represent only one state of affairs (*L* R.37).

4.3   Truth possibilities of elementary propositions mean [bedeuten] possibilities of existence and nonexistence of states of affairs.

4.4   A proposition is an expression of agreement and disagreement with truth possibilities of elementary propositions.

So if p is an elementary proposition representing one state of affairs and q represents another, the sense of the molecular proposition p and q will be the agreement of p and q with the possible existence or nonexistence of p and q. In tabular form:

p	*q*	*p & q*	*not-(p & q)*
T	T	T	F
T	F	F	T
F	T	F	T
F	F	F	T

The two columns on the left represent all possible combinations of the existence and nonexistence of p and q. With a convention for representing these possibilities, we could replace "p and q" with the sign "(TFFF)(p,q)" and "not-(p and q)" with "(FTTT)(p,q)" (*TLP* 4.442). This is the symbolism that comes to replace the a-p-b notation. They are alike in indicating that propositions can be true or false. They embody the principle of excluded middle.

This symbolism also helps us recognize two limiting cases of propositions: those that are always true (tautologies) and those that are always false (contradictions).

p	*q*	*p & q* **OR** *not-(p & q)*	
T	T	T	
T	F	T	**TAUTOLOGY**
F	T	T	
F	F	T	

p	*q*	*p & q* **AND** *not-(p & q)*	
T	T	F	
T	F	F	**CONTRADICTION**
F	T	F	
F	F	F	

Wittgenstein's view is that tautologies and contradictions are senseless [sinnlos] but not nonsensical [unsinnig] (*TLP* 4.461–4.4611). "They do not represent any possible situations" the way propositions with sense do (*TLP* 4.462). They are not pictures of reality (*TLP* 4.462). "Tautology and contradiction are the limiting cases—indeed the disintegration—of the combination of signs" (*TLP* 4.466). But they are not gibberish, for they are part of the symbolism that does permit sensible propositions to represent possible situations (*TLP* 4.611). So:

6.1   The propositions of logic are tautologies.

6.11   Therefore the propositions of logic say nothing.

6.12   The fact that the propositions of logic are tautologies *shows* the formal—logical—properties of language and the world.

   The fact that a tautology is yielded by *this particular way* of connecting its constituents characterizes the logic of its constituents.

   If propositions are to yield a tautology when they are connected in a certain way, they must have certain structural properties. So their yielding a tautology when combined *in this way* shows that they possess these structural properties.

"P or not-p" is a tautology that is clearly related to the law of the excluded middle, but it says nothing. Rather it is a condition of making sense at all that all sensible propositions say nothing when put into this schema. It is not a generalization about propositions.[69] It is not the pure foundation of sense. It is the first glimpse of its opposite: senselessness. And that the opposite of sense is first glimpsed in this way makes manifest the limits of any world we might know or imagine, dream, or dread.

   And again, we are near to forgetting that the objects we have been concerned with are outside of the world, and outside of the world there is nothing to talk about. So although the elementary propositions are introduced as pictures of simple objects, this is not something that—if we get the point of the *Tractatus*—we will find understandable, at all. The anxieties about logic that launched the *Tractatus* are not answered in that book. The book is metaphysical poison (nonsense/Unsinn) to end the explanatory metaphysical impulse.[70]

   What were Wittgenstein's logical cares (*L* R.2)? In part they were his fear that the nonaccidental, the essential, would masquerade as the accidental. We saw this in his comparison of "all propositions are true or false" with "all roses are red or yellow," "All theories that make a proposition of logic appear to have content are false" (*TLP* 6.111). Wittgenstein's logical cares concerned the nonaccidental, and the *Tractatus* protects the nonaccidental by revealing that there is nothing that can be said about it. Nevertheless, the fact of determinate sense assures us that this nothing is there.[71]

> 6.522 There is indeed the inexpressible. This *shows* itself; it is the mystical.

That the inexpressible exists is itself inexpressible. There is nothing we cannot say. Remember:

> 3.221 Objects can only be *named.* Signs are their representatives. I can only speak *about* them: I cannot *put them into words.* Propositions can only say *how* [wie] things are, not *what* [was] they are.

I have already interpreted this proposition as an instance of the general impossibility of explaining why just these were the sensible propositions, the possible facts of the world. The limits of sense show themselves. My favorite way of imagining this is to imagine that one was required to determine the anatomy of another's hand solely by determining the ways the fingers can and cannot move. Someone places their hand in mine. I look it over, almost as if it were not a hand, but a thing. This way it moves easily, and that way, but when I pressure it to move in certain directions, it refuses. I cannot see the bones of this hand, but its anatomy is made manifest by the particular ways the fingers can, and cannot, move. Like the bones of another's hand, the limits of sense show themselves in what does and does not make sense.

> The aim of the book is to draw a limit to thought, or rather—not to thought, but to the expression of thoughts: for in order to be able to draw a limit to thought, we should have to find both sides of the limit thinkable (i.e., we should have to think what cannot be thought).
>
> It will therefore only be in language that the limit can be drawn, and what lies on the other side of the limit will simply be nonsense [Unsinn]. (*TLP* preface)

Thus it is Wittgenstein's "Fundamental principle ... that whenever a question can be decided by logic at all it must be possible to decide it without more ado" (*TLP* 5.551). There can never be any question of resolving a logical problem, a question about what makes sense, by appeal to what is (accidentally) the case. "Logic must take care of itself" (*NB* p. 2; *TLP* 5.473).

The mysticism of the *Tractatus* is motivated, in part, by the fact that if we are to understand anything we must be related to objects, things. Wittgenstein speaks of objects as being "given" [geben] to us, and of our "knowing" [kennen] objects (*TLP* 2.0124, 2.0123). But since the objects are the unchanging structure of logical space (*TLP* 2.027), and since whatever we could experience could be otherwise (*TLP* 5.634), there can be no experience of objects. So how are we to understand the givenness of objects, the givenness of the world? It is an experience not of HOW the world is but THAT it is, at all (*TLP* 6.44).

5.552   The "experience" that we need in order to understand logic[72] is not that something or other is the state of things [sich etwas so und so verhält], but that something *is*: that, however, is *not* an experience.

It is *prior* to every experience—that something is *so*.

It is prior to the question "how?," not prior to the question "What?" [Sie ist vor dem Wie, nicht vor dem Was.]

6.44   It is not *how* the world is that is mystical, but *that* it is. [Nicht *wie* die Welt ist, ist das Mystische, sondern *dass* sie ist.]

Logic is before the How, not before the What. But how the world is, is what is the case. So the experience we need, if we are to understand logic, is not an experience of what is the case, of what has happened in the world.

6.45   To view the world *sub specie aeterni* is to view it as a whole—a limited whole.

Feeling the world as a limited whole—it is this that is mystical.

In a letter to Ogden, Wittgenstein notes that in 6.45 (but not 6.44) he is talking about a mystical *feeling*.[73] In his notes for October 7, 1916, he had written that "The usual way of looking at things sees objects as it were from the midst of them, the view *sub specie aeternitatis* from outside" (*NB* p. 83; see *CV* p. 33). The mystical wonder at the bare existence of things—the what not the how—this is the experience we need to understand logic.

When we do understand logic, we realize that it is senseless [sinn-los]. Beside the world there is nothing, and nothing is precisely what logic "treats" of (*TLP* 6.124). Understanding something is, in every case, understanding something against the background of logic, against the background of nothing. In July 1929, Heidegger had tried to understand the deepest form of anxiety in terms of his belief that "human existence can relate to beings only if it holds itself out into the nothing."[74] In December of that year Wittgenstein said, "To be sure, I can imagine what Heidegger means by being and anxiety" (*WVC* p. 68).

Wittgenstein had logical worries. He was worried that Russell, for example, would mistake the realm of logic for an empirical realm amenable to the methods of science. Logic, he thought, must be the background of every scientific investigation of the world. The final background of science is what permits us to understand anything at all—in the *Tractatus* these are the objects in logical space—and about these nothing at all can be said, period. So we were worried about the foundations of sense and discover that there is nothing that can be said about the foundations of sense. And this is the balm for his logical cares. "When the answer cannot be put into words, neither can the question be put into words" (*TLP* 6.5). And so Wittgenstein's anxieties about the necessity of logic were calmed, not by the answer to his questions, but by the silencing of his questioning. Metaphysics sublimes.

(4) Science, Showing, and (Existential) Sense

In the last section, I tracked the grounds of propositional sense into silence. In this section, I will do the same with the grounds of existential sense. Wittgenstein approaches the question of the meaning of life, the meaning of the world with all the (subliming) machinery that we saw disappear from the world in the last section. He may be unique in using a concept of meaning inspired by the philosophical logic of Frege and Russell to solve the question of Nihilism.

It is widely known that while Wittgenstein was in the war he was sometimes called "the one with the Gospels," because he carried Tolstoy's *Gospel in Brief* with him at all times, even under fire.[75] He discovered the book by accident and started reading it on September 1, 1914; in a letter dated July 24, 1915, he recommended it to von Ficker saying "at its time, this book virtually kept me alive ... you cannot imagine what an effect it can have upon a person."[76] A few months later, in October of 1915, Wittgenstein wrote to Russell that he was busy summarizing his work and "writing it down in the form of a treatise" [Abhandlung] (L R.32). The *Tractatus* was therefore first organized while Wittgenstein was still under the spell of Tolstoy's *Gospel in Brief*. These externals are relevant to the position of the "riddle of life" and the "sense of the world" in the *Tractatus*, for Tolstoy wrote in the preface to his *Gospel*: "I regard Christianity neither as an exclusive divine revelation nor as an historical phenomenon, but as a teaching which gives us the *meaning of life*"[77] (my emphasis; see *TLP* 6.41, 6.4312).

I have already traced the numbering system of the *Tractatus* to Russell and Whitehead's *Principia Mathematica*, but here is the place to draw out the tantalizing similarities of structure shared between Wittgenstein's book and Tolstoy's *Gospel*. First, the two books have very similar tasks: to summarize and organize a collection of remarks of varying value. Tolstoy begins with the scattered tales of the gospels themselves. He eliminates those aspects of the gospels he thinks unimportant—in effect this means all those parts of the gospels that Tolstoy understands simply as attempts to prove the divinity of Jesus. Of the remaining remarks, he weaves one story. Wittgenstein's task is also to select the best of his thoughts from what Engelmann described as seven "large office-books bound in black and green striped cloth, of the kind used in Austria as ledgers."[78] So again we have a process of culling and organizing.

Second, the *Prototractatus* (1918) begins with the remark: "All the good propositions from my other manuscripts have been fitted between these propositions."[79] And then follow the six main propositions of the *Tractatus*, and nine subpropositions.[80] So it seems that Wittgenstein first determined the systematic structure of his subliming thoughts and then placed all his "good" remarks at those places in the structure where they belonged. Tolstoy's *Gospel* is organized similarly. Tolstoy writes: "The division of the Gospel into twelve chapters (or six if each two be united) came about of itself from the sense of the teaching"[81] (Tolstoy's parentheses). Tolstoy then lists twelve numbered propositions that easily form six pairs since each pair is connected by a "Therefore." Moreover Tolstoy heads each of his 6 x 2 chapters with the appropriate thesis from his master list, and then the relevant bits of the gospels are supplied under that heading. The thought is inescapable—but probably unconfirmable—that Wittgenstein organized his treatise according to principles absorbed equally from *Principia Mathematica* and *The Gospel in Brief.*

I float this speculation here because the connection to Tolstoy is a connection with the centrality of the meaning of life, which is the subject of this section. Indeed I shall suggest that Tolstoy's discovery of the meaning of life is also Wittgenstein's—though, like objects, Wittgenstein's discovery will sublime. Tolstoy writes:

5. The service of the will of that Father of life gives life.

6. Therefore the gratification of one's own will is not necessary for life.[82]

The key to what Tolstoy calls peace, joy, and security is to renounce one's personal desires and make one's own will a great mirror of the will of God[83] (see *TLP* 5.511, 6.13). My interpretive edge is two sided: first this is one way of troping what Wittgenstein says about the propositions of logic and, second, this is one way of troping what Wittgenstein says about the good life. Happy is the person whose life has become a great mirror of what is higher, the true life. In the rest of this section I will bring out the way Tolstoy's traditional path to peace is followed in the *Tractatus,* first concerning propositional sense and, second, concerning existential sense.

Propositional sense. Despite its obscure number, there can hardly be a more important passage for understanding the *Tractatus* than 6.41, I will quote it as a whole:

6.41 The sense [Sinn] of the world must lie outside the world. In the world everything is as it is, and everything happens as it does happen: *in* it no value exists—and if it did exist, it would have no value.

If there is any value, it must lie outside the whole sphere of what happens and is the case [alles Geschehens und So-Seins]. For all that happens and is the case is accidental.

What makes it nonaccidental [nicht-zufällig] cannot lie *within* the world, since if it did it would itself be accidental.

It must lie outside the world.

This number tells that the sense of the world, value, and what is nonaccidental [nicht zufällig] are all equally outside the world. They are part of what he calls the "higher" [das Höhere] (*TLP* 6.432). There is no reason not to think that the things beyond being that guarantee the determinacy of sense should be any less part of the higher than the sense of the world. Tolstoy follows Christian tradition in linking the meaning of life with making one's own will coincide with the will of the father. So one pauses at the realization that Tractarian objects (things) are sometimes described in terms of an alien will. The *Notebooks* have:

> The world is *given* me, i.e. my will enters into the world completely from outside as into something that is already there. . . . That is why we have the feeling of being dependent [abhängig sind] on an alien will. (*NB* 74)

In this passage, the givenness of the world is either its accidental arrangement or its nonaccidental form (the space structured by Tractarian objects). It is not likely to be the accidental existence of what is the case, for being accidental this won't have the structural physiognomy of a will. It would make more sense if the alien will on which we find ourselves to depend were the subliming Tractarian objects. These thoughts are confirmed by remarks written three days later (*NB* p. 76) that appear in the *Tractatus* as:

> 5.524   If objects are given, then at the same time we are given *all* objects.

What is *given*, first of all, is the logical space of what is the case. The givenness of the world that feels like an alien will is the givenness of logical space, the givenness of objects. On the one hand, every proposition whether accidentally true or accidentally false depends [abhängen] on logical space for its sense. On the other hand, "Substance [i.e., objects] is what subsists independently [unabhängig] of what is the case" (*TLP* 2.024).

Every proposition is dependent on the logical space of states of affairs, one or more of which it represents as existing. But there are some that represent the structure of logical space more perspicuously than most. As we saw, these are the propositions of logic: tautologies (*TLP* 6.1). "The propositions of logic describe the scaffolding of the world, or rather they represent it [sie stellen es dar]. They 'treat' of nothing" (*TLP*

6.124). The propositions of logic are not really propositions (*TLP* 4.462), but they are a kind of nonproposition that can—as the last section demonstrated—make the structure of logical space manifest.

This much is uncontested. My own extension of these commonplace remarks is to suggest that we think of the propositions of natural science as having a will of their own. Their "wills" are their own individual truth-conditions, their own individual "agreement and disagreement with truth possibilities of elementary propositions" (*TLP* 4.4). By contrast, tautologies and contradictions have no wills of their own. They have no truth-conditions:

> 4.461 Propositions show what they say: tautologies and contradictions show that they say nothing.
>
> A tautology has no truth-conditions, since it is unconditionally true: and a contradiction is true on no condition.
>
> Tautologies and contradictions lack sense [sind sinnlos].

If we could trust my assimilation of having truth-conditions to having a will of one's own, then we should find Wittgenstein writing as if tautologies and contradictions had given up their own will for the will of logic itself, the nothing of which logic treats. And this is what we do find. It is the decisive point:

> 6.124 . . . It is clear that something about the world must be indicated by the fact that certain combinations of symbols— whose essence involves the possession of a determinate [Frege] character—are tautologies. This contains the decisive point. We have said that some things are arbitrary in the symbols that we use and that some things are not. In logic it is only the latter that express: but that means that logic is not a field in which *we* express what we wish with the help of signs, but rather one in which the nature of the absolutely necessary signs *speaks for itself.* If we know the logical syntax of any sign-language, then we have already been given all the propositions of logic. (second emphasis mine)

Thus Wittgenstein explicitly indicates that the propositions of logic have no will of their own, the nonaccidental structure of the world speaks for itself through them. At 4.462, Wittgenstein remarks that the propositions of logic do not represent any possible situation because the conditions of agreement with the world [Übereinstimmung mit der Welt] cancel each other out. But the passage just cited from 6.124 suggests that this very cancelling out of any particular agreement with what happens to be the case means that the propositions of logic are in agreement with the scaffolding of the world as a whole. Relinquishing any will to agree with a particular HOW of the world, they can agree with the WHAT of the world as a whole, a limited whole (*TLP* 6.44, 6.45). In his notebooks, Wittgenstein wrote:

> In order to live happily I must be in agreement with the world. And that is what "being happy" *means.*
>
> I am then, so to speak, in agreement with an alien will on which I appear dependent. That is to say: "I am doing the will of God." (*NB* 75)

I find that this passage confirms the interpretation of the propositions of logic I have just articulated. I linked the realm of objects to the notion of an alien will, and I have suggested that we think of the propositions of logic as being in agreement with the scaffolding of the world as a whole: the realm of objects. This is already to have said that the propositions of logic have relinquished their own wills, their own truth-conditions, and thus they let the logical structure of the world speak for itself (*TLP* 6.124).

Existential sense. One superficial difference between what the *Tractatus* says about propositional sense and what it says about existential sense is that whereas we are told a good deal about the "propositions of logic" we are told that "it is impossible for there to be propositions of ethics" (*TLP* 6.42). But this distinction will not last. "A proposition is a picture of reality" (*TLP* 4.01). But "tautologies and contradictions are not pictures of reality" (*TLP* 4.462). So, just as there are no ethical propositions there are also no logical propositions, and for the same reason: "Propositions can express nothing that is higher" (*TLP* 6.42). The ethical life, the happy life of which the *Tractatus* speaks, is the existential analog of the tautology. Tautologies have just as peculiar *truth-conditions* as the happy life has *satisfaction-conditions* (though not, of course, in Tarski's sense).

Wittgenstein discusses ethical laws and logical laws. About the former he writes: "When an ethical law of the form, 'Thou shalt . . .', is laid down, one's first thought is, 'And what if I do not do it?'" (*TLP* 6.422). Set this next to one of the things he says about logical laws: "Clearly the laws of logic cannot in their turn be subject to laws of logic" (*TLP* 6.123). He appears to be addressing a similar point. If a logical law said "Thou shalt form sentences that . . ." we might equally think: "And what if I don't?" Frege suggested that for a while we might appeal to other laws:

> The question why and with what right we acknowledge a law of logic to be true, logic can answer only by reducing it to another law of logic. Where that is not possible, logic can give no answer.[84]

This is the familiar position of all those who tend to think of justification in terms of axiomatic systems, the axioms have no justification. Wittgenstein's approach was not to provide a justification for the axioms but to deny that logical laws could be understood in terms of axiomatic systems and so as needing, but not being able to receive, a justification. The question about the justification of logical laws, the question about why we must obey them, is not to be answered; but neither are we to be left speechless, no: the question itself is to be silenced.

According to the *Tractatus*, "Frege says that any legitimately constructed proposition must have a sense. And I say that any possible proposition is legitimately constructed" (*TLP* 5.4733). Wittgenstein does not attempt to restrict the possible combinations of signs so that all legal constructions would have a sense. He would have asked: "And what if I do not obey these laws of logic, these laws of logical syntax?" The answer is clear: the combination of signs would not make sense. But if the combination of signs is nonsense, then we don't need a law to tell us that we should not combine the signs in that way.[85] What we need is a logical syntax that makes the logical structure, which is already there, clear. Logic must take care of itself (*NB* p. 2, *TLP* 5.473).

As we saw, one consequence of this approach to what others would call "logical laws" or "laws of thought" is that these so-called laws are no longer properly conceived as generalizations. I recite and continue:

6.123 Clearly the laws of logic cannot in their turn be subject to laws of logic.

6.1231   The mark of a logical proposition is *not* general validity. To be general means no more than to be accidentally valid for all things.

According to Wittgenstein, the so-called laws of logic are built into the unspeakable structure of logical space. They are called upon by every proposition because any individual proposition reaches through the whole of logical space (*TLP* 3.42). But they were most perspicuously apparent in such sentences as

p or not-p

IF p and (if p then q), THEN q.

So logical laws are not empirical generalizations about propositions but neither are they normative constraints, restricting the domain of sense from the outside. They are manifest in the fact that some combinations of signs but not others make sense.

Russell misconstrued the task of logic as the installation of rules obedience to which would keep our propositions within the realm of sense. The theory of logical types was of precisely this nature. Moralists make the same error. They attempt to construct a set of moral rules obedience to which will give our lives meaning. But if disobedience deprives life of meaning and meaninglessness is a self-exhibiting property of a life, then moral rules can serve no purpose. Violate logical laws and your marks will *make no sense*, violate ethical laws and your life will *make no sense*.

These thoughts are prompted by the following passage, the first part of which has already been cited:

6.422   When an ethical law of the form, "Thou shalt . . . ," is laid down, one's first thought is, "And what if I do not do it?" It is clear, however, that ethics has nothing to do with punishment and reward in the usual sense of the terms. So our question about the *consequences* of the action must be unimportant.—At least those consequences should not be events. For there must be something right about the question we posed. There must indeed be some kind of ethical reward and ethical punishment, but they must reside in the action itself.

(And also it is clear that the reward must be something pleasant and the punishment something unpleasant.)

It could not be the acquisition of a prize or the avoidance of a specific sanction. Within the circle of the *Tractatus*, this is obvious. The realm of value is part of what is higher, so it will not be able to be part of the world; thus ethical reward and punishment could not be events *in* the world (*TLP* 6.41). But should we agree?

Wittgenstein can seem blind to the virtues of any form of utilitarian or more generally naturalistic ethics.[86] That is because professional ethics is not concerned with the meaning of life, but with distributive justice, political justice, the liberation of the oppressed, and so on. These are not simple and certainly not unimportant matters. But the author of the *Tractatus* does not seem to use "ethics" to refer to them. Sharing another resonance with Spinoza, he seems to use ethics to refer to the inquiry into the meaning of life. In August 1916, he asked himself "Can there be any ethics if there is no living being but myself?" and immediately answered "If ethics is supposed to be something fundamental, there can" [ja!] (*NB* p. 79e). On this account, ethical concerns would be living concerns even if there were only one person alive on the earth, so even when political philosophy would be merely academic, that is, dead. Some ten years after the *Tractatus*, in his "Lecture on Ethics," he wrote that ethics is equally an inquiry into the "good," the "valuable," the "really important," the "meaning of life," "what makes life worth living," and the "right way of living."[87] If we think of Wittgenstein's concern as being with the meaning of life, then it is easier to accept his denying that ethical reward and punishment are anything like prizes and sanctions. It is almost a commonplace of thinking about the meaning of life that one may have all the economic, political, and social success one could desire and still feel one's life to be empty, meaningless. It is at least hard, if not impossible, to think of any acquisition or accomplishment, possession of which would be incompatible with the sense that one's life was without value. It is not so much surprising as obvious that one's life cannot be given meaning simply by receiving a prize or avoiding a sanction.

My approach to Wittgenstein's reflections on the meaning of life will be modelled on Wittgenstein's presentation of tautologies and contradictions as revealing the scaffolding of the world as a (limited) whole. So I must locate something like the propositional structure of a life. Some help is provided in a letter Wittgenstein wrote to Engelmann in January 1921 (*TLP* was completed in August 1918): "My life has really become meaningless [sinnlos][88] and so it consists only of futile episodes" (E.38). Thus a meaningless life is a life that consists of nothing but episodes, futile episodes. I will suppose that the units of a life that are analogous to the names of simple objects will be these episodes, these individual actions. In what are we to imagine their futility to consist? It cannot be right to think of their futility as consisting in anything like not succeeding. For—as Peter Shaffer's Salieri reminds us—the despair of meaninglessness might actually be deepened by our having succeeded. The futility must consist in the failure to find or to give life meaning, and this failure is perfectly consistent with success, more narrowly construed.

Tolstoy's traditional view was that the meaning of life requires relinquishing of one's own will in favor of an alien will he called the Father's. In the *Tractatus*, we discover that "the will as a phenomenon is of interest only to psychology," not to ethics (*TLP* 6.423). This fits. The will of interest to psychology is the will as the contingent source of our desires. Actions motivated by the psychological will have certain definite conditions of satisfaction and dissatisfaction. These actions are motivated by specific desires and are satisfied only in specific situations, temporary situations. Even if you were fortunate enough to get your every wish, like Midas, that would not guarantee that your life had meaning—quite the reverse. Life's meaning cannot be found by supernatural good fortune. Life's meaning is not an accident.

Life would be meaningful if it were in tune with the logical structure of the world, the alien will. If we model this on the peculiar truth-conditions of propositions of logic (tautologies), we should expect a meaningful life to have no particular satisfaction-conditions (see *TLP* 4.461). But what kind of life would that be? A meaningful life is unconditionally satisfied. What if one simply lived, not for this or that personal end (selfish or altruistic), but simply lived, *hence* lived simply? What if one did not eat fine food, but simply ate? What if one did not wear fine clothes, but simply dressed? What if one did not clothe one's dwelling in ornament, but simply dwelt? Perhaps this would be a tautological life, a life in search of nothing more than itself. "There must indeed be some kind of ethical reward and ethical punishment, but they must reside in the action itself" (*TLP* 6.422). "Or again we could say that the one who fulfills the purpose of existence is he who needs no further purpose other than life. That is to say, who is satisfied [befriedigt]" (*NB* p. 73).[89] This makes of life a kind of tautology in the same extended sense that Wittgenstein spoke of tunes: "A tune is a kind of tautology, it is complete in itself; it satisfies itself [sie befriedigt sich selbst]" (*NB* p. 40; see *TLP*

3.141).[90] And at this precise point, his notebooks include: "And *now* if I ask myself: But why should I live *happily*, then this of itself seems to me to be a tautological [!] question; the happy life seems to be justified, of itself, it seems that it *is* the only right life" (*NB* p. 78).

What kind of satisfaction might be achieved by the quasi-tautological life just described?

> 6.43   If the good or bad exercise of the will does alter the world, it can alter only the limits of the world, not the facts—not what can be expressed by means of language.
>
> In short the effect must be that it becomes an altogether different world. It must, so to speak, wax and wane as a whole.

This picture of the world expanding and contracting can find a home in the Tolstoyan direction of my interpretation of these concluding pages of the *Tractatus*.[91] If we center our desires on the psychological will, then the world shrinks to those satisfaction-conditions that are cued to our specific desires. This makes our satisfaction very vulnerable, like the lives of birds that feed on only one species of insect. The rest of the world is in shadow. On the other hand, when personal desires are relinquished, and the world as a whole is accepted as it is for what it is—a kind of love of fate, *amor fati*—then the world can wax. Details formerly shadowed by what we thought was so important, can suddenly, wonderfully, come into view. Where had I been? Recall Nietzsche from 1886:

> It seems to him as if his eyes are only now open to what is *near*. He is astonished and sits silent: where *had* he been? These near and nearest things: how changed they seem! what bloom and magic they have acquired.[92]

The satisfaction-conditions of such a life are like the truth-conditions of a tautology, unconditional.

> In order to live happily I must be in agreement with the world. And that is what "being happy" *means* [*heisst*].
>
> I am then, so to speak, in agreement with that alien will on which I appear dependent. That is to say: "I am doing the will of God." (*NB* p. 75)

The will that is the subject of ethical properties (*TLP* 6.423) is, as Wittgenstein suggests, "an attitude to the world" [eine Stellungnahme zur Welt] (*NB* pp. 86, 87). It is an attitude of acceptance, and that is why it is the solution to the meaning of life. It wants nothing more than it has, and whatever it finds, is enough (Sophocles, *Oedipus at Colonus* ll 5–6). Life itself, is enough (*NB* p. 73). Ethical life does not embody a doctrine, it is a mirror image of the world, not of our desires (see *TLP* 6.13, 5.511).

It might be thought that this interpretation of the tautologous nature of the happy life must be wrong because I have endorsed a particular way of life: a simple life.[93] This seems to conflict with the view that ethics is not part of the world, but part of what is higher. This is not a serious objection because logic too is part of what is higher, and yet the *Tractatus* provides a way of telling from the signs themselves which sentences are either tautologous or contradictory and which sentences are not (*TLP* 6.113). There is no reason why the happy life might not also be described. The propositions of logic are not fully propositions. The actions that make up a happy life are not fully actions, for they do not serve the interests of the psychological will. Thus the happy life has no particular satisfaction-conditions in much the way that a tautology has no particular truth-conditions. The actions of the happy man are no more easily called actions than the propositions of logic are called propositions. They may be discerned by their differences.

In sum, logical laws and ethical laws work the same way. Violation is punished by the loss of sense. This is not punishment from without, but from within the practices of thinking and living, respectively. The question of how to construct thoughts that make sense cannot be framed. For we cannot think the unthinkable and then exclude it with laws to the purpose (see *TLP* 5.61). Wittgenstein may have thought that the question of how to give life meaning is likewise not able to be posed. This would be the case if a meaningless life were no life at all, but death—suicide. Death by one's own hand is figuratively what happens when we throw away our lives on things that don't matter. Literal suicide is the ultimate failure to make life itself goal enough (*NB* p. 73). Wittgenstein wrote in his notebook that "suicide is, so to speak, the elementary sin," because if there were no ethical "laws" then suicide would be permitted and if suicide were not permitted then there would be ethical laws (*NB* p. 91). Both the question about how to avoid senselessness in language and the question about how to avoid senselessness in life are equally impossible to pose.

And if the question can't be posed then there is no question to answer. This is the way to avoid the logical and existential anxieties that gave us the *Tractatus*. "The solution of the problem of life is seen in the vanishing of the problem" (*TLP* 6.521). What people have tried to say in providing theories of logical types and theories of the ethical life cannot be said, but makes itself manifest in the fact that some sentences and lives make sense, and others don't. What is higher takes care of itself.

(5) ... *sind Eins*

At the start of this chapter, I noted that the arc of the *Tractatus* moved from dejection to peace, and I suggested that this book traced the same arc as the 1872 *Birth of Tragedy*. This is not as gratuitous a comparison as it must at first have appeared. I am only suggesting that the book of Nietzsche's that is closest to Schopenhauer has points of contact with the book of Wittgenstein's that is closest to Schopenhauer. The structure of Nietzsche's book is this. First, the appearance that the principle of sufficient reason has suffered exception is terrifying. This is marked by what Nietzsche calls the wisdom of Silenus that the best thing is never to have been born, and the second best is to die young. Second we discover that beneath the realm characterized by the principle of sufficient reason—the realm of science—there is a primordial unity [Ur-Eine] that links the essence of the individual with the essence of the world. Discovering this primordial unity deep within our selves and nature, restores our ability to live. It overpowers the terrifying anxiety marked by Silenus, and gives us peace. The *Tractatus* has versions of both of these stages.

Wittgenstein's first book discusses the principle of sufficient reason while it is discussing science. His view is that scientific descriptions of the world all presuppose the principle of sufficient reason (nothing without reason) and the "law of causality" (no event without a cause), but that these laws are not discovered by scientific investigations.

6.34   All such propositions, including the principle of sufficient reason, the laws of continuity in nature and of least effort in nature etc. etc.—all these are a priori insights about the forms in which the propositions of science can be cast.

But as with the rest of the *Tractatus*, these a priori laws cannot even be put into words.

> 6.35   Laws like the principle of sufficient reason etc. etc. are about the net and not about what the net describes.
>
> 6.36   If there were a law of causality, it might be put in the following way: There are laws of nature.
>
>   But of course that cannot be said: it makes itself manifest.

The principle of sufficient reason is a feature of the net we use to understand the world; it is not a discovery about the world. The discovery that it is *not* a discovery about the world could easily be disturbing. If it is not part of the world then where is it? Could just anything happen? This anxiety, this care, afflicts Wittgenstein's thinking about logic (*L* R.2). If logical laws were empirical generalizations about brain meat, the hardness of logic would disappear. If the sum of 2 and 2 were only 4 *for us*, the hardness of arithmetic would disappear. Wittgenstein's response to these cares was not to firm up the foundations of logic or arithmetic, "my method is not to sunder the hard from the soft, but to see the hardness of the soft" (*NB* p. 44).[94] Logic treats of nothing (*TLP* 6.124).

Throughout this chapter I have occasionally used the word *care* to name the anxiety that characterizes Wittgenstein's philosophizing. This was Wittgenstein's own term in an early letter to Russell. On June 22, 1912, Wittgenstein wrote:

> Whenever I have time I now read James's "Varieties of Religious Exp." This book does me a lot of good. I don't mean that I will be a saint soon, but I am not sure that it does not improve me a little in a way in which I would like to improve *very much*; namely I think that it helps me to get rid of the *Sorge* (in the sense in which Goethe used the word in the second part of Faust). (*L* R.2)

Very likely Wittgenstein is thinking of the speeches of a "grey woman" named "Sorge [Care]." Here is one of them, delivered to Faust at Midnight, which it concerns cares so deep they could survive the acquisition of every treasure:

Care: He whom I have conquered could
        Own the world and not feel good:
        Gloom surrounds him without end,
        Sun shall not rise nor descend;
        Though his senses all abide,
        Darknesses now dwell inside,
        And though he owned every treasure,
        None should give him any pleasure;
        Luck and ill luck turn to anguish,
        In his plenty he must languish;
        Be it rapture or dismay,
        He will wait another day,
        Worry lest it vanish,
        And so he can never finish.[95]

There is no evidence that Wittgenstein linked care, in this sense, to the discovery that the principle of sufficient reason could not be a scientific discovery. But if you had counted on there being nothing without reason and then discovered that this principle could not be proved on the basis of science, this might easily appear to weaken the principle. It is the task of the *Tractatus* to reveal how this in fact strengthens it, thereby calming care.

The second feature of the *Birth of Tragedy* that we might find in the *Tractatus* is Nietzsche's way to peace through the primordial unity of the world—the discovery that all of what appear to be individuals are in fact part of the same primordial unity [Ur-Eine]. In the *Tractatus* this appears as the impossibility of thinking that there are differences in the realm of what is higher. The higher cannot be thought, so it cannot be thought to involve differences. Yet the higher is the source of all that is nonaccidental in the sense of propositions and in the sense of life. So the *Tractatus* rests the solution to its logical and existential cares on a unity beyond thought, a primordial unity. There are no thinkable distinctions in the realm of the higher. So the transcendental is not many, it is one.

2.027   Objects, the unalterable, and the subsistent are one [sind Eins].

6.421   (Ethics and aesthetics are one [sind Eins].)

5.621   The world and life are one [sind Eins].

2.027 says that the higher source of the realm of propositional sense is one. 6.421 says that the higher source of the realm of existential sense is one. 5.621 says that these two higher sources are themselves one. The unity of the transcendental. Above the world that divides into contingent facts, there is a higher realm beyond being in which all the individuality of the world of facts sublimes. The higher source of facts is a unity that must be divided into facts. Division is appearance held in place by a unity beyond being, beyond thought. The metaphysics of the *Tractatus* are designed to be the last metaphysics, they are designed to destroy the impulse to speak what must not be spoken.

This means that the *Tractatus* does not take its own methodological advice. Wittgenstein had written:

> 6.53   The correct method in philosophy would really be the following: to say nothing except what can be said, i.e., propositions of natural science—i.e. something that has nothing to do with philosophy—and then, whenever someone else wanted to say something metaphysical, to demonstrate to him that he had failed to give a meaning to certain signs in his propositions. Although it would not be satisfying to the other person—he would not have the feeling that we were teaching philosophy—*this* method would be the only strictly correct one.

The *Tractatus* does not follow this method; that is why Wittgenstein describes what the correct method would *really* be. He has not in fact followed it. Why not? One suspects that the reason is that the correct method is less satisfying in virtue of not seeming like it is the teaching of philosophy. The method of the *Tractatus* is to present one self-destroying metaphysical answer to all of our problems. Gesturing to Derrida, I have described this as a poison to cure us of metaphysics; James Conant provides the figure of a "vaccine."[96] Vaccines can be kept barely alive or killed. Those that are barely alive actually give the recipient a weak case of the disease: sufficient to acquire immunity but not to cause death. This seems to have been the strategy of the *Tractatus*: to vaccinate its readers with a metaphysics of meaning injured, but not killed, by irony.

> 6.54   My propositions serve as elucidations in the following way: anyone who understands me eventually recognizes them as

nonsensical [unsinnig], when he has used them—as steps—to climb up beyond them. (He must, so to speak, throw away the ladder after he has climbed up it.)

He must transcend these propositions, and then he will see the world aright.

The Tractarian metaphysics of the primordial unity is presented with irony, and when you come to see that, you will see the world aright. The nonaccidental scaffolding of the world cannot be put into any words at all, not even those of the *Tractatus.*

In his mature philosophy Wittgenstein sticks more closely to what even the *Tractatus* calls "the only strictly correct" method in philosophy (*TLP* 6.53). He may have come to think that the *Tractatus* was too ironic, too devious, too self-conscious, not plain enough to bring peace to our worries, calm to our cares. The danger with live vaccines is that you may kill the patient. In the *Philosophical Investigations* peace is more fragile, more precious, and the world more wonderful. There are still moments of security—freedom from care, but he is no longer of the opinion that all the essential problems of logical and existential meaning can be, and have been, solved. Fully, finally, solved (*TLP* preface).[97]

Chapter 3

Superficial Essentialism:
Wittgenstein's Turn from the Sublime

These considerations bring us up to the problem: in what sense is logic something sublime [etwas Sublimes]. (*PI* par. 89).

For we are under the illusion that what is sublime [das Sublime], what is essential, about our investigation consists in its grasping one comprehensive essence. (*Z* par. 444: c. 1937–38; see *PI* par. 97)

The more narrowly we examine actual language, the sharper becomes the conflict between it and our requirement. (For the crystalline purity of logic was, of course, not a result of investigation: it was a requirement.). . . . The preconceived idea [Vorurteil] of crystalline purity can only be removed by turning our whole examination around. (One might say: the examination must be turned, but around the fixed point of our real need.) (*PI* par. 107, 108)

The aspects of things that are most important for us are hidden because of their simplicity and familiarity. (One is unable to notice something—because it is always before one's eyes.) (*PI* par. 129)

(1) The Other Nietzsche and the Other Wittgenstein

"The break between *Tractatus* and *Philosophical Investigations* is of the same kind as that between Nietzsche's *The Birth of Tragedy* (1872) and his *Human, All-Too-Human* (1878)."[1] Although Erich Heller published this sentence in 1959, my efforts to read Nietzsche and Wittgenstein together have often been greeted with surprise or incredulity. Here, again, is my version of the story.

When Nietzsche republished *The Birth of Tragedy* in 1886, he repositioned his first book to suppress its most metaphysical moments. In the first chapter I argued that while retaining the Dionysian terror, Nietzsche tried to write the Dionysian ecstasy out of *The Birth.* He distanced himself from the ecstasy he had once found waiting on our confrontation with a lapse in the principle of individuation. But he continued to think there was no way to avoid the terror waiting on the suggestion that the principle of sufficient reason was itself groundless.

In Nietzsche's first account of the dynamics of tragedy, the terrifying thought that it would be best never to have been born is overcome by the realization that we (even we) and the pulsing power of the world are one [sind Eins]. Distinguishing his position from Schopenhauer's, this realization was to give us the courage *to live,* even in the face of the terrifying wisdom of Silenus. It was to give us peace. The mature Nietzsche continued to be motivated by the "question mark concerning the value of existence," but turned decisively against his earlier reliance on the primal unity [Ur-Eine] to restore the value of existence (*BT* SC par. 1).

Quite unexpectedly, by rejecting the metaphysics of primal unity, terror can be overcome. The very groundlessness of the things nearest to us renders them wonderful, fills them with a bloom and magic we had thought lost, forever (*HH* I, P par. 5). Peace is now ours, not thanks to the metaphysical Ur-Eine of the world, but thanks to nothing. Thanks only to our acceptance of the things nearest, with all their bloom and magic; so thanks only to our thankfulness.[2] "Oh, those Greeks! They knew how to live. . . . Those Greeks were superficial—*out of profundity!* [oberflächlich—*aus Tiefe*!]" (*GS* P, par. 4; see *PI* par. 92). Nietzsche's project rotated around the fixed point of our real need (see *PI* par. 108). Peace no longer arrives up from our ecstatic union with the darkest one; if we can muster the strength, peace will come right off the spots of sunlight on the downy surface of the things nearest. This is the vision of the great health of the free spirit.

> Only the *ennobled man may be given freedom of the spirit,* to him alone does the *easing of life* draw near and salve his wounds; only he may say that he lives for the sake of *joy* and for the sake of no further goal;[3] and in any other mouth his motto would be perilous: *Peace [Frieden] all around me and goodwill to all things nearest.* (*HH* II *WS* par. 350: 1880; Nietzsche's emphases)

Wittgenstein, too, was concerned with giving our restlessness peace. Moreover, he seems never to have relinquished his conviction that the way to ease our cares is to understand the grammar or logic of our language. Throughout his life he was convinced that once the grammar of our language was clarified, our cares would, by themselves, calm themselves. That is to say, his conception of philosophy persisted throughout the changes that brought the *Philosophical Investigations* to the surface from the esoteric depths of the *Tractatus*. Around the fixed point of his existential and logical cares, Wittgenstein turned his whole investigation around (*PI* par. 108). In the *Tractatus*, the grammar of our language was hidden beneath our actual use of words. Deep under the surface of language, the author of the *Tractatus* discerned only one kind of grammatical connection: truth-functional connections. In the *Investigations*, the grammar of our language—like the purloined letter—is hidden in plain view (see *PI* par. 129). The trick is to see what, from the very beginning, in all its exuberant variety, had been there on the surface.

The other Nietzsche and the other Wittgenstein resist the temptation to ground the sense of the sentences and of the world on a noncontingent reality behind, beyond, or beneath what is the case. My interpretation of the unwritten *Birth of Tragedy*, the one imagined by Nietzsche's never quite actualized book *Seven Prefaces* (1886), tracked this turn in Nietzsche's philosophy. This chapter begins to chart the same trajectory in Wittgenstein's mature philosophy. We will watch him turn his whole investigation around, thus—as he well knew—threatening not only its sublimity, but the very idea of logic itself. In this picture, our real needs are not to be altered, but to be acknowledged. The happy surprise—our good fortune—is that the absence of what we thought essential to their satisfaction can itself satisfy. Coming face to face with the dumb fact that some things do and some things do not make sense can incite the feeling that one is in Wittgenstein's words: "walking on a mountain of wonders."[4]

(2) Orientation

The *Tractatus* had begun with a motto and a preface that served to orient the reader to the peculiar nature of the book to follow. The *Investigations* continues this practice, and shares the somewhat pained tone of the *Tractatus*'s preface. But it shares none of the philosophical confidence of that earlier preface. It seemed to the author of the *Tractatus* that the truth of the thoughts there communicated was "unassailable and definitive" (*TLP* P). He was of the opinion that "on all essential points" he had found the "final solution" to the logical and existential problems his book addressed (*TLP* P). This philosophical confidence is completely absent from the preface to the *Investigations*: "I make them [my remarks] public with doubtful feelings. It is not impossible that it should fall to the lot of this work, in its poverty and in the darkness of this time, to bring light into one brain or another—but, of course, it is not likely" (*PI* P).

How are we to understand this loss of philosophical confidence? Perhaps in this way. Perhaps Wittgenstein's mature approach to philosophy leaves no room for permanent solutions to philosophical problems, philosophical unease. This makes it very difficult to write a treatise of logic or philosophy, even one that, like the *Tractatus*, treats the untreatable ground of sense ironically. But the author of the *Investigations* is as yet unreconciled to the fact that his new investigations were incompatible with the idea of a treatise or a book. Thus we find that author writing a preface that raises some puzzling questions about whether the text that follows should properly be described as a book, at all.

Wittgenstein's first book was not a book in two obvious senses. Its numbering system asks that its sentences be read in an order determined in part, and variously, by its various readers; this is what makes it resemble what is today called a hypertext. Moreover, each of the sentences in that book is described by that very book as gibberish, Unsinn. So in the previous chapter, I stole the first sentence of Derrida's *Dissemination* for the *Tractatus*: This (therefore) will not have been a book.[5] This Derridean sentence might equally—but for different reasons—characterize the *Investigations*.

The preface of the *Investigations* ends on a note of regret: "I should have liked to produce a good book. This has not come about, but the time is past in which I could improve it" (*PI* P). So this is not a good book; but what is a good book?

> It was my intention at first to bring all this together in a book whose form I pictured differently at different times. But the essential thing, it seemed to me, was that the thoughts should proceed from one subject to another in a natural order and without breaks [natürlichen und lücklosen Folge]. (*PI* P)

What was the problem? Why was he unable to present his thoughts in a natural order, without breaks? Here is his reason: "my thoughts were soon crippled if I tried to force them on in any single direction against their natural inclination" [ihre natürliche Neigung] (*PI* P). He seems to be explaining the appearance of his text. Rather than breaking the bones of his thoughts by forcing them into the form of a book, Wittgenstein presented them ordered according to their natural inclination. But this is puzzling, for the "essential thing" about a good book is just such a natural arrangement. So is this a bad book, because the thoughts do NOT proceed in a natural order? Or: is it a good book after all, because the thoughts DO proceed according to their natural inclination?

Wittgenstein's difficulty in presenting his work as a "good book" may be the result of his work representing a break with the tradition of the book. The natural inclination of his thoughts would not permit being cast in the form of a traditional philosophy book: a book with a theory or a thesis to defend, objections to be answered, further research to be sketched.[6] And Wittgenstein tells us that his failure to weld his thoughts together into such a book was not a personal failing of his, but "was, of course, connected with the very nature of the investigation" (*PI* P). So it begins to look as though these investigations are essentially unbookable, their apparently digressive, haphazard form is their own kind of rigor. This preface argues that the text to come could not have been a good book, so why the closing note of regret? I don't know. Perhaps, realizing how much his writing demands from its readers, realizing how strange and difficult it would appear (especially to philosophers), he never finally gave up the hope of making his work seem more traditional, the hope of writing what the world would recognize as a "good book."

But if not even able to take the form of a good book, what is the nature of Wittgenstein's philosophical investigations? In the preface, he characterizes them as attempting to give an overall picture of an entire landscape (language)[7] by means of sketches of particular features of the terrain from particular vantage points. And the difficulty, he concedes, is not simply that his intention is to construct an aerial photograph (a "synoptic view")[8] from a pad full of sketches of particular rocks and trees, but also that these sketches are not always terribly good. At other times, he spoke about philosophy in different terms.

G. E. Moore reports that in lectures delivered in 1930–31, Wittgenstein said his mature philosophical methods were similar to the methods of housekeeping. Moore:

> He said . . . that the "new subject" [he taught] consisted in "something like putting in order our notes as to what can be said about

> the world," and compared this to the tidying up of a room where you
> have to move the same object several times before you can get the
> room really tidy.[9]

Wittgenstein emphasizes that tidying up a room is the kind of activity
that involves addressing the couch a number of different times for a
number of different purposes before the couch and environs are clean.
So too his philosophical investigations will approach the same or almost
the same points from a number of different directions before the source
of our confusion, our disquietude, can be healed. Equally important is
another feature of housework that is shared by Wittgenstein's later
vision of philosophy: it is never done. Tidy rooms untidy themselves. So
too in philosophy, the bothered individual can be calmed, but time
uncalms all things (Sophocles, *Oedipus at Colonus*, l. 695). Philosophy
and housework are never finished, but sometimes we stop, survey the
site of our previous discomfort, and are content. These passing
moments of peace are the ambition of Wittgenstein's philosophical and
existential investigations (*PI* par. 133).

The preface to the *Investigations* also remembers that when Wittgenstein returned to philosophy after a hiatus of almost ten years, he
was "forced to recognize grave mistakes in what [he] . . . wrote in that
first book" (*PI* P). What are these "grave mistakes"? How shall we bring
them to light? My approach will be to focus on the *Investigations'* own
picture of these grave mistakes. Much of the attraction and difficulty of
this topic derives from the fact that Wittgenstein's two most influential
books are so wholly different and yet so utterly the same. The later one
has an uncanny resemblance to the earlier one.[10]

First, early and late Wittgenstein recognized that his problems, like
those of Hertz, would not be touched by further scientific investigations
(*TLP* 4.111; *PI* par. 109).[11] Second, early and late he thought the way to
calm our cares was to provide a perspicuous representation of the logic
or grammar of our language (*TLP* 3.325; *PI* par. 90, 122). Third, early
and late he thought that the grammar of language was hidden (*TLP*
3.323; *PI* par. 90). But fourth, early on he thought the grammar was all
of one sort and hidden beneath the surface of language (*TLP* 4.002).
Only later did he come to believe that the grammar of language was
multiform and distributed on the surface of language; only later did he
come to believe that the grammar of language was hidden, because it
was "always before one's eyes" (*PI* par. 129). The change, I want to say,

is from a sublime to a superficial conception of grammar and of what grammar expresses: essence (*PI* par. 371).

Some will remember that Wittgenstein once said just the opposite; namely, that the *Investigations* were concerned to uncover depth grammar. Wittgenstein writes:

664. In the use of words one might distinguish "surface grammar" from "depth grammar." What immediately impresses itself upon us about the use of a word is the way it is used in the construction of the sentence, the part of its use—one might say—that can be taken in by the ear. And now compare the depth grammar, say of the word "to mean," with what its surface grammar would lead us to suspect. No wonder we find it difficult to know our way about. (*PI* par. 664)

In this paragraph, Wittgenstein is using the difference between surface and depth grammar to mark the difference between features of the use of a word which are easily recognized and those which are not. But what are the aspects of the use of language that are difficult to recognize? The superficial aspects: "The aspects of things that are most important for us are hidden because of their simplicity and familiarity" (*PI* par. 129). The work of Wittgenstein's mature philosophical investigations is "to bring words back from their metaphysical to their everyday use" (*PI* par. 116). I shall attempt to display the fact that Wittgenstein more usually uses the figure of the surface as something he wishes he had the strength to accept than, as at paragraph 664, something to be seen beneath. The apparent inconsistency is a consequence of the fact that Wittgenstein follows a long tradition in describing the peculiar difficulty and importance of philosophy as its depth [Tiefe] (*Z* par. 456). His hope—to return from the metaphysical to the everyday—is one he shares with many others, not only Nietzsche and his recovery of the near, but also Walt Whitman:

Perhaps indeed the efforts of the true poets, founders, religions, literatures, all ages, have been, and ever will be, our time and times to come, essentially the same—to bring people back from their persistent strayings and sickly abstractions, to the costless average, divine, original concrete.[12] *Copyrighted Material*

(3) Grave Mistakes: The Sublime as Critique

Although Wittgenstein sometimes speaks of where he wants to bring us back from as metaphysics, he also refers to this extraordinary place as sublime. So it is not unusual to remark that the "grave mistakes" Wittgenstein came to find in the *Tractatus* may all derive from what the *Investigations* suggests we think of as a "tendency to sublime the logic of our language—as we might put it" (*PI* par. 38). But the force of "sublime" as a term of criticism remains obscure. Here is Rorty, voicing his version of the mature Wittgenstein's criticisms of the *Tractatus*:

> Why, [Wittgenstein] comes to ask himself, did I think that logic—the outmost frontier of language, looming over the abyss beyond—was something sublime? Or even if it were, what is the sublime to me? Why did I hope that there was something like a "limited whole" to be felt? Why did I think that language had a limit, that there was a single problem called "the problem of life," that to grasp that problem one must teeter over an abyss? Not, he concluded, because deep philosophical researches showed such limits to exist, but because an ascetic, obsessively self-purificatory attitude toward ordinary human life had demanded that there be such limits, such a problem, and such an abyss.[13]

In this passage, Rorty associates the tendency to sublime the logic of our language with the (eighteenth-century) paradigms of the aesthetic sublime: ravines, chasms, gorges, and abysses. To the extent that people have attempted to understand the force of *sublime* as a term of criticism, this is the way they have approached it. Even Cavell, who is less sure than Rorty that Wittgenstein outgrew his fascination with these dizzying ideas, provides an aesthetic interpretation of Wittgenstein's talk of the sublime.[14]

I share Cavell's interest in the *positive* connection between what Burke (for example) might have called the sublime and the writings of the mature Wittgenstein. But if Rorty is right in reading the "tendency to sublime the logic of our language" as a reference to just this aesthetic tradition, then the positive ties binding the *Investigations* to the aesthetic notion of the sublime (e.g., the role in that book of groundlessness) would be in conflict with Wittgenstein's criticism of the *Tractatus* as sublime. We would therefore do well to look for a new, nonaesthetic interpretation of the tendency to sublime. "Sublime" appears in the title of my own chapter on the *Tractatus,* but I there lent this word a more chemical than aesthetical force, and that is the way I will read Wittgenstein's use of "sublime" as a term of criticism.

The word for the aesthetic concept of the sublime, *das Erhabene,* does not appear once in the *Concordance* to the *Investigations.*[15] When Wittgenstein asks, "In what sense is logic something sublime?" (*PI* par. 89), his word is *sublimes,* and the central uses of this word are not aesthetical but chemical. It corresponds to our verb *to sublime,* which refers, for example, to the ability of dry ice at room temperature to change directly from solid to gas. In chemical contexts, to sublime is to pass from a solid state directly to a gaseous state, without passing through a liquid state. If this were the slant of Wittgenstein's use of *sublime,* then there would be less tension in Cavell's defense of the relevance of the aesthetic sublime to the *Investigations.* But the prospects for linking the criticism gathered by the term *sublime* to dry ice will not, at first, seem very promising.

At least not until we remember that one of the illusions Wittgenstein hopes to overcome is parenthetically parodied in this way: "(The conception of thought as a gaseous [pneumatische] medium)" (*PI* par. 109). So we should not be surprised to discover the *Blue Book* discussing gasses at some length:

> But let me remind you here of the queer role which the gaseous and the aetherial play in philosophy,—when we perceive that a substantive is not used as what in general we should call the name of an object, and when therefore we can't help saying to ourselves that it is the name of an aetherial object. I mean we already know the idea of "aetherial objects" as a subterfuge, when we are embarrassed about the grammar of certain words, and when all we know is that they are not used as names for material objects. (*BlB* p. 47)

Gas does indeed figure in Wittgenstein's genealogy of (queer) philosophical theorizing. To construe significant conversation as requiring—for its possibility—more than persons using words, as requiring in addition propositional contents accompanying the words in an invisible gaseous realm of thought, would be to sublime—in the chemical sense—the functioning, the logic, of our language.

This is one of the ways in which Wittgenstein uses the sublime as critique. It appears in a Wittgensteinian genealogy of the exasperated exclamations: "A proposition is a queer thing!"; "Thought must be something unique" (*PI* par. 94, 95). Grant this thought: "When we say, and *mean*, that such-and-such is the case, we—and our meaning—do not stop anywhere short of the fact, but we mean: *such-and-such—is—so-and-so*" (*PI* par. 95). The problem is that not only can we speak about what is the case (the material world), we can also speak about what is not the case (*PI* par. 95). And then, our thought cannot—so we think—acquire its meaning in the same way that it does when we speak about what is the case, for now there is no fact for our thought to take us all the way to. So we suppose that thought can never take us more than half way. We can think about what is not the case as well as about what is the case, so our significant utterances must acquire their significance from a world *between* what we say and what is the case: a gaseous world. Wittgenstein:

> "A proposition is a queer thing!" Here we have in germ the subliming of the whole account [Sublimierung der ganzen Darstellung]. The tendency to assume a pure intermediary between the propositional *signs* and the facts. Or even to try to purify, to sublime [sublimieren], the signs themselves. (*PI* par. 94)

Unfortunately, even if these remarks are adequate as a criticism of the aesthetical interpretation of Wittgenstein's use of "sublime" as a term of criticism, the mere fact that one interprets this term as a chemical metaphor does little to bring that criticism into focus.

Some further help is provided by the following remark included in a 1937–38 version of the *Investigations*,[16] where he is discussing why philosophers sometimes have theories without recognizing them to be theories:

> For it is the characteristic thing about such a [hidden] theory that it looks at a special clearly intuitive case and says: "*That* shows how things are in every case; this case is the exemplar [Urbild] of *all* cases."—"Of course! It has to be like that" we say, and are satisfied. We have arrived at a form of expression [Darstellung] that *strikes us as obvious*. But it is as if we had now seen something lying *beneath* the surface [*unter* der Oberfläche liegt].
>
> The tendency to generalize the clear case seems to have a strict justification in logic: here one seems *completely* justified in inferring: "If *one* proposition is a picture, then any proposition must be a picture, for they must all be of the same essence." For we are under the illusion that what is sublime [das Sublime], what is essential about

our investigation consists in its grasping *one* comprehensive essence [Wesen]. (*Z* par. 444; see *PI* 92)

If there is a tendency to sublime the logic of our language, this passage articulates two aspects of this tendency:

1. Digging beneath the surface of language, hoping to unearth

2. The one, comprehensive essence of whatever has caused our philosophical unease.

Let these aspects define the tendency to sublime the logic of our language.[17] This two-pronged interpretation of the tendency to sublime already suggests that, whereas the *Tractatus* sought a sublime essence of language underneath the superficial features of our life with signs, the later work looked for the essence of language in the surface of our lives. Like the later work of Nietzsche, Wittgenstein's *Investigations* is superficial, not out of hastiness, but out of profundity (see *GS* P par. 4). Let us see whether we can understand the *Investigations'* criticism of the *Tractatus* in terms of this account of the "sublime" as a term of criticism.

(4) Turning from the Tendency to Sublime

The commonplace observation that Wittgenstein understood the *Tractatus* to have sublimed the logic of our language is correct. If the *Investigations* has one opponent, this tendency is it. But it is a Protean enemy. In this section, I will discuss three paragraphs of the *Investigations,* each of which manifests Wittgenstein's opposition to subliming accounts of language. I begin with two paragraphs concerned more or less explicitly with the *Tractatus,* and conclude with a reading of the very first paragraph of the book. An opposition to subliming accounts of language orients the whole of Wittgenstein's mature philosophizing: both his explicit discussion of linguistic meaning and his implicit discussion of existential meaning.

(a) *Investigations:* Paragraph 98

Almost citing the discussion of the sublime in *Zettel* 444, the *Investigations* confesses: Copyrighted Material

> We are under the illusion that what is peculiar, profound [Tiefe], essential in our investigation, resides in its trying to grasp the incomparable essence [Wesen] of language. . . . On the one hand it is clear that every sentence in our language "is in order as it is." That is to say, we are not *striving after* an ideal, as if our ordinary vague sentences had not yet got a quite unexceptionable sense, and a perfect language awaited construction by us. On the other hand it seems clear that where there is sense there must be perfect order [vollkommene Ordnung]. So there must be perfect order even in the vaguest sentences. (*PI* par. 97–98)

These lines suggest the following simple argument:

1. ". . . every sentence in our language is 'in order as it is.'" (*PI* par. 98)

2. ". . . where there is sense there must be perfect order." (PI par. 98)

SO

3. ". . . there must be perfect order even in the vaguest sentence." (*PI* par. 98)

The quotation in (1) is a paraphrase of part of *Tractatus* 5.5563. (2) is a paraphrase of *Tractatus* 3.23. These connections suggest that we might read this passage as offering the following diagnosis of the "grave errors" of the *Tractatus* (*PI* P). It is a genealogy by subtraction: Take the *Tractatus*, subtract the Fregean requirement that sense be explained in terms of a perfect order, and you will have the *Investigations* (see chap. 2, sect. 3). The demand for a perfect order is the tendency to sublime the logic of our language. Beneath the confusing superficial similarities of language we were to find the one truth-functional essence of the proposition (*TLP* 6).

The mature Wittgenstein disrupts this pattern of thinking by denying that "where there is sense there must be perfect order" (*PI* par. 98). Consider his immediate response to the argument of *PI* par. 98. In the last chapter I discussed Frege's use of the analogy between a concept and an area on a plane surface.[18] Wittgenstein recalls this Fregean analogy when, in the *Investigations*, he observes:

> An indefinite boundary is not really a boundary at all. Here one thinks perhaps: if I say "I have locked the man up fast in the room—

there is only *one* door left open"—then I simply haven't locked him in at all; his being locked in is a sham. One would be inclined to say here: "You haven't done anything at all." An enclosure with a hole in it is as good as *none*. (*PI* par. 99; see *Z* par. 441)

And these are indeed the kind of considerations that incite the tendency to sublime. The author of the *Investigations* simply asks, "—But is that true?" (*PI* par. 99). It is not true. We forget that if the man does not think that perhaps one of the doors is open, then he may very well be locked in a room with an open door. Of course there is no proof that nobody could ever get out of such a room, but—all the same—some won't, ever.

Analogous considerations were in play during Wittgenstein's discussion of ostensive definition. Wittgenstein is very well known for having observed that, when you explain the word *tove* by pointing to a pencil and saying "This is tove," your ostensive definition might be variously interpreted to mean "this is a pencil," "this is thin," "this is yellow," "this is one," and so on down all the properties of the pencil (*BlB* p. 2: 1933). He is less well known for having observed that ostensive definitions can be perfectly exact.

Now one can ostensively define a proper name, the name of a color, the name of a material, a numeral, the name of a point of the compass, and so on. The definition of the number two, "That is called 'two'"—pointing to two nuts—is perfectly exact [vollkommen exakt]. (*PI* par. 28)

He has not forgotten that, as this very paragraph has it, "an ostensive definition can be variously interpreted in *every* case" (*PI* par. 28). So how can this definition be "perfectly exact"? It is clear that as Wittgenstein is using the expression "perfectly exact" in this paragraph, an ostensive definition does not have to be protected from *every possible misinterpretation* in order to be perfectly exact. All that is required is that the person to whom the definition is given takes the definition in the right way (*PI* par. 29).

The ease with which we sublime the logic of our language is the ease with which we think, "But this is not *really* perfectly exact. It is just lucky that it worked. What we really need is a mode of ostensive definition that it is impossible to misinterpret. Anything less is not perfectly exact." The expression "'perfectly exact'" is here subliming. It is turning into the sublimed notion of perfection that we discovered in *Investigations* par. 98. Wittgenstein offers a brief diagnosis of the tendency.

> It can also be put like this: we eliminate misunderstandings by mak-ing our expressions more exact; but now it may look as if we were moving toward a particular state, a state of complete exactness [vollkommenen Exaktheit]; and as if this were the real goal of our investigation. (*PI* par. 91)[19]

It is true that we can sometimes remove misunderstanding by adding sortal terms. Instead of "This is called 'two,'" we say "This *number* is called 'two,'" "This *color* is called 'red,'" "This *length* is six inches." So it can appear that we are moving toward a perfectly exact definition: one that nobody could possibly misunderstand. But this sublimes the prac-tice here truly described. The sortals are added where and when needed, but they are in no better position—in point of possible misunderstand-ing—than the original ostensive definition.[20] Wittgenstein:

> That is to say: misunderstandings are sometimes averted in this way. But is there only *one* way of taking the word "color" or "length"? (*PI* par. 29)

Another voice suggests:

> —Well, they just need defining. (*PI* par. 29)

Wittgenstein replies:

> Defining, then, by means of other words! And what about the last def-inition in this chain? (*PI* par. 29)

And suspecting the other voice would be inclined to say that there was no last definition because the series of definitions *could* go on forever, Wittgenstein warns:

> (Do not say: "There isn't a 'last' definition." That is just as if you chose to say: "There isn't a last house in this road; one can always build an additional one.") (*PI* par. 29)

The "real goal" (*PI* par. 91) of Wittgenstein's investigation is to resolve misunderstandings of our language, and there is no magical form of words that will accomplish this—always and inevitably. In particular, the *Investigations* turns away from the Fregean approach to sense embodied by the *Tractatus*: the fantasy of a perfect logical order:

> When I give the description: "The ground was quite covered with plants"—do you want to say that I don't know what I am talking about until I can give a definition [Definition] of plant? . . . Frege compares a concept to an area and says that an area with vague boundaries cannot be called an area at all.[21] This presumably means that we cannot do anything with it.—But is it senseless to say "Stand roughly there"? (*PI* par. 70–71)

No. In different circumstances different strategies will relieve our philosophical cares. "There is not *one* [*eine*] philosophical method, though there are indeed methods, like different therapies" (*PI* par. 133). The emphasis here, and the change from the *Tractatus,* is on the *plurality* of methods.

(b) *Investigations*: Paragraph 23

The first time the *Investigations* invokes the name of Wittgenstein's first book is in a final parenthesis appended to a paragraph that begins by asking,

> But how many kinds of sentence [Satz] are there? Say assertion, question, and command? (*PI* par. 23)

This is the start of a recognizable list needing only the addition of exclamations to fill out a list I vaguely remember from elementary school. And it fits a familiar picture of language as first of all a formal structure of signs with sense, which is then employed to accomplish a variety of things in our lives: to assert, to command, etc. Wittgenstein's paradigm of this approach to language is "Frege's idea that every assertion contains an assumption, which is the thing asserted" in an assertion, commanded in a command, queried in a question, and so forth (*PI* par. 22).[22] Wittgenstein elaborated Frege's idea on a slip of paper inserted into the typescript at this point:

> Imagine a picture representing a boxer in a particular stance. Now, this picture can be used to tell someone how he should stand, should hold himself; or how he should not hold himself; or how a particular

man did stand in such-and-such a place; and so on. One might (using the language of chemistry [!]) call this picture a proposition-radical. This will be how Frege thought of the "assumption." (*PI* page 11e, bottom)

On this account, which would fit the *Tractatus* picture of language equally as well,[23] there will be a unitary account of the senses of propositions and then a variety of ways of employing these: to make assertions, commands, and so on. We owe to Dummett the currency of Frege's marking this distinction with the terms *sense* and *force*, and Dummett correctly notices that this is a distinction Wittgenstein does not take to be basic.[24]

In this Fregean/Tractarian scheme it would be important to decide how many different kinds of forces a proposition might be given. Dummett concedes: "if no definitive list of types of force can be made, then no complete account of language can ever be arrived at by Frege's strategy."[25] And it is true that when Wittgenstein does ask himself how many kinds of sentence there are, an authoritative voice replies:

—There are *countless* kinds: countless different kinds of use of what we call "symbols," "words," "sentences." And this multiplicity is not something fixed, given once for all; but new types of language, new language-games, as we may say, come into existence, and others become obsolete and get forgotten. . . . Here the term "language-*game*" is meant to bring into prominence that the *speaking* of language is part of an activity, or of a form of life. (*PI* par. 23; Wittgenstein's emphases)

According to Dummett, the "real point" of paragraph 23 "is to deny that there is any 'language-game' of such generality as that of assertion; and if there is not, then, it seems to me [Dummett], there is no general distinction between sense and force."[26] This worries Dummett, because if there is no such distinction, then it may simply be impossible to give a "systematic account of how a language functions, or of what we know when we know a language. . . . [And Dummett exclaims] But how can this be? . . . How can it be impossible to say what it is that we do, what it is that we learn?"[27]

Dummett has great admiration for the *Investigations*. He says this passage criticizing Frege's doctrine of assertion sticks out like a gasometer in a classical landscape.[28] For Dummett, a "systematic account of how language functions" means a determination of the particular content of each utterance in terms of some central notion such as truth or verification, set against the background of some uniform explanation of the significance of an utterance with some arbitrary given content, so determined.[29]

If that is what a "systematic account of how language functions" means, then Wittgenstein's opposition to such an account—so far from being, like the gasometer, incidental and occasional—is the beating heart of the *Investigations*.

This is one way of receiving Wittgenstein's self-interpretation of his use of "language-game."

> Here the term "language-*game*" is meant to bring into prominence the fact that the *speaking* of language is part of an activity, or of a form of life. (*PI* par. 23; Wittgenstein's emphases.)

In an earlier paragraph, one of the uses of this expression was introduced this way: "I shall also call the whole, consisting of language and the actions into which it is woven, the 'language-game'." (*PI* par. 7). Thus the term "language-*game*" serves, by itself, to mark Wittgenstein's distance from the Fregean approach to language just described. On Wittgenstein's mature account, language is first of all something people do, it is part of an activity. The Fregean/Tractarian approach requires that we divide our knowing what Patrick asserted into our knowledge of the semantic content of the utterance and our knowledge of the conversational force or use to which Patrick was putting that content. I take Cavell to be elaborating the *Investigations'* alternative approach when he wrote:

> To know what a person said you have to know [1] that he or she has *asserted* something, and [2] know what he or she has asserted. What difficulty is there in that? No difficulty, nothing is easier. But what is easy, then, is to understand the point of his words; for that is essential to knowing that he has asserted something and knowing what he has asserted. And that is what is left out when we look upon what he means as *given* by, or derived from, the meanings of the words he used. . . . If the connection between "our words" and "what we mean" is a necessary one, this necessity is not established by universals, propositions, or rules, but by the form of life which makes certain stretches of syntactical utteran

If I understand what Patrick has said, I must have understood Patrick. It is not enough to be able to imagine a different context in which the words in that order might have made sense. That might be an acoustical illusion, similar to the illusion of understanding a parrot when it "speaks" (see *PI* par. 525, *OC* par. 10). To understand what Patrick has said, I must understand Patrick's actions as part of an activity, or form of life. That is why there are countless kinds of sentences. For how many kinds of things do people do? Countless kinds, and this multiplicity is not something fixed, given once for all; but new kinds of thing come into existence and others become obsolete and get forgotten. Wittgenstein's "countless kinds" is not the groundless, European hyperbole it has seemed to the friends of Austin.[31] It is a simple truth.

Paragraph 23 continues with a command: "Review the multiplicity of language-games in the following examples, and in others" (*PI* par. 23). And Wittgenstein then lists more than fifteen different language-games. The reader is supposed first to consider how very different are the contextual homes of these different linguistic practices, and then to continue the comparison with other cases.[32] Wittgenstein's hope is that this exercise will confront us with the variety of ways that language bubbles up out of our lives, and make us suspicious of the value of Dummett's dream: a systematic "account of the particular content of each utterance in terms of some central notion such as truth or verification."[33] Finally the paragraph closes and recalls the *Tractatus*:

> —It is interesting to compare the multiplicity of the tools in language and of the ways they are used, the multiplicity of kinds of word and sentence, with what logicians have said about the structure of language. (Including the author of the *Tractatus Logico-Philosophicus*.) (*PI* par. 23)

According to Wittgenstein, one of the "grave mistakes" (*PI* P) of the *Tractatus* was to deny the countless kinds of sentences, to deny the unbounded variety of things we do (with words): to sublime the logic of our language, the logic of our lives.

(c) *Investigations*: Paragraph 1

The *Investigations* opens with a criticism of Augustine's account of the essence of language, a sublime essence. Wittgenstein introduced his mature thoughts with his opposition to the tendency to sublime.

Augustine's words come first: a brief account—purportedly from memory—of how he learned his mother tongue.[34] Wittgenstein then remarks:

> These words, it seems to me, give us a particular picture of the essence [Wesen] of human language. It is this: the individual words in a language name objects—the sentences are combinations of such names. (*PI* par. 1)

Right at the start we are concerned with the a rough picture of the *essence* of language, according to which what makes a sound or a mark linguistic is that it names objects. Of course Augustine's is not yet a systematic theory of meaning in Dummett's sense, but it does already display an impressive obliviousness to the countless ways language works. So the first mouthful of the investigations already exhibits a version of the grave mistake that *PI* par. 23 attributes to the author of the *Tractatus*.

In the spell of this picture, we may construct a more robust, more philosophical theory (*Z* par. 444). Wittgenstein asserts:

> —In this picture of language we find the roots of the following idea: [1] Every word has a meaning. [2] This meaning is correlated with the word. [3] It is the object for which the word stands. (*PI* par. 1, my numbers)

The picture of language provided by Augustine is the soil in which this more systematic theory of meaning roots itself. Wittgenstein's immediate response to this "philosophical concept of meaning" (*PI* par. 2) is that if you are tempted by such a conception you are

> thinking primarily of nouns like "table," "chair," "bread," and of people's names, and only secondarily of names of certain actions and properties; and of the remaining kinds of word as something that will take care of itself [als etwas, was sich finden wird]. (*PI* par. 1; compare *Z* par. 444; contrast *NB* p. 1)

According to this conception, the meaning of a word is construed as the object for which it stands, and so it should be no surprise that it is most satisfying when we are concerned with words for relatively independent *objects*. It is rather less satisfying with actions, like playing. What is the object for which "playing" stands or means"? It is not very satisfying when applied to properties, like being red or being five inches long. Ironically, the cited passage from Augustine is itself a rich source of words that do not happily fit the idea that *every* word stands for an *object* that is its *meaning*. Just looking at the first two lines of the passage, we find: "when," "some," "and," "accordingly," "saw," "grasped," "the," "was." *None* of these words—out of Augustine's own mouth—is very happily construed as standing for an object that is its meaning.

The first paragraph proceeds to tell the story of what can appear to be a sort of zombie shopping trip.[35] Without saying a word, a man passes a slip of paper to a shopkeeper. The paper has been marked "five red apples." After looking at the paper, the shopkeeper

> opens the drawer marked "apples"; then he looks up the word "red" in a table and finds a color sample opposite it; then he says the series of cardinal numbers—I assume that he knows them by heart—up to the word "five" and for each number he takes an apple of the same color as the sample out of the drawer. (*PI* par. 1)

Wittgenstein comments:

> —It is in this and similar ways that one operates with words. (*PI* par. 1)

You will be thinking: it certainly is not! It is not the way I buy five red apples from a shopkeeper. I simply say "five red apples" and then the grocer puts five red apples in a bag for me; there is no trace of any silent looking up colors in a table or of reciting the cardinal numbers out loud.

But sometimes we do behave like this. I look over the paint samples and circle the color I want: Pine Forest Green. When I hand the color sample to the shopkeeper I say, "two gallons please." Then he looks up the formula for mixing Pine Forest Green in a book and proceeds to mix so many drops of this with so many drops of that. He does it twice, once for each gallon. Again, we might think of Wittgenstein's story "as one of those games by means of which children learn their native language" (*PI* par. 7). Small children *might* play at shopping more or less according to Wittgenstein's story. Thus with modest effort, we can place Wittgenstein's story in our lives. Still we may not be ready to concede that "it is in this and similar ways that one operates with words" (*PI* par. 1).

The difficulty is that Wittgenstein's shopper and shopkeeper seem mindless. True: words are presented by one and the other reacts in an unusual but recognizable way. But we may feel that this is only the external side of our operations with words. There is something missing: the inside, the understanding. That, we may feel, is the essential thing, and it is absent.

Another voice now asks, "But how does he [the shopkeeper] know where and how he is to look up the word 'red' and what he is to do with the word 'five'?" (*PI* par. 1). The two persons involved don't show any signs that there is anything particular going on in their minds. Hence, the trancelike appearance. Although there are many ways that this could come to seem a problem, one of them is closely related to the conception of meaning that Wittgenstein introduced in this very paragraph. Later in this book, Wittgenstein will argue that when I respond understandingly to a linguistic act, my understanding does not consist in anything particular (or perhaps at all) going on in my head (see *PI* par. 150–55). To suspect otherwise is to show oneself bound by the spell of the Augustinian picture of the essence of language and the idea that *every* word stands for an *object* that is its *meaning*.

The shopkeeper does indeed understand what to do upon receipt of a slip marked "five red apples." But if "understanding" must stand for an object, which objects will be the likely candidates? Running a finger along a table to find the color sample marked "red"? Scanning the drawers for one marked "apples"? There is much that is unappetizing about these suggestions. For one thing they are not very much like objects, for another they don't seem to be the kind of thing that *understanding* should—or could—consist in. They seem too material: not spiritual enough. Far more tempting will be mental states, interior thoughts. I suspect it is the absence of these from Wittgenstein's description that originally gives these characters the attributes of zombies. In this first paragraph, Wittgenstein doesn't argue against those who would identify understanding with a mental state. He satisfies himself with drawing a connection between the urge to make that identification and the Augustinian picture. Wittgenstein nowhere describes his shopper and shopkeeper as zombies. Their trancelike appearance was contributed by us, in particular, by our commitment to the Augustinian picture of the essence of language.

Wittgenstein's positive account of what their understanding does consist in must—at least at first sight—seem impossibly slight.

"But how does he [the shopkeeper] know where and how he is to look up the word 'red' and the word 'five'?"—Well, I assume that he *acts* [*handelt*] as I have described. Explanations come to an end somewhere. (*PI* par. 1)[36]

There it is. In the opening paragraph of the *Investigations*, Wittgenstein is already opting for the non-Fregean approach to language that we discovered in paragraph 23, where the *Tractatus* will have first been mentioned. In the *Investigations*, language is not first of all to be understood in terms of a theory of semantic content, but simply as a part of the countless things that people do: the way they act [handeln].

Later in the book, Wittgenstein asks himself: How am I able to obey [folgen] a rule? and he replies:

—if this is not a question about causes, then it is about the justification for my following the rule in the way I do [das ich *so* nach ihr handle].

If I have exhausted the justifications I have reached bedrock, and my spade is turned. Then I am inclined to say: "This is simply what I do" ["So handle ich eben"]. (*PI* par. 217)

Explanations come to an end somewhere. We could have figured that out. It is just that we thought they wouldn't end at the very beginning, in the first paragraph. In 1950, Wittgenstein was still writing: "It is our *acting* [*Handeln*], which lies at the bottom of the language-game" (*OC* par. 204). From the *Tractatus*'s unutterable substance of the world, the *Investigations* turns to what we just do (from Nietzsche 1872 to Nietzsche 1886). From necessity to contingency. From an unutterable explanation to no explanation at all.

Barely two lines remain of this first paragraph of the *Investigations*. They radicalize the point just made about action.

—But what is the meaning of the word "five"? No such thing was in question here, only how the word "five" is used. (*PI* par. 1)

Demanding a meaning for the word *five*, no less than demanding a mental state to account for the shopkeeper's understanding, is incited by the Augustinian idea that *every* word stands for an *object* that is its *meaning*. The word *five* was apparently used with meaning, so we hunt for an object. None is ready to hand, so we decide we don't, or don't fully, understand (even) this shopping story. Yet it should be the easiest thing in the world to understand, we make it difficult for ourselves because, under the spell of the Augustinian picture, we think we must find what we can't find. "What one ought to shun is found attractive. One puts to one's lips what drives one ever faster into the abyss."[37]

Far from offering a theory of meaning as use, Wittgenstein contrasts a concern for the meaning of words with a concern for their use. Certainly he would discard the general concept of meaning that he associates with the Augustinian picture of the essence of human language.

> If we look at the example in paragraph 1, we may perhaps get an inkling how much this general notion of the meaning of a word surrounds the workings of language with a haze which makes clear vision impossible. It disperses the fog to study the phenomena of language in primitive kinds of application in which one can command a clear view [klar übersehen kann] of the aim and functioning of language. (*PI* par. 5)

The problem is that while the general notion of the meaning of a word as the object for which it stands is sometimes helpful, it is not generally helpful. A commitment to a systematic account of the workings of language in terms of this or some other unitary or even a regulated plurality of concepts of meaning shipwrecks on the countless variety canvassed in *PI* par. 23. Of course nothing prevents us from *forcing* the explanation of the use of every word into this Augustinian mold. In each case we would find some (possibly queer) object for each word to refer to; but Wittgenstein asks, "Would anything be gained by this assimilation of expressions?" (*PI* par. 10). No. It would mask real differences between the uses of various words. It would make us expect the same kinds of features to characterize the use of every word and when we discovered that these analogies fail, we would be perplexed. The use of our language is right before our eyes, and yet when we try to understand it we can't. "When we believe we must find that order, must find the ideal, in our actual language, we become dissatisfied with what are ordinarily called 'propositions', 'words', 'signs'" (*PI* par. 105). We are lost (*PI* par. 123).

Ironically, Wittgenstein's account of the genealogy of this anxiety about language is verified by Dummett's own discussion of paragraph 23. Confronting himself with Wittgenstein's opposition to a systematic account of meaning, Dummett writes:

> But, now, what is supposed to be the alternative? Is it just that a systematic account of how a language functions, or of what we know

when we know a language, is impossible? But, then, how can this be?
It is something that we do, something that we learn to do: how can it
be impossible to say what it is that we do, what it is that we learn?[38]

These are the characteristic expressions of someone captive to Augustine's picture of the essence of human language (*PI* par. 1 and 115). There is nothing easier than to describe what we do. "I assume he *acts* [er *handelt*] as I have described. Explanations come to an end somewhere" (*PI* par. 1). But Dummett will not count a ragged description of the superficial activities of the shopper and the shopkeeper as an adequate account of what Wittgenstein would describe as the "ways that one operates with words" and Dummett as what it is that we learn when we learn a language (*PI* par. 1). Wittgenstein once wrote: "What's ragged should be left ragged" (*CV* 45e: c. 1944). On Dummett's account, what is missing from the account in the *Investigations* is the systematicity, parsimonious grounds yielding exuberant capacities. The task of a theory of meaning would be to provide a theoretical representation of the way one operates with words that relies only on the concepts essential to accounting for linguistic sense, for example, truth, verification, assertability, and so on. Wittgenstein turns from precisely this task when he turns from the Augustinian picture of the essence of human language, a picture that sublimes the logic of our language.

(5) The Sublime Source of Our Disquiet

One of the most disappointing features of teaching the *Investigations* is that the book seems to be so thoroughly about language. But as I read the book, it is equally—if not more so—about the meaning of life. This section therefore is an interlude during which I will try to make persuasive the still surprising Wittgensteinian claim that the Augustinian picture of the sublime essence of human language is the source of many of our logical and existential cares.

(a) Logical Cares

I begin by demonstrating the Augustinian sources of the *Tractatus*'s picture of the substance of the world. From the Augustinan picture of language consisting of words that name objects and sentences that are combinations of such names, we derive a philosophical concept of meaning according to which *every* word is correlated with an *object* that is its *meaning* (*PI* par. 1). An immediate result of this is that words that are not correlated with objects have no meaning. Every meaningful mark must be correlated with an object, and an apparently meaningful word that is not correlated with an object cannot, on this account, really be meaningful. Accepting this much, whenever we tried to understand a (philosophical) concept that is not obviously correlated with an object, we would discover ourselves at a philosophical impasse. At the start of notes he dictated in 1933, we can read:

> The questions "what is length?", "what is meaning?", "what is the number one?" etc., produce in us a mental cramp. We feel that we can't point to anything in reply to them and yet ought to point to something. (We are up against one of the great sources of philosophical bewilderment: a substantive makes us look for a thing that corresponds to it.) (*BlB* p. 1: 1933–34)

The "ought" is a consequence of an uncritical acceptance of the Augustinian picture of the essence of language. That picture is one of the great sources of philosophical bewilderment, philosophical disquiet, "philosophische Beunruhigung" (*BigT* p. 174).

The previous chapter emphasized that the objects of the *Tractatus* were not like chairs, brooms, or swords. The world divides into facts, not objects. Tractarian objects are beyond what is the case; so beyond the world. But since the world is all, objects aren't. Or better, they are beyond being and nonbeing. They are not tinier than quarks. They are not bigger than galaxies. When you divide the world, you discover quarks and galaxies, but the world doesn't divide into objects, only facts.

> What does it mean to say that we can attribute neither being nor nonbeing to elements?—One might say: if everything that we call "being" and "non-being" consists in the existence and non-existence of connections between elements, it makes nonsense to speak of an element's being (non-being); just as when everything that we call "destruction" lies in the separation of elements, it makes no sense to speak of the destruction of an element. (*PI* par. 50)

This passage appears in the *Investigations*. The Tractarian position it epitomizes is there traced to the Augustinian picture of the essence of language. Here's how.

Showing their acceptance of that picture, Russell and Whitehead's *Principia Mathematica* (1910) endorsed a maxim to constrain their analysis of puzzling expressions; that is, expressions such as "the square circle," which are correlated with no object at all. This is the maxim:

> Whenever the grammatical subject of a proposition can be supposed not to exist without rendering the proposition meaningless, it is plain that the grammatical subject is not a proper name, i.e., not a name directly representing some object. Thus in all such cases, the proposition must be capable of being so analyzed that what was the grammatical subject shall have disappeared.[39] (see *PI* par. 95)

The Augustinian picture produces this Russellian maxim; and now, in turn, the maxim can present us with Tractarian objects. Accepting this maxim, the fact that the sentence "Excalibur [Nothung] has a sharp blade" makes sense even if Excalibur does not exist proves that "Excalibur" is not a proper name, that is, not a name directly representing some object (*PI* par. 39). So there must be some other object (call it "E-calibur") that is the meaning of "Excalibur." But since the meaningfulness of "E-calibur" must satisfy the same maxim, we might find that "E-calibur" suffers the same fate as its parent "Excalibur." It too would disappear in analysis. In the final analysis, we will discover simple elements of Excalibur: simple because if they were complex they could become unhinged and so would not provide an adequate semantic ground. The existence of these simple elements—unlike either Excalibur itself or what we normally think of as its subatomic parts—is ontologically secure. The *Tractatus* has this:

    2.02   Objects are simple.

    2.021   Objects make up the substance of the world. That is why
            they cannot be composite.

    2.022   It is obvious that an imagined world, however different it
            may be from the real one, must have *something*—a form—
            in common with it.

    2.023   Objects are just what constitute this unalterable form.

Wittgenstein may easily have thought that in the face of philosophical bewilderment brought on by acceptance of the Augustinian picture there were only two options: living with bewilderment and confusion or accepting a Tractarian philosophy. The *Investigations* attempts to rid us of this picture.

(b) Existential Cares

Perhaps it was to be expected that Wittgenstein could make a case for the connection between the Augustinian picture of the essence of language and a battery of philosophical problems. It is more surprising to discover that this picture of the essence of human language is also one of the great sources of existential bewilderment. Misinterpretations of our forms of language "are deep disquietudes [tiefe Beunruhigungen]; their roots are as deep in us as the forms of our language and their significance is as great as the importance of our language" (*PI* par. 111).

It is not just adolescents who are confused about love. Daydreaming, you suddenly realize you were somewhere else reviving the thrill—tinged with the erotic—of being with your new friend. But it is the wrong friend. Without having said anything, you and someone else had given up seeing other people about a month ago. Still living separately, you were already—but privately—wondering why you didn't move in together. Now you're having syncopated daydreams about two different people. It feels wrong. Had you ever really loved the first one? Are you falling in love with the second? Is it just the momentary dizziness of kissing someone for the first time? Is all of this just varying degrees of what your more worldy friends dismiss as infatuation, or is it love? But can you love two people at once? It is not just adolescents who can be bewildered by love.

How do you decide if you love the one or the other? As this should not be left to chance, you check. First you imagine the one, and look inside yourself to see. Next you imagine the other, and look again. But this never helps. There is nothing to see. There are oil lights on the dashboards of cars; they are either on or off, and when they are on, you need oil. Sometimes I think I used to act as though there were a lovelight on the dashboard of my soul. I would look in to see if it was on or off, but I was never satisfied. I could never find the dashboard. So our strategy for finding our way out of existential bewilderment doesn't work. And trying and failing hardly makes things better. What has gone wrong?

It will not seem like much of an answer to be told that we have misunderstood the grammar of the word *love*.[40] But if we are in the grip of the Augustinian picture of language, how would we respond to the question "What is love?" *By looking for an object with which "love" could be correlated.* And where will we find this object? Not in any particular action: you can hug anyone. So we should turn inside (see *PI* par. 598). And that is just what we do. And that is just what does not help. Is it any wonder that when you and your friends bumped into "What is love, anyway?" you turned away, trying to laugh. Wittgenstein had harsh words for this pattern of thinking:

> There is a general disease of thinking which always looks for (and finds)[41] what would be called a mental state from which all our acts spring as from a reservoir. Thus one says, "The fashion changes because the taste of people changes." The taste is the mental reservoir. But if a tailor today designs a cut of dress different from that which he designed a year ago, can't what is called his change of taste have consisted, partly or wholly, in doing just this? (*BrB* p. 143: 1934–35)

Wittgenstein rehearses the thoughts that drive us inside: any external action might occur even if there has been no change in one's taste. Conceding this truth, he continues:

> But it doesn't follow that what distinguishes a case of having changed one's taste from a case of not having done so isn't under certain circumstances just designing what one hasn't designed before.... That is to say, we don't use the word "taste" as the name of a feeling. To think we do is to represent the practice of our language in undue simplification. This, of course, is the way in which philosophical puzzles generally arise. (*BrB* p. 144: 1934–35)

This is old ground. The source of the "general disease of thinking" is an overly simplified picture of human language as consisting of names for things: the Augustinian picture. My brief discussion of being bewildered about love was meant to show that this picture cannot only produce philosophical confusion but existential unrest as well. In this regard, "love" is not unique; similar genealogies might be found for the existential unrest that accumulates around "desire," "want," "need," "wish," "happiness," "pleasure," "cruelty," "resentment," "respect," "anxiety," "fear," "the meaning of life," and so on. The Augustinian picture of the essence of human language can pervert our understanding of these concepts, and so disturb our understanding of ourselves. I have only to read such a list of words to realize how little I know of the concepts which are already central to the way I already think about my life. That we do not recognize this perversion and this disturbance contributes to the difficulty of philosophy.

However, we do not want to undertake an investigation of our use of these words because we are so sure it is unnecessary (*PI* par. 52). If anything would help, it is sure to look less like lexicography and more like psychopharmacology. Our emotional life is all chemistry. Human behavior is all sociobiologically encoded in the human genome. What is the attraction of these reductionist explanations? In his 1938 lectures on aesthetics, Wittgenstein is reported to have observed that explanations like this have a certain "peculiar charm" (*LCA* p. 25: 1938).[42]

> The attraction of certain kinds of explanation is overwhelming. . . . In particular, explanations of the kind "This is really only this." . . . The picture of people having subconscious thoughts has a charm. The idea of an underworld. A secret cellar. Something hidden, uncanny. Cf. Keller's two children putting a live fly in the head of a doll, burying the doll and then running away. (Why do we do this sort of thing? This is the sort of thing we do do.) A lot of things one is ready to believe because they are uncanny. (*LCA* pp. 24–25 and 24–28)[43]

Under the spell [die Verhexung] (*PI* par. 109), charmed by the Augustinian picture of the essence of language, we think: the surface grammar of *game* is an unholy mess, but our use of the word *game* is determinate, there are correct and incorrect ways to use *game*, so there must be something that is the meaning of the word *game*, the essence of all games. Right now, we don't know what this essence is. All we can produce are pale imitations of that essence, each of which can be counterexampled with little difficulty. Still, we think there must be this essence, for otherwise our use of the word could not be determinate. There must exist an essence of game; it thwarts every attempt at understanding, but it must exist. That's the charm of the Augustinian picture: an order hidden beyond present comprehension which—though now invisible—must exist.[44]

In his 1939 lectures on the foundations of mathematics, Wittgenstein again uses the English word *charm* to explain the attraction of what he opposes.

> The difficulty in looking at mathematics as we do is to make one particular section—to cut pure mathematics off from its application. It is particularly difficult to know where to make this cut because cer-

> tain branches of mathematics have been developed in which the charm consists in the fact that pure mathematics looks as though it were applied mathematics—applied to itself. And so we have the business of a mathematical realm. (*LFM* p. 150)[45]

Here again the charming charms on account of the suggestion of an ordered realm beyond every ordinary mode of access—yet one whose existence seems—at least to those in the Augustinian spell—to be secure. As Wittgenstein uses and opposes *charm*, what is charming is an explanatory order, which is hidden—more than empirically hidden.

In his own view: "Since everything lies open to view there is nothing to explain. For what is hidden is of no interest to us" (*PI* par. 126; see par. 435). His concern was with seeing the differences lying right before his eyes, not with discovering hidden unifying essences. "'This is *really* this' . . . There are certain differences which you have been persuaded to neglect'" (*LCA* p. 27). Wittgenstein's own philosophical method is one of "finding and inventing *intermediate cases*" [*Zwischengliedern*] (*PI* par. 122). And the point of such intermediate cases is to confront us with the differences between things, the lack of any underlying characteristics: the lack of sublime essences. The task is to break the spell, the charm, of the Augustinian picture. Wittgenstein's mature philosophical method does indeed turn away from the conception of essences as sublime, but it does not turn away from essences.

(6) Wittgenstein's Superficial Essentialism

Wittgenstein's opposition to sublime essences is not a global anti-essentialism. His mature work retains a place for essences. It retains a place for superficial essences. It retains a place for grammar.

The critique of Augustine's picture of the sublime essence [Wesen] of human language in the very first paragraph of the *Investigations* displays Wittgenstein's negative concern with essences. But his positive concern, later in the book, is equally plain:

371.   *Essence* [Das *Wesen*] is expressed by grammar.

373.   Grammar tells what kind of object anything is. (Theology as grammar.) (*PI* par. 371, 373)

These thoughts seem to conflict with a famous discussion of games. Earlier in the book, he observes that he has come up against "the great question that lies behind all these [i.e., LW's] considerations" (*PI* par. 65). And then one of the other voices loses its temper and shouts:

> You take the easy way out! You talk about all sorts of language-games, but have nowhere said what the essence [Wesentliche] of a language-game, and hence of language, is: what is common to all these activities and what makes them into language or parts of language. (*PI* par. 65)

Wittgenstein replies: "And this is true" (*PI* par. 65). The usual way of reading this reply is as a very blunt expression of what Rorty and others have taught us to call Wittgenstein's anti-essentialism.[46] But it is already a mark against this reading that it makes it difficult to understand how the same book could speak so naturally of essences (e.g., in *PI* par. 371). Moreover, simply taking paragraph 65 on its own, it is not clear what precisely Wittgenstein is agreeing to when he writes "And this is true" (*PI* par. 65). Is he agreeing that he has nowhere said what the *essence* of language is? Or is he simply agreeing that he has nowhere said what is *common* to all these activities? Wittgenstein's reply continues:

> —Instead of producing something common to all that we call language, I am saying that these phenomena have no one thing in common which makes us use the same word for all—but that they are *related* to one another in many different ways. And it is because of this relationship, or these relationships, that we call them all "language." I will try to explain this. (*PI* par. 65)

The key to this exchange is to permit Wittgenstein to retain a concern with the great question as to the essence of language while rejecting the sublime Augustinian picture of essences as the common element hidden beneath the surface effects of linguistic life. So the passage does not read "Instead of producing the essence of language, I will . . ." Rather, it reads, "I did indeed produce the essence of language, but because you expected essences to be common elements hidden under the surface effects of linguistic life, you didn't recognize what I produced as an essence." I will try to explain this.

Immediately after replying in this way, Wittgenstein introduces a discussion of games, especially of the fact that there is no one thing that all games have in common. The usual way to read this is as a denial that there is anything like the essence of a game, and that is just what is at issue here; namely, whether the absence of an essence construed as sublime is the same as the absence of an essence, period. How does Wittgenstein, himself, characterize the result of his examination of games?

> And the result of this examination is: we see a complicated network of similarities overlapping and criss-crossing: similarities in large respects and in small. (*PI* par. 67)[47]

The result of this examination is that we will have learned our way around some of that part of our language in which "game" appears. We will have an overview [übersichtliche Darstellung (*PI* 122)] of the "grammar (the use)" (*BlB* p. 23) of the word *game*. My suggestion is that we interpret this not as an expression of Wittgenstein's anti-essentialism, but rather as an expression of his *Superficial Essentialism*. His anti-essentialism was directed only at sublime essences. If the result of the examination of the variety of what we call games is that they are *united* by a "complicated network of similarities," then the point is not the separateness of different games, but their togetherness as games. The fact that there is no common property of all games does not mean that games have no essence.

"*Essence* is expressed by grammar" (*PI* par. 371). Grammar? Wittgenstein's use of the word *grammar* is notoriously problematic, the source of countless sneerings, proof of his desperate need to be evasive, obscure.[48] But Wittgenstein's conception of philosophy was intimately linked to his conception of grammar. The proper way to respond to philosophical questioning was with grammatical investigations, because grammatical investigations would uncover superficial essences. We are going around in a small circle. Let's start again, first by distinguishing two kinds of essence and next by determining how superficial essences might be expressed by grammar.

One of Wittgenstein's discussions of the nature of philosophy begins by confronting the question, In what sense is logic something sublime [etwas Sublimes]? Logic seems to be sublime because there seems to pertain to logic a "peculiar depth" (*PI* par. 89). But why does logic, philosophy, seem (peculiarly) deep? Wittgenstein does not think that this is *flatly mistaken*. One reason that philosophy seems deep is that "we want to *understand* something that is already right before our eyes" (*PI* par. 89; W's emphasis). So whatever is right before our eyes must not be enough. This is why "we feel as if we had to *penetrate* phenomena" [die Erscheinungen *durchschauen*] (*PI* par. 90; W's emphasis). Wittgenstein is convinced that this is a temptation to be resisted. It is in fact the very temptation to sublime the logic of our language that I have been discussing. The positive task is to receive the logic of our language without subliming it.

The subliming movement of Augustine's *Confessions* is cited for a second time[49] to exemplify the kind of question that makes philosophy or logic seem to be sublime. These questions seem to (but in fact do not) require looking beneath the surface of language or experience to the pure essence of whatever disturbs us.

> "What then is time? If nobody asks me, I know; if I am asked to explain what it is, I don't know."—This could not be said about a question of natural science ("What is the specific gravity of hydrogen?" for instance). (*PI* par. 89)

The suggestion is that a philosophical problem is any problem that can be put into Augustine's schema: "What then is _____? If nobody asks me, I know; if I am asked to explain what it is, I don't know." And this is a schematic demand for the essence of _____. Moreover, since there is a sense in which time is both in plain view and confusing, the way out of our confusion will naturally seem to require the uncovering of what is *not* in plain view. The solution to our concerns—so we willingly think—will be discovered by science: either by board-certified sciences like psychology or physics or sociology, or else by very careful description of our experiences, themselves: "the present experience that slips quickly by . . ." (*PI* par. 436).

Another question that fits the Augustinian schema is, How do sentences manage to represent? (*PI* par. 435.) The question assumes that sentences do manage to represent; it asks, how? And—since we know how to speak and write—we have all the evidence we could want. But how do our sentences manage to represent? Where do we turn? Again: "We feel as if we had to *penetrate* phenomena" (*PI* par. 90).

During his discussion of why logic seems sublime, Wittgenstein draws a distinction between *durchschauen*—which has some of the force of penetrating beneath the surface to see into the heart of the matter—and *nachschauen*—which has rather the force of looking to see if. Wittgenstein uses these two verbs to distinguish looking through [durchschauen] the surface of language to the sublime essence of what concerns us, and looking at [nachschauen], or in, those surfaces for those essences. The mature Wittgenstein will find essences distributed in our uses of words, so it is a nice feature of nachschauen that it can mean to look something up, as in a dictionary.[50]

Recalling precisely the question as to the essence of language that initiated the previous discussion of games, Wittgenstein observes that the urge to look through [durchschauen] language for its completely exact core "finds expression in questions as to the *essence* [*Wesen*] of language, of propositions, of thought" (*PI* par. 92). And Wittgenstein comments:

—For if we too in these investigations are trying to understand the essence of language—its function, its structure . . . (PI par. 92)

But for the "if," this is clear evidence that Wittgenstein took his investigations to be concerned with understanding the essence of language. The passage continues:

—yet *this* is not what those questions have in view. (W's emphases)

This is a bit of a puzzle. Wittgenstein says that if he too is interested in essences, then this is *not* what the question as to the essence of language has in view. The solution is to see him as concerned with essences distributed in the surface of our lives, rather than with sublime simplicities hidden beneath that surface. The passage continues:

For they see in the essence, not something that already lies open to view [offen zutage liegt][51] and that becomes *surveyable* by rearrangement [durch Ordnen *übersichtlich* wird]. (W's emphasis restored)

This is Wittgenstein's account of the kind of essences he is concerned with: like the purloined letter, these essences are hidden in plain sight. Superficial essences. Distributed essences. "The aspects of things that are most important for us are hidden because of their simplicity and familiarity (one is unable to notice something—because it is always before one's eyes)" (*PI* par. 129).

The paragraph concludes with a description of the rejected conception of essences. Picking up the start of the sentence again, we read:

For they see in the essence . . . something that lies *beneath* the surface [*unter* der Oberfläche]. Something that lies within, which we see when we look into [durchschauen] the thing, and which analysis digs out.

"The essence is hidden from us": this is the form our problem now assumes. We ask: "*What is* language?", "*What is* a proposition?" And the answer to these questions is to be given once for all; and independently of any future experience. (*PI* par. 92; W's emphases)

On the rejected picture, sublime essences are hidden under the surface of language. When analysis digs them out, the answer to our questions will be given. Our problems will be finally and completely solved: like in the *Tractatus* (*TLP* P).

So the search for sublime essences belongs to a conception of a philosophical problem as being able to be solved—once and for all. And we should expect that a different conception of the essences to be discovered by philosophical investigations might belong with a different conception of the ending of philosophical investigations. They will not end once and for all, but variously in response to various disturbances, various disquietudes [Beunruhigungen]. "The work of the philosopher consists in assembling reminders for a particular purpose" (*PI* par. 127).

Thus when Wittgenstein writes that "the real discovery is the one that makes me capable of stopping doing philosophy when I want to" (*PI* par. 133), he is excluding not the endlessness of philosophy, but stopping when philosophy (not the philosopher) wants to. He is excluding an approach to philosophy that sees it as solving philosophical problems by looking through the surface of our lives, of our langaguge, to discover the substance of the world (see *PR*, foreword, *CV* 7e). The *Tractatus* embodied this now rejected sense of philosophy, even though the substance unearthed sublimed, leaving no sensible substance at all. The *Investigations* takes its problems from our own troubles, deep disquietudes [tiefe Beunruhigungen] (*PI* par. 111). "The real discovery . . . is the one that brings philosophy peace" [Ruhe] (*PI* par. 133). But where peace is brought by rearrangement of a variously contoured surface, there will be no end to philosophy, only endings. And beginnings.[52]

Paragraph 92, which I have been reciting, is followed by one which gives an account of how we might be able to discover superficial essences in the grammar of our language.

One person might say "A proposition is the most ordinary thing in the world" and another: "A proposition—that's something very queer!"— And the latter is unable simply to look and see [nachschauen] how propositions work. The forms that we use in expressing ourselves about propositions and thought stand in his way. (*PI* par. 93)

Wittgenstein's mature account of essences involves denying that the essence of "language" or "game" is one thing that is common to everything we call a language or a game. Rather, the various uses of these words "are *related* to one another in many different ways. And it is because of this relationship, or these relationships, that we call them all 'language'" [or "game"] (*PI* par. 65). Superficial essences are distributed in the surfaces of our linguistic life, in grammar.

The surface Wittgenstein concerns himself with is the surface of language. Philosophical distress is—on this account—a consequence of our turning from this surface.

> A main source of our failure to understand is that we do not *command a clear view* [*übersehen*] of the use of our words.—Our grammar is lacking this sort of perspicuity [Übersichtlichkeit].—A perspicuous representation [übersichtliche Darstellung] produces just that understanding which consists in "seeing connections." Hence the importance of finding and inventing *intermediate cases.* (*PI* par. 122; W's emphases)

The importance of intermediate cases is not that they permit us to see continuities, similarities between widely separated parts of our linguistic practices. Quite the reverse. They reinforce the differences. They stop the tendency to sublime the logic, the grammar, of our language: the use of our words. Wittgenstein suggests that Augustine's puzzles concerning time were generated by a misleading assimilation of two different parts of the grammar of "measurement":

> Solving this puzzle will consist in comparing what we mean by "measurement" (the grammar of the word "measurement") when applied to a distance on a traveling band with the grammar of that word when applied to time. The problem may seem simple, but its extreme difficulty is due to the fascination which the analogy between two similar structures in our language can exert on us. (*BlB* p. 26)

And to confirm the thought that his concern is with suppressed differences between different aspects of the grammar of the same word, Wittgenstein adds: "It is helpful here to remember that it is sometimes almost impossible for a child to believe that one word can have two meanings" (*BlB* p. 26).

Grammatical investigations are investigations of the uses of words in various situations. Hence these investigations are not concerned with language in a narrow sense; they include or touch upon every aspect of our life with words. For instance, Wittgenstein says, "It is part of the grammar of the word 'chair' that *this* is what we call 'to sit on a chair'" (*BlB* p. 24). The force of the italicized demonstrative is to invoke the way we move our body when we sit. So too the grammar of "explanation" will include how and where we turn up our noses at dubious explanations. It is simply a mistake to think that Wittgenstein's philosophical method is hypnotized by words, needing further elaboration in terms of the patterns of activity manifest in different parts of our lives.[53] Wittgenstein's grammatical investigations were already investigations of the forms of our lives.

(7) Grammar and Philosophy

Grammatical investigations—even in this sense—will still not seem like philosophical investigations. We would seem to be wasting our time by investigating the details of our uses of a given word (*PI* par. 52). Since, however, Wittgenstein believes his grammatical investigations can solve philosophical problems, some will suspect that he must have a rather idiosyncratic idea of what a philosophical problem is. But this is not so. He has a perfectly familiar conception of a philosophical problem. "A philosophical problem has the form: 'I don't know my way about'" (*PI* par. 123). We don't know our way about because the grammar of the words/concepts that concern us is bewildering (*PI* par. 664). "The man who is philosophically puzzled sees a law in the way a word is used, and, trying to apply this law consistently, comes up against cases where it leads to paradoxical results" (*BlB* p. 27). The attempt to force our linguistic life into agreement with a simple law is the source of our puzzlement, our disquiet. This is one reading of the difficult remark in the *Investigations*: "A simile that has been absorbed into the forms of our language produces a false appearance, and this disquiets us [beunruhigt uns]. 'But *this* isn't how it is!'—we say. 'Yet *this* is how it has to *be*'" (*PI* par. 112; see *CV* p. 30: 1937). We expect a concept always to function according to a law for special cases and then are bewildered by its failure to adhere to that law in general. And this incites—not a turn away from the construction of laws—but the search for a better law, a better defi-nition. The search for a sublime essence.

The *Blue Book* describes this familiar sequence at some length:

> Very often the way the discussion of such a puzzle runs is this: First the question is asked "What is time?" This question makes it appear that what we want is a definition. We mistakenly think that a defini-tion is what will remove the trouble (as in certain states of indigestion we feel a kind of hunger which cannot be removed by eating). The question is then answered by a wrong definition; say: "Time is the motion of celestial bodies." The next step is to see that this definition is unsatisfactory. But this only means that we don't use the word "time" synonymously with "motion of celestial bodies." However in saying that the first definition is wrong, we are now tempted to think that we must replace it by a different one, the correct one. (*BlB* p. 27)

Wittgenstein's understanding of the great questions is perfectly tradi-tional. It is a demand to look for essences, for what hope, time, knowledge, and so on are. The demand for essences seems to be a demand for sublime essences (definitions) hidden under the various features of our use of lan-guage. To some naturalized philosophers this will seem to be a demand for scientific investigation and to other, supernaturalized philosophers this will seem to be a demand for transcendental phenomenological inves-tigation. Wittgenstein's original discovery was to see that our philosoph-ical disquiet, which is never settled by these two techniques, might be calmed by a third battery of techniques: grammatical investigations.

The trouble is that it is very difficult to resist the urge to dig beneath the surface, to resist the temptation to discover deep, sublime essences.

> Here it is difficult as it were to keep our heads above water,[54]—to see that we must stick to the subjects of our everyday thinking, and not go astray and imagine that we have to describe extreme subtleties, which in turn we are after all quite unable to describe with the means at our disposal. We feel as if we had to repair a torn spider's web with our fingers. (*PI* par. 106)

But our problems will not be resolved by science or superscience. Witt-genstein says it neatly:

> They are solved, rather, by looking into [eine Einsicht] the workings of our language, and that in such a way as to make us recognize those

workings: *in despite of* an urge to misunderstand them. The problems are solved, not by giving new information, but by arranging what we have always known. Philosophy is a battle against the bewitchment of our intelligence [Verhexung unseres Verstandes] by means of language. (*PI* par. 109)

The urge to misunderstand the workings of our language is the urge to discover—deep beneath the unruly surface of the exuberance of our life with language—one common essence.

A syntactical sign that one has confronted a philosophical problem is that one is facing a question that stammers: what makes ____ ____. For example: what makes hope hope, or love love, or knowledge knowledge.[55] According to Wittgenstein, these philosophical questions seem to demand an account of the *sublime* essence of hope, love, knowledge. Definitions. But this is not so. *Superficial* essences are distributed in our use of words. What makes hope hope and not expectation is distributed in the multiply various uses of the verbs "to hope" and "to expect." There is no single thing—simple or complex—which hope *consists in*, but if you have a clear view of the grammar of these words then you will know what hope is, you will not be disquieted by questions like "What is hope?"

One negative reaction to this Wittgensteinian position is that this gives too much power to the particular language one happens to speak. For instance, where English has one word for love, Greek has a few, so it would seem to be a gross mistake to move in on the superficial essence of love by investigating the grammar of the English word *love*.[56] The familiarity, and naturalness, of this objection marks the extent of our bewitchment by language. The assumption is that where you have one word you have one grammar: "It is helpful here to remember that it is sometimes almost impossible for a child to believe that one word can have two meanings" (*BlB* p. 26). But it is essential to Wittgenstein's approach that the grammar of some bits of *love*'s use might be like that of *eros* and other bits might be like *agape*. But we should be careful not to assume that the Greek lexicon carved nature at its joints any more than the English lexicon does.

Since Wittgenstein is constantly reminding us of different uses of words, it would be easy to think that he was dreaming of an ideal language that had a different word for every grammatical pattern. But this is not his aim.

> Such a reform for particular practical purposes, an improvement in
> our terminology designed to prevent misunderstandings in practice,
> is perfectly possible. But these are not the cases we have to do with.
> The confusions which occupy us arise when language is like an engine
> idling, not when it is doing work. (*PI* par. 132)

It comes as a surprise to Wittgenstein's speed-readers that he even permits the invention of specific terminology to accomplish specific tasks,
but Wittgenstein has no specific tasks. He explains why his aim is not to
refine the grammar of our language: "For the clarity we are aiming at is
indeed *complete* [*vollkommen*] clarity. But that simply means that the
philosophical problems should *completely* disappear" (*PI* par. 133; W's
emphases). But what does this mean? Wittgenstein is concerned with
details of our uses of words, but he is not concerned with specific,
detailed, practical problems. His aim is to change a pattern of thinking
[Denkweise], to turn us from the subliming thoughts introduced in the
first paragraph of the *Investigations* (*PI* preface; *CV* p. 48: 1946). "We
want to understand what lies right before our eyes. For *this* is what we
seem in some sense not to understand" (*PI* par. 89). His notebooks left
the following sentence: "God grant the philosopher insight into what
lies in front of everyone's eyes" (*CV* p. 63: 1947). Wittgenstein is praying
for the courage to bring words back to their everyday homes (*CV* p. 52:
1946; *PI* par. 116) This is the sense in which he wants to leave everything
as it is (*PI* par. 124). He is praying for the courage to accept the unruly
grammar of our language: "What's ragged should be kept ragged" (*CV*
p. 45: 1944). The real discovery would give philosophy "peace" because
the real discovery would stop the quest for sublime essences. To find the
courage to accept the language we speak, the life we lead. To discover
peace.[57] Logical and Existential peace.

"Thoughts that are at peace [Friede]. That's what someone who
philosophizes yearns for."[58] But this peace, if it comes, remains mysterious: "The solution of philosophical problems can be compared with a
gift in a fairy tale: in the magic castle it appears enchanted and if you
look at it outside in daylight it is nothing but an ordinary bit of iron (or
something of the sort)."[59] If peace [Ruhe, Friede] sets Wittgenstein's
goal, disquiet [Unruhe, Unheimlichkeit] is its inseparable shadow, so
Wittgenstein's could not possibly be a "Perpetual Peace."[60]

Chapter 4

The Wonder of Linguistic Meaning: Don't Take It as Obvious

Don't take it as a matter of course [selbstverständlich], but as a remarkable fact, that pictures and fictitious narratives give us pleasure, occupy our minds.

—Wittgenstein, *PI* par. 524

It is an impediment to looking at the picture [e.g., the oil painting], if you are struck with the conviction that you must either extract the picture from the description of the color of each color patch in a fine grid laid upon it, or that you must have a theory of what the picture is apart from what that description describes. If you forswear both inclinations you may get to look at the picture, and doing so you may find yourself full of amazement. Or, as Wittgenstein once put it, you may find yourself "walking on a mountain of wonders."

—G. E. M. Anscombe[1]

Suppose you go about to explain the number 1. You show someone your fore-finger, then another finger, then another. Then he "counts" groups of three things. How does this happen, seeing that all I've done is show him my fingers; and I'm not sure if he looks in the right direction; and I don't know what other technique he has; and I can't be sure he doesn't only seem to have any technique. Nevertheless it happens. Is this a mystery? If you like: but it's one of the sort that can't be removed.

—Wittgenstein 1946, as reported by A. C. Jackson[2]

119

(1) The Depth of Philosophy, and Jokes

In 1886, Nietzsche closed the preface to the second edition of *The Gay Science* exclaiming:

> Oh, those Greeks! They knew how to live. What is required for that is to stop courageously at the surface. . . . Those Greeks were superficial—*out of profundity* [oberflächlich—*aus Tief!*]. (*GS* P par. 4).

In the last chapter I articulated Wittgenstein's own turn to the surface [Oberfläche] of our life with language from the depths of the *Tractatus* (*PI* par. 92). But there remains in Wittgenstein's mature work a sense of the depth of philosophical disquietudes [tiefe Beunruhigungen] (*PI* par. 111). This depth appears in Wittgenstein's distinguishing his concerns from scientific problems: "we are not doing natural science . . ." (*PI* p. 230e, par. 109). It also appears in his criticism of other philosophers:

> Some philosophers (or whatever you like to call them) suffer from what may be called "loss of problems." Then everything seems quite simple to them, no deep problems [keine tiefen Probleme] seem to exist any more, the world becomes broad and flat and loses all depth [Tiefe]; and what they write seems immeasurably shallow and trivial. (*Z* 456)[3]

The terms in which Wittgenstein criticizes this kind of philosopher—or whatever you like to call them—recall the terms in which Nietzsche describes the colder phase of his convalescence from nihilism: a bird's-eye view that sees a tremendous number of things broad and flat below (see chap. 1 and Nietzsche, *HH* I, P par. 4). Moreover, Nietzsche's praise of the Greeks as "superficial—out of profundity" gives us hope of reconciling Wittgenstein's own turn to *surfaces* with his aim of calming cares which Wittgenstein himself describes as *deep*. The reconciliation—better, acceptance—of these two perspectives on our logical and existential cares is what I will call Wittgenstein's wonder.

The task of this chapter is to come to defend the suggestion that the superficiality of the *Investigations* is compatible with an acknowledgment of the depth of philosophy. But we may wonder whether anything enlightening can be said about this so-called depth. Occasionally Wittgenstein does try to help his readers understand what philosophical depth [die philosophische Tiefe] is (*PI* par. 111). In the *Investigations*, for example, there is one, but only one, such passage:

111. The problems arising through misinterpretations of our forms of language have the character of *depth* [*Tiefe*]. They are deep disquietudes [Beunruhigungen]; their roots are as deep in us as the forms of our language, and their significance is as great as the importance of our language.—Let us ask ourselves: why do we feel a grammatical joke [einen grammatischen Witz] to be *deep*? (And that is what philosophical depth [philosophische Tiefe] is.) (*PI* par. 111)

The "misinterpretations of our forms of language" mentioned in the first sentence of this paragraph are misinterpretations deriving from our having succumbed to the tendency to sublime the logic of our language: misinterpretations caused, in part, by the naturalness of the Augustinian picture of language. Although these misinterpretations are said at first to cause problems [Die Probleme], the next sentence rather characterizes these problems and their depth as "disquietudes" [Beunruhigungen] (*PI* par. 111). It is such disquietudes—logical and existential—that motivate Wittgenstein's work. In 1933, he wrote: "In my way of doing philosophy, its whole aim is to give an expression such a form that certain disquietudes [Beunruhigungen] disappear" (*BigT* p. 181).[4] Wittgenstein, realizing that "misinterpretations of our forms of language" will sound as unimportant as mixing up right and left, asserts that the importance of these disquietudes is as important as our language. I take this to remind us that we think about our lives in language.[5] So getting clear about our lives presupposes that we are clear about our language. Hence there is no part of our life whose understanding is not endangered by our misunderstanding of the grammar of our language. The previous chapter broached this ground by way of the grammar of "love." The next chapter will take this theme further.

The long dash at the end of *PI* par. 111 introduces a new topic: philosophical depth. It is hard to know how to take this. Can Wittgenstein seriously mean that—yes—philosophy is deep—like a *joke?!* Well, he doesn't quite compare it to all jokes. He doesn't say that the depth of philosophy is like the mean sort of jokes named by nationalities, or races. Philosophical depth is like the depth of a grammatical joke. But what is that? "Grammatical joke" ["einen grammatischen Witz"] is not defined by English [or German] dictionaries. We are left to work out what Wittgenstein's expression might mean from the examples that were originally a part of this paragraph. Baker and Hacker report that in an early version of this paragraph (originating in 1937 or 1938) Wittgenstein

considers two jokes: Lewis Carroll's "We called him 'tortoise' because
he taught us" (from *Alice in Wonderland*, Ch. IX) and an instance
from Lichtenberg's "Letters from a Maid on Literature" in which one
hundred is written "001."[6]

The first of these is a pun—one that I rather suspect is better understood
nearer London. People scorn puns and punsters; they groan. It seems as
if the pun is somehow tinged with immorality. According to Pope, "a
great Critic formerly ... declared He that would pun would pick a
Pocket."[7] This "great Critic" suspects that there is something rather like
picking a pocket about punning. Picking a pocket is theft, but generally
minor theft. Moreover, though immoral, one can still admire the skill
required to pick a pocket. I am not (I hope) unique in being somewhat
amazed by the smoothness with which successfully picking a pocket
must be accomplished. I remember actually attempting it with members of my family: could I be that delicate, could I act with such finesse?
The "great Critic" seems to have found a real transgression about which
we feel just as conflicted as we do about the pun: simultaneously awed
and offended. But what is the pun's transgression? What tinges it with
immorality?

Perhaps we can make a beginning out of the bare observation that
puns turn on the fact that some words with different meanings and perhaps different spellings are nevertheless pronounced in the same or
nearly the same way. The pun's transgression might be to turn from the
content of the text, away from what is essential, to what is accidental:
from content conveyed to the material of conveyance. I suspect that this
makes the pun's transgression like that of playing with your food. Food
is variously enjoyable. At various times we may enjoy (or not) our food's
aroma, its appearance, its taste, its texture, its contribution to our
health. But we are not supposed to investigate whether the relative stick-
iness and malleability of, for example, spinach, makes it the perfect pro-
jectile for "spinach tennis." Those who have tasted the illicit pleasures of
"spinach tennis" know whether it does. But playing with your food
addresses one of food's accidental features. This is why it is frowned on.
(Not just because it is messy; eating lobster is messy too.) This is why we
are expected to mature from spinach tennis to lawn tennis. "Stop playing with your food—grow up!"

Wordplay [das Wortspiel], like foodplay [das Speisespiel], addresses
itself to an accidental feature of our language. And it, too, is popular

with children. Even children so young, they are at least as much disquieted as amused that a single sound can have two different meanings are happy to play word games. My four-and-a-half-year-old daughter, Alice, just yesterday giggled herself dizzy as she ran through a longer sequence than the following: what if you had red lipstick? what if you had potato lipstick? what if you had bowl lipstick? what if you had eye lipstick? And like playing with your food, playing with words is frowned on. Legions of students have been taught that when reasoning turns on a pun they should turn away shouting: "Equivocation!" So puns are familiar examples of philosophical disaster, yet Wittgenstein treats them as examples of philosophical depth. "Grow up!" Well, Russell almost reacted to Wittgenstein's mature philosophy with this exclamation:

> Its positive doctrines seem to me trivial and its negative doctrines unfounded. I have not found in Wittgenstein's *Philosophical Investigations* anything that seemed to me interesting. . . . The later Wittgenstein . . . seems to have grown tired of serious thinking and to have invented a doctrine which would make such an activity unnecessary. . . . If it is true, philosophy is, at best, a slight help to lexicographers, and at worst, an idle tea-table amusement.[8]

But there is more that can be said on behalf of the comparison of philosophical depth and puns. Wordplay is deeper than foodplay.

In one important way, punning is unlike playing with your food. The material conveyance of semantic content, the sounds or shapes of words, is—we were told—obviously [selbstverständlich] irrelevant to the content conveyed (*PI* par. 524). But puns threaten this obvious truth, for the punning connection, irrelevant as it is, is also relevant. This would be as if you might make a meal well balanced by playing with your food: making the spinach not only more fun but better for you by sailing it across the table to your sister's plate. But puns do just this: Lady Macbeth, returning their daggers and announcing her plan to frame Duncan's guards, observes:

> If he do bleed
> I'll gild the faces of the grooms withal;
> For it must seem their guilt.[9]

Here the irrelevant connection between "gilt" and "guilt" is found relevant. We can be surprised by this relevance. This is why people can suddenly find themselves punning: "Pardon the pun." Here, the amazement that characterizes my reaction to picking pockets can strike punsters themselves. Where did that connection come from? It shouldn't be there—it is irrelevant—and yet it is there—and it is relevant. There is something a little uncanny about the aptness of the pun, the accidental pun. From irrelevance, relevance; from accident, essence; from contingency, necessity.

"—Let us ask ourselves: why do we feel a grammatical joke to be *deep* [*tief*]? (and that is what philosophical depth is)" (*PI* par. 111). My discussion of the pun has come to focus on the boundary between contingency and necessity. So it might seem as if the depth of the pun and the depth of philosophy were both derived from our recognition that linguistic signs are arbitrary. But when Wittgenstein discussed the tortoise/taught-us joke, he explicitly denied that interpretation. Baker and Hacker report that he thought that "the depth of a grammatical joke is lost if one thinks that since signs are arbitrary one could, e.g., use 'taught us' as a substantive . . . or '001' for '100'."[10] We can see that this is correct if we imagine someone so constitutionally sober that they appear pun-deaf. To the pun-deaf, the fact that one sound has two meanings is a flat fact about language. Words are arbitrary signs and any sign can have any number of semantic values as long as context is adequate to disambiguate. So much is obvious [selbstverständlich]. "God" is "dog" spelled backwards, but funny? Surely not. Only children play with their words and their food. Grow up. Thus, the pun-deaf.

The depth of the grammatical joke derives not from its confronting us with something arbitrary or contingent in the usual sense: "Fido"'s being my faithful dog's name. The depth of the joke comes from confronting us with the contingency of the division between the contingent and the necessary. The contingency not simply of the name of this dog, but the contingency of language itself. So the contingency revealed by grammatical jokes and grammatical investigations is not ordinary contingency. In fact it is not clear that we have any words at all for the contingency of the split between the contingent and the necessary, the accidental and the essential.[11] Baker and Hacker—still reporting, not citing, Wittgenstein—continue:

> The depth of absurdity is only revealed if one keeps in mind the correct use of the appropriate signs, sees what their consequences are, and notes the conflicts and incongruities which would stem from a

Copyrighted Material

change in notation, e.g., if "001" replaced "100," but everything else remained the same. We have the feeling of depth when we thus look at the system of language, it is as if we could see the whole world through its net.[12]

We have the feeling of depth when language as a whole—embodying necessities and contingencies—is discovered in its naked contingency. So the contingency confronting us in a pun might be called a meta- or philosophical contingency (if we could—but we can't—make those words mean anything). That is the pun's depth.

"And that is what philosophical depth is" too (*PI* par. 111). In the *Big Typescript* (c. 1933), Wittgenstein asked—point blank: "Where does the feeling that our grammatical investigations are fundamental [Fundamentalen] come from?" (*BigT* p. 167). He is sure we do experience a feeling of depth when concerned with philosophical or grammatical questions, a depth we do not feel with questions like "'What is the specific weight of this body', 'Will the weather stay nice today', 'Who will come through the door next', etc." (*BigT* p. 167). And he writes, "And now I say: if we have this experience, then we have arrived at the limits of language" [der Grenze der Sprache] (*BigT* p. 167). My "contingency of language itself" was meant to anticipate Wittgenstein's more evocative use of the "limits of language." He associated running up against the limits of language with a certain experience. Here he is in conversation on December 30, 1929, at Schlick's house:

Man feels the urge to run up against the limits of language [die Grenzen der Sprache]. Think for example of the astonishment [das Erstaunen] that anything at all exists. This astonishment cannot be expressed in the form of a question, and there is also no answer whatsoever. Anything we might say is *a priori* bound to be mere nonsense [Unsinn]. Nevertheless we do run up against the limits of language. (*WVC* p. 68)[13]

In the text of a lecture he prepared at about the same time, he wrote, in English, of his "*wonder at the existence of the world*" ("LE," p. 8; Wittgenstein's emphasis).

Two moments—confronting the limits of language and awaking to wonder—are at work both in the *Tractatus* (finished c. 1918) and in the *Investigations* (finished c. 1945). In the earlier work, the limits of language, of propositions, are marked not by puns but by tautologies and contradictions.

> Contradiction, one might say, vanishes outside all propositions: tautology vanishes inside them.
>
> Contradiction is the outer limit of propositions [die äussere Grenze der Sätze]: tautology is the unsubstantial point at their center. (*TLP* 5.143)

In his first book, Wittgenstein's wonder at the existence of the world appears as the mystical. On October 20, 1916, he wrote in his notebooks: "Aesthetic wonder [Das künstlerische Wunder] is: that the world exists. That what exists does exist" (*NB* p. 86). A few years later, in the *Tractatus*, this wonder is no longer specifically associated with art, and it is renamed the mystical:

> 6.44   Not *how* [*wie*] the world is, is the mystical, but *that* [*dass*] it is. (cf. *TLP* 5.552)

The passage cited above from the *Big Typescript* (c. 1933) implicitly contrasts scientific questions and philosophical questions.[14] And if science is concerned with *how* the world is, then philosophy's "depth" is what the *Tractatus* presented—equally gnomically—as the mystical.

Both moments—first confrontation with limits and second wonder—survive Wittgenstein's maturation. In the earlier work, we are *charmed* by the existence of something mysterious, an order beyond understanding, while the feeling of *depth* in the *Investigations* is incited by the bare fact of confronting the absence of understanding—with no glimmer of an order in the beyond[15] (see *PI* par. 209). So this distinction recalls that between Nietzsche's two solutions to the problem of existence: 1872's, which posited something—the primordial unity—beyond understanding that redeems, and 1886's, in which existence is redeemed by nothing, in which the very absence of a redeemer is itself redemptive. This is our always theme.

To open this chapter, it remains to sketch the manner in which the *Investigations*, first, confronts the limits of language and, second, discovers the wonder of existence. There is only one section in the *Investigations* that speaks of die Grenze der Sprache:

> 119. The results of philosophy are the uncovering of one or another piece of [1] plain nonsense [eines schlichten Unsinns] and of [2] bumps [Beulen] that the understanding has got by running up against the limits of language [die Grenze der Sprache]. These, the

> bumps, make us see the value of the discovery. (*PI* par. 119, my
> numbering)

These bumps, bruises, boils, were once limited only to contradictions
and tautologies. Failed attempts at making sense: senseless [sinnlos]
combinations of words that were still not gibberish [nicht unsinnig]
(*TLP* 4.461–4.4611). In the *Investigations* running up against the limits
of language produces plain nonsense (gibberish?) that is not understandable; but this urge to run up against the limits of language sometimes only leaves the understanding bruised. What are these bruises?
Some of them are our deep disquietudes (*PI* par. 111): this is the way it
must be—but it can't be—but it must be (*PI* par. 112).

> In the course of our conversations Russell would often exclaim
> "Logic's hell!" And this *perfectly* expresses the feeling we had. ... I
> believe that our main reason for feeling like this was the following
> fact: that every time some new linguistic phenomenon occurred to
> us, it could retrospectively show that our previous explanation was
> unworkable. ... But that is the difficulty Socrates gets into in trying
> to give the definition of a concept. Again and again a use of the word
> emerges that seems not to be compatible with the concept that other
> uses have led us to form. We say: but that *isn't* how it is!—it *is* like
> that though! and all we can do is keep repeating these antitheses. (*CV*
> p. 30: 1937)

We bruise our understanding by looking for charming elegance underneath the multifarious diversity of linguistic and other practices.

Our understanding is bruised also in wordplay. Puns were my first
pass at this point. Remember that I was discussing puns simply because
Wittgenstein mentions one of Lewis Carroll's while trying to tell us what
a grammatical joke is. But I am not entirely happy with the pun as the
paradigm of the bruising grammatical joke. I would be happier with
almost any of these jokes recently circulating in my neighborhood. They
are due to the comedian Steven Wright:[16]

- If you shoot a mime, should you use a silencer?
- I made wine out of raisins so I wouldn't have to wait for it to
  age.
- I saw a subliminal advertisement alternative, but only for a second.

- Cross-country skiing is great if you live in a small country.
- I went to a restaurant that serves "breakfast at any time." So I ordered French Toast during the Renaissance.

These are not puns. They trade on contingent grammatical connections: between mimes and silence, between aged wine and aged grapes, and so on. This kind of grammatical joke, like the pun, trades on the contingency of language, more particularly the contingency of grammar: the contingency of the grammar that divides whatever is necessary from whatever is contingent. So again, we have to do with the depth of philosophy. The deep abyss[17] facing our discovery that the division between the necessary and the contingent is itself contingent—or meta-contingent (if we could—but we can't—make that expression mean anything). Coiled in the heart of being, is a worm.

Wittgenstein worked hard to face us with the naked contingency of the distinction between the contingent and the necessary, and Wright's jokes are just as deep. So the following recollections should not be surprising:

> A curious thing, which I observed innumerable times, was that when Wittgenstein invented an example during his lecture in order to illustrate a point, he himself would grin at the absurdity of what he had imagined. But if any member of the class were to chuckle, his expression would change to severity and he would exclaim in reproof, "No, no; I'm serious!" . . . It is worth noting that Wittgenstein once said that a serious and good philosophical work could be written that would consist entirely of jokes.[18]

The reason a serious philosophical work could consist entirely of jokes is that some jokes, grammatical jokes, play with the same grammatical confusions that disquiet philosophy. Perhaps this is one reason that "For a philosopher there is more grass growing down in the valleys of silliness [den Tälern der Dummheit] than up on the barren heights of cleverness" (CV p. 80: 1949). Sometimes grammatical differences show up in jokes. Laughter can be a criterion of having crossed a grammatical threshold.

But confronting contingency is just the first moment of Wittgenstein's project. Since I should have put scare quotes around "contingency," I am tempted to steal the sound of Heidegger and speak of confronting nothing. Perhaps I should. Wittgenstein almost does (*WVC* p. 68: 12–30–29). The second moment of Wittgenstein's project discovers a new—to him—form of the mystical. The wonder that we can communicate at all. Coming to feel as if one is walking on a mountain of wonders.[19] Wittgenstein wants us to be struck, amazed, that we can talk to one another, at all. He warns his other voice: "I should like to say: you take it much too much as a matter of course [selbstverständlich] that one can tell anything to anyone" (*PI* par. 363). And then, later, about an equally fundamental matter:

> 524. Don't take it as a matter of course [selbstverständlich], but as a remarkable fact that pictures and fictitious narratives give us pleasure, occupy our minds.
>
> ("Don't take it as a matter of course" [selbstverständlich]. —that means: find it surprising [Wundere dich daruber] as you do other things that trouble [beunruhigt] you. Then the puzzling aspect of [our life with pictures and fictions] will disappear, by your accepting this fact as you do the others.)

This is the plan: first to bring us face to face with the abyssal contingency, the beyond comprehension of our life with language, and then to show how acceptance of that life, as it is, wanting nothing different— Nietzsche's *amor fati*—can be our salvation. Oh, those Greeks! They knew how to live. What is required for that is to stop courageously at the surface. . . . Those Greeks were superficial—*out of profundity* (*GS* P par. 4).

(2) Does Meaning Consist in Something, Like a Picture?

What does meaning something consist in? In the philosophical arm of the advance guard of cognitive psychology, this is a pressing and important question. Its difficulty explains the confidence of vocal critics of the foundations of this field, such as Searle, and the pessimism of those who attempt answers, such as Fodor. But when the first paragraph of the *Investigations* looks at the written request "five red apples," this pressing question disappears. "But what is the meaning of the word 'five'?—No such thing was in question here, only how the word 'five' was used" [gebraucht wird] (*PI* par. 1). Almost immediately, we are told that the author of these investigations would like to convince us that the "general notion of the meaning of a word surrounds the working of our language with a haze" (*PI* par. 5). Wittgenstein does not have a single answer to the question "what does meaning something consist in." On his account, the question itself is the problem: "The mistake is to say that there is anything meaning something consists in" [Der Irrtum ist zu sagen, Meinen bestehe in etwas] (*Z* par. 16).[20] The mistake is not to have signed on with the wrong account of what meaning something consists in, say with an individualistic as opposed to a communitarian or neurocomputational account. The mistake is deeper. The mistake is to have signed on to any such account, at all. The mistake is to say "This is what meaning consists in: _____."

My discussion of Wittgenstein's mature approach to linguistic meaning proceeds in two phases. *First* to confront us with the contingency of the fact that we can speak with each other, and *second* to see how this contingency can, when accepted, reveal the wonder of human communication. "If I say: here we are at the limits of language, then it always seems ... as if resignation were necessary, whereas on the contrary complete satisfaction [Befriedigung] comes, since *no* question remains" (*BigT* p. 183). But to discover that some questions are gone is not like discovering that there is no more flour in the flour bin, or that heat doesn't come in particles of caloric. How could it be *easy* to give up questions that seem the most important?

> It can be difficult not to use an expression, just as it is difficult to hold back tears. . . . What has to be overcome is not a difficulty of the intellect [des Verstandes] but of the will. Work on philosophy is—as work in architecture[21] frequently is—actually more a work on oneself. On one's own conception. On the way one sees things. (And what one demands of them.) (*BigT* p. 161; see *PI* par. 144)

I will describe these difficulties of the will, first, as they confront the question of linguistic meaning and, in the next chapter, as they confront existential meaning.

If there were something that meaning *did* consist in, what kind of thing might it be? How might it settle our cares, logical and existential? This is a difficult question simply because the expression "consists in" [bestehen in] is not that familiar. Moreover, Wittgenstein is, at times, perfectly willing to concede that linguistic activity consists in various facts. Concerning the relation between a name and a thing named he writes (in his own voice):

This relation may also consist [darin bestehen], among many other things, in the fact that hearing the name calls before our mind the picture of what is named; and it also consists [besteht], among other things, in the name's being written on the thing named or being pronounced when the thing is pointed at. (*PI* par. 37; see par. 197)

But notice that Wittgenstein doubly underlines the lack of systematicity in the sort of fact in which this relation consists, first by listing three separate kinds of fact and, second, by reiterating that these three are some "among many other things" that the relation can consist in. The connection between a particular name and what it is a name for consists in the various, unsystematic ways that name enters our life with it. In a similar vein, he writes:

—Where is the connection effected between the sense of the expression "Let's play a game of chess" and all the rules of the game?—Well, in the list of rules of the game, in the teaching of it, in the day-to-day practice of playing [Praxis des Spielens]. (*PI* par. 197)

So if we are willing to say that these connections consist in the multitudinous details of our life with these words, then even Wittgenstein will speak of what these connections consist in. (Of course, such details hold no theoretical interest, which is either a reason to reject Wittgenstein or an occasion to learn something about the position of theory in philosophy.) The mistake that the passage from *Zettel* (*Z* par. 16) invokes is to think that there is some one thing that meaning, even of a single word, always consists in, some one thing beneath our linguistic practice. "Consists in" is essence talk, and we have already seen (in chapter 3) that it is important to distinguish the essence talk which Wittgenstein endorses from that which he does not endorse. Wittgenstein's opposition is to a certain systematic account of what meaning is, not to saying what, in a given case, meaning something consists in.

If there were something—an Ur-something—deep beneath our linguistic practice that made it meaningful, then it would be the key to the proper account of the grammar of every word of our language and hence also of our understanding of ourselves and everything else. By paragraph 138, it is already clear that the *Investigations* is offering an alternative account according to which we should release the general notion of the meaning of a word (*PI* par. 5), and concern ourselves with the use [Gebrauch] of the word in the linguistic practice itself (*PI* par. 43).

> When philosophers use a word ... and try to grasp the *essence* [*Wesen*] of the thing, one must always ask oneself: is the word ever actually used [gebraucht] this way in the language which is its original home?
>
> What *we* do is to bring words from their metaphysical back to their everyday use [Verwendung]. (*PI* par. 116)

One problem for this alternative approach is that some of the everyday uses of "meaning" seem to require (in opposition to Wittgenstein) that meaning *be something*, that meaning consist in something, something singular. We speak, for example, of finding the right word for a given sentence, a word whose meaning "fits" right there. Wittgenstein himself raises this problem:

> Of course, if the meaning is the *use* [der *Gebrauch*] we make of the word, it makes no sense to speak of such a "fitting." But we *understand* the meaning of the word when we hear or say it; we grasp it in a flash [mit einem Schlage], and what we grasp in this way is surely something different from the "use" ["Gebrauch"] which is extended in time! (*PI* par. 138)[22]

These uses of "meaning" and "understanding" suggest that there *must be* something that meaning consists in, something that—unlike the temporally extended use—might be understood, at a shot. It seems that there *must be* something that can come before our minds—all at once: if not, then how could we explain our ability to grasp a meaning in a moment?

But what comes before the mind all at once? What sort of thing could possibly come before the mind like that, and could it possibly perform its appointed purpose of being that in which meaning consists? Before I present some of Wittgenstein's particular ripostes to particular suggestions as to what "all at once" thing meaning might consist in, I will try to say something at a level of generality he does not normally permit his writing to reach. There is a reason why he does not. The attractions, the charms,[23] that Wittgenstein is trying to dispel are such that any general argument against the theoretical demand for something in which meaning consists would, very likely, lose its persuasive force immediately we succumbed—as surely we would—to the charms of explanation. The general considerations are like medicine we cannot bring ourselves to swallow: they have no actual therapeutic value. Nevertheless these general considerations might bring the details to follow into better focus.

The goal is to see that we misconstrue the grammar of our language—hence our understanding of ourselves and everything else—by trying to construe meaning as consisting in something (*Z* par. 16). Sensitive as he is to the contexts in which each of these attempts turns up, Wittgenstein doesn't always say the same thing, but his first move is almost always of the same type: raising unusual possibilities. Picture our problem like this: given something or other that comes all at once when we grasp the meaning of a word, we are to generate, derive, produce the correct use of the word. This introduces something like a "gap" separating what is grasped (all at once) from the use of the word (extended in time).[24]

(A)   Something (which we grasp all at once)

———(*GAP*)———

(B)   The actual hurly-burly use of the word (extended in time).[25]

Wittgenstein drives home the existence of the gap by reminding us of unusual possibilities. Someone might naturally react to or naturally understand [versteht von Natur] (A) by not performing (B) (*PI* par. 185). Wittgenstein's strategy rests on the existence of this gap. For if there is a gap, then *simply* having or exemplifying or grasping the whatever it is that meaning consists in will not—*all by itself*—ensure that our use of the word will be what we call correct. There is a gap to hurdle. Suppose we introduced a third thing to hurdle the hurdle (perhaps a third man). That thing will either be different from the hurly-burly of our linguistic practice [Praxis der Sprache] or not (*PI* par. 51)—that is, this third thing will either be different from (B) or not. If it is different from (B), the gap remains. If it is not different, then there is nothing less than the hurly-burly for meaning to consist in. In which case, just as Wittgenstein said, "to imagine a language means [heisst] to imagine a form of life" (*PI* par. 19). And again:

—To obey a rule, to make a report, to give an order, to play a game of chess are *customs* (uses, institutions). [*Gepflogenheiten* (Gebräuche, Institutionen)]

> To understand a sentence means [heisst] to understand a language. To understand a language means to be master of a technique [Technik]. (*PI* par. 199)

And how is it possible to master a technique as hurly-burly as (linguistic) life? Here is where Wittgenstein's wonder arrives. For he offers nothing more than this: the possibility of (linguistic) life dangles from our reactions (*PI* par. 143 and 145). No explanation is offered (*PI* par. 217)—not even a naturalistic explanation (*PI* p. 230). Sometimes we may even find ourselves trying to believe explanations that serve only architectural purposes, like ornamental moldings [Scheingesims] or false pediments, which support nothing (*PI* par. 217; see *RFM*3 p. 135: 1938).

Wittgenstein works through this pattern of thinking for a variety of possible instances of (A): mental pictures, real pictures, states of the brain, rules, and so on. He doesn't lend these various possibilities any systematic structure because his writing is so close to the details of the particular problem on his plate, and because he is trying to let his remarks proceed "from one subject to another in a natural order and without breaks" (*PI* preface). Nevertheless, in the end he will have canvassed an instance or two of most of the possible versions of (A): mentalistic, materialistic, and mathematical. In the rest of this section, we will look at one of them: "something, like a picture" (*PI* par. 139).

Wittgenstein had asked himself what really comes before the mind when we understand a word all at once: "Isn't it something, like a picture?" [Ist es nicht etwas, wie ein Bild?] (*PI* par. 139). (The "etwas" recalls, "Der Irrtum ist zu sagen, Meinen bestehe in etwas" [*Z* par. 16].) And the particular "all at once" something that surfaces here is something like a picture. *Like* a picture, because we will probably think of this not as a real three-dimensional painting but as a *mental* picture (*PI* par. 141). This will be important, for the illusion that the appeal to a picture explains something is encouraged by our placing it in the gaseous (hence, I suppose, intrinsically explanatory) realm of spirit (*BlB* p. 5). Wittgenstein gives his opponent a favorable example. He doesn't consider a mental picture of the meaning of "requirement," whatever that might be. He considers a mental picture of the meaning of the word *cube*, which is pretty easy to imagine.

Imagine that the meaning of the word *cube* consists in something, like a picture. Still, the use of a word must also be connected to the meaning of a word (*PI* par. 139). So we face a more defined question: does the something that comes before the mind all at once—in one present moment—trump the use that we make of the word, or contrariwise? We are tempted (are we?) (why?) to say that what comes before the mind all at once is what the meaning of a word consists in. Hence, we may think that the use—extended in time—will be correct/incorrect, if it fits/fails to fit the meaning (picture) of the word that we grasp—all at once.

On this account then, we must know what it is to fit or fail to fit the picture that comes into (something like) view when we understand a word. And it is here that Wittgenstein raises an unusual possibility that reminds us of the gap between (A) and (B):

> In what sense can this picture fit or fail to fit a use [Verwendung] of the word "cube"?—Perhaps you say: "It's quite simple;—if that picture occurs to me and I point to a triangular prism for instance, and say it is a cube, then this use of the word doesn't fit the picture."—But doesn't it fit? I have purposely so chosen the example that it is quite easy to imagine a *method of projection* [*Projectionsmethode*] according to which the picture does fit after all.
>
> The picture of the cube did *suggest* a certain use to us, but I could also use it differently [aber ich konnte es auch anders verwenden]. (*PI* par. 139)

In the next paragraph Wittgenstein tells us that the essential [das Wesentliche] thing about these considerations—which he calls "my argument"—is that "the same thing can come before our minds when we hear the word and the application [Anwendung] still be different" (*PI* par. 140). In such a case he thinks we will say that the word is differently understood, so that the hurly-burly use of the word trumps the picture that comes before our minds, *not* contrariwise (*PI* par. 140). This seems true. Imagine that Chad has been telling you all about how strange Summit Street looks, now that his porch has been painted magenta. Every porch on the street is now magenta. You climb up to his street and are stunned by the sight of four teal blue porches, all in a row. If Chad's use of *magenta* was more or less exactly like the normal use of *teal*, then wouldn't we say that by *magenta*, Chad meant teal? But what if, even though he used *magenta* just as we use *teal*, a magenta mental patch still came before Chad's mind when he heard the word *magenta*? If you can use one series of letters to mean what a different series of letters means, why can't you use a patch of one color to mean a different color? So it looks like Wittgenstein is correct: the actual use [Anwendung] of the word would trump the picture associated with the word, and not contrariwise (*PI* par. 140). But however we stand on that issue, the unusual possibility reveals that if meaning consists in something, it can't be a (mental) picture.

Wittgenstein is intrigued by the very fact that there is something for his "argument" to point out. Although it is "quite easy" [ganz leicht] to imagine a different method of projection of the (mental) picture of a cube, we seem not to be able to remember this possibility. We seem to have thought that a particular picture (A) made a particular use (B) *inevitable* (*PI* par. 140). Wittgenstein is incredulous:

> How could I think that? What *did* I think? Is there such a thing as a picture, or something like a picture, that forces a particular application [Anwendung] on us; so that my mistake lay in confusing one picture with another? (*PI* par. 140)

There are no pictures like that. But this is not news. What were we thinking? What weren't we thinking? Why is the gap between (A) and (B) invisible?

Paragraph 140 lofts another account of the mistake made. Perhaps we were mislead because although we are under a *psychological* compulsion to apply the word *cube* in a certain way, we are not under any *logical* compulsion. Wittgenstein has his doubts about whether we really do know two kinds of case, logical and psychological compulsion.[26] But the force of this distinction, here, can come into focus in this way. Maybe the reason for the failure of the picture account of meaning is that pictures all by themselves need to be interpreted, projected, if they are to be applied to objects (even other pictures) in the world. Different people might be psychologically inclined to project *this* picture in different ways, hence they are under no more than a psychological compulsion to apply the word *cube* to cubes. But if hearing the word brought before our minds not just a picture but also a method of projecting that picture, then the gap would be hurdled and psychological compulsion would mature into logical. This is the suggestion that appears in *PI* par. 141.

Wittgenstein supposes that when the correct method for projecting (what we call) the picture of a cube comes before the mind, it will be a schema: something like "a picture of two cubes connected by lines of projection" (*PI* par. 141). So we are to imagine the picture of a cube and the schema both coming before the mind when we grasp the meaning of a word, all at once. This pair is now the something in which meaning consists. This pair is to hurdle the gap. The presence of this new version of (A) will now—so we suppose—make the presence of (B) inevitable. But the problem remains (the third man). Wittgenstein: "But does this really get me any further? Can't I now imagine different applications [Anwendungen] of this schema?" (*PI* par. 141). So we are really back at the same place. "For the ground keeps on giving us the illusory image of a greater depth, and when we seek to reach this, we keep on finding ourselves on the old level" (*RFM*3 p. 333: c. 1943–44).

Naturally, Wittgenstein next imagines that another thing comes before the mind when we hear a word and grasp its meaning at a shot. This will be the application [Anwendung] of the schema of the method of projection (*PI* par. 141). This seems to be something new. No longer obviously something that must be interpreted, but a kind of doing [handeln]. In terms of the

(A) . . . . . . (GAP) . . . . . . (B)

picture, we are now close to simply identifying (A)—the something meaning consists in—with the hurly-burly of (B). This would be a pyrrhic victory for Wittgenstein's other voice. Either: the application of a schema is just another quasi-pictorial something—which *still* gets us no further, for it too might be reacted to differently by different people. Or: the application just is the hurly-burly of our use of the word, which is a pyrrhic victory for those who want to say that meaning consists in something (*Z* par. 16). And this is familiar:

> The essential thing is to see that the same thing can come before our minds when we hear the word and the application [Anwendung] still be different. Has it the *same* meaning both times? I think we shall say not. (*PI* par. 140)

The something, which comes all at once, drops out of our account of meaning and we are left with the use [Gebrauch] of the word (*PI* par. 43, par. 142). Of course there can be a collision between the (picture + schema) and its application. Why?

> There can, inasmuch as the picture makes us expect a different use, because people in general apply *this* picture like *this*.
>
> I want to say: we have here a *normal* [*normalen*] case and abnormal cases. (*PI* par. 141)

We seemed to have, it had seemed there must be, two cases: logical and psychological compulsion (*PI* par. 140). And these have turned into two kinds of case: the normal human reaction, and abnormal reactions.

Why is the gap between (A) and (B) invisible? The gap is invisible because, when we suppose that meaning consists in a picture—or something like it—coming before our eyes, we unthinkingly and invisibly suppose that our reaction to that picture is *the* normal *one*. Thus the gap disappears. But it is so easy to imagine a different reaction. What do we gain from hiding this possibility from ourselves? (Wittgenstein's investigations often turn, in this way, back on the philosopher.)[27] What anxiety does this willful blindness cover? Well, what has philosophy's motivation been? Escaping fate.

The turn to philosophy (as also to empirical science) can be conceived as a turn away from fate and its dangers. On Dewey's account, the philosophical project is rooted in the escape from disaster: "man who lives in a world of hazards is compelled to seek for security."[28] In *The Birth of Tragedy*, the world of hazards is figured as tragedy, so it tells us that philosophy begins by turning away from tragedy, fate, and darkness, to justice, reason, and light. What does Nietzsche imagine Socrates to have thought of tragedy?

> Let us now imagine the one great Cyclops eye of Socrates fixed on tragedy. . . . What then did it see. . . . Something rather unreasonable, full of causes apparently without effects and effects apparently without causes; the whole, moreover, so motley and manifold that it could not but be repugnant to a sober mind, and . . . dangerous tinder for sensitive and susceptible souls. (*BT* par. 14, p. 89; see par. 11, p. 80)

Some, at least, of the philosophical quest has been an effort to overcome our dependence on fate, mere contingency, to turn to the light of reason, transcendent necessity.

Wittgenstein's discussion of sentential and existential meaning moves in just the opposite direction. Toward unreason: "My reasons will soon give out. And then, without reasons, I shall act" [handeln] (*PI* par. 211). Toward darkness: "I obey the rule *blindly*" (*PI* par. 219). Back to the cave. There may be some peace, some security, in the offing here, but it will never be a perpetual peace (*PI* par. 133). The peace to be attained will be as exposed to the hazards that cause disaster as any other feature of our lives. Is it any wonder then that we find ourselves working to hide the contingency of language from our own eyes? Supposing the philosophical drive answers to widespread cares—not first of all technical ones—then it is no surprise that we veil from ourselves just those possibilities that threaten the effort to place meaning beyond fate.

"Meaning" here is in the same position as any other attempt to describe a domain that we think to involve necessary connections. So the fear of letting fate back into philosophy may be the fear that there will be no more room for necessary connections at all.

> —But what becomes of logic now? Its rigor [Streng] seems to be giving way here.—But in that case doesn't logic altogether disappear?— For how can it lose its rigor? Of course not by our bargaining any of its rigor out of it.—The *prejudice* [*Vorurteil*] for crystalline purity can only be removed by turning our whole examination round. (*PI* par. 108)

The point here is that if we chip away at the rigor of logic, then, naturally, logic will completely disappear. The problem, however, is not with logic, it is with our confident assumption [Vorurteil] that we know what logical rigor must look like. For it is that picture of rigor that is threatened, not logic. I will pick up this thread again after briefly looking at another failed attempt to say that meaning consists in something (*Z* par. 16).

(3) Does Meaning Consist in Something, like a Rule?

I have been surprised how weak the previous considerations have seemed to Wittgenstein's readers. Many people react to Wittgenstein's discussion of pictures protesting that *nobody*, or perhaps nobody *any longer*, believes that meaning something consists in a picture coming before your mind; Bishop Berkeley—they say—might even have known better than *that*. Perhaps it is my un-Wittgensteinian characterization of this discussion in terms of the (A)...(GAP)...(B) picture that makes it easy to see how the discussion of pictures might be turned against any account of (A). In any case, as soon as his discussion of pictures reaches the importance of the one normal and the many abnormal reactions, Wittgenstein finds himself writing about meaning and understanding without mentioning pictures. His topic returns to one he had already discussed at *PI* par. 81–87; namely, conceiving of language as a calculus of rules. On this account, the meaning of a word is not the picture that swims before our mind when we hear it, but the rule for its correct use. On this account the meaning of a word consists in something, like a rule or law.[29]

Imagine, then, that when we grasp the meaning of a word—all at once—we grasp something, like a rule. This is our new (A). Now we will want to know whether the correct rule can come before our mind and yet our use of the word still not be what we would call "correct." This is the same question we faced when we asked: Does the something that comes before the mind all at once—in one present moment—trump the use that we make of the word, or contrariwise? But things are a bit more complicated, for when shall we say that someone has grasped the rule for the use of word?

Wittgenstein addresses this question:

> Let us imagine the following example: A writes series of numbers down; B watches him and tries to find a law for the sequence of numbers. If he succeeds he exclaims: "Now I can go on!" (*PI* par. 151)

So for example when A writes "6, 12, 18, 24, . . .," B might say "You're counting by sixes, 30 is next." This game is an experimental system to determine if there is anything that *does always* come before our minds when—all at once—we understand a rule. Wittgenstein's discovery here is that "various things may have happened" (*PI* par. 151). For instance: (i) If A was counting by sixes, we might have just seen that 6 was separated from 12 by 6 and then a little less quickly seen that 6 separated 12 from 18, and 18 from 24 too; (ii) if the series were a bit more devious we might actually have to try out algebraic formulae before we settled on how to continue; (iii) if the series were 6, 6, 6, 6, we might just laugh and say "six" with nothing much in our heads at all. Various things may happen when we suddenly understand the rule for the series.

So what are the criteria for having grasped the law of the series? Not having a mental something in mind. Apparently we accept as such a criterion adding the next one or two numbers to the series with the appropriate manifestations of confidence and release of tension. But that will not seem enough, for "There is a general disease of thinking which always looks for (and finds) what would be called a mental [or neurophysiological] state from which all our acts spring as from a reservoir" (*BrB* p. 143: 1934–35). This general disease of thinking issues in this thought (see *PI* par. 146): "My grasping the law of the series *can't* consist in my having continued the series another one or two (or an infinity) of numbers further; continuing the series correctly is rather a manifestation of my having grasped the law of the series; this prior grasping is a (mental or neurophysiological) state which is the source of my correct behavior." And to thoughts like this—from his own pen—Wittgenstein reacts:

> What is one really thinking of here? Isn't one thinking of the derivation of a series from its algebraic formula? Or at least of something analogous?—*But this is where we were before.* The point is, we can think of more than *one* application [Anwendung] of an algebraic formula; and every type of application can in turn be formulated algebraically; but of course [selbstverständlich] this does not get us any further.—The application [Anwendung] is still a criterion of understanding. (*PI* par. 146; first emphasis mine)

Where were we before? We had supposed meaning to consist in something, like a picture. Then we discovered that one picture could be applied according to different methods of projection. Then we discovered that one schema for a method of projection might be applied differently too. The method of projection had gotten us no further. Now we are supposing meaning to consist in something, like a rule or law. And we have discovered that one rule can have various applications, and that each of these can be construed algebraically. So although we keep thinking we have found something short of the hurly-burly of our use of a word for its meaning to consist in, nothing works. We keep finding ourselves back at the surface of language: "For the ground keeps on giving us the illusory image of a greater depth, and when we seek to reach this, we keep on finding ourselves on the old level" (*RFM*3 p. 333: c. 1943–44).

Later in the book Wittgenstein tries to put his finger on the problem with the appeal to rules, any rules, to hurdle the gap from (A) to (B). One of Wittgenstein's voices asks, "But how can a rule show me what I have to do at *this* point? Whatever I do is, on some interpretation [Deutung], in accord with the rule" (*PI* par. 198). The idea here is that if the rule for the correct use of a word requires that at *this* point I say this, then—as long as I provided an idiosyncratic interpretation of the rule—

I might claim that anything I said at that point was in accord with that rule. So what good is the rule? It seems not to be restricting my actual use of the word, at all.

But another, more authoritative, voice reacts to these worries about the power of rules:

> —That is not what we ought to say, but rather: every interpretation, together with what is being interpreted, hangs in the air [hängt . . . in der Luft],[30] and cannot give it any support. Interpretations by themselves do not determine meaning. (*PI* par. 198)[31]

The mistake the first voice made was to suppose that (rules plus) interpretations are any better able to hurdle the gap between (A) and (B) than rules alone. We learned this when we remembered that the same picture may be used with different methods of projection (*PI* par. 139). Interpretations are not the answer to our search for that in which meaning consists.[32]

Whereupon what seems to be the previous voice asks:

> Then can whatever I do be brought into accord with the rule? (*PI* par. 198)

The concern is that if interpretations do not determine meaning, then perhaps it is not even true that we can make any application of a word fit a given rule by the selection of an appropriate interpretation of the rule. The other voice then changes the subject. I think we can see why. If (1) we are seriously trying to bridge the gap between (A) and (B), if we are seriously trying to avoid even such difficulties as are posed by persons with abnormal natural reactions, and if (2) we are supposing that our use of a word will fit/not fit its rule only if the rule is interpreted, then (3) the powerlessness of interpretation to determine meaning will mean that the very idea of agreement with the rule will disappear. As Wittgenstein soon says: "if everything can be made out to accord with the rule, then it can also be made out to conflict with it. And so there would be neither accord nor conflict here" (*PI* par. 201).

Thus, Wittgenstein's first move is to change the subject. To ask us just how we thought we were going to bridge the gap between (A) and (B) with a rule:

—Let me ask this: what has the expression of a rule—say a sign-post[33]—got to do with my actions [Handlungen]? What sort of connection is there here?—Well perhaps this one: I have been trained to react to this sign in a particular way, and now I do so react to it. (*PI* par. 198)

This is where the discussion of pictures led us as well. We begin looking for something very special—a superfact (*PI* par. 192)[34]—to take us from what meaning consists in to our linguistic practice (from A to B), and we end up with just our normal and abnormal reactions. And this is nothing like what we were looking for. As the other voice says, or shouts:

But that is only to give a causal connection; to tell how it has come about that we go by the sign-post; not what going-by-the-sign really consists in [worin . . . besteht]. (*PI* par. 198)

So what is missing is the normativity, the necessity that if you apply this word this way, then you will have made a mistake—not simply that *we* were trained to say that it is incorrect, but that it *is* incorrect. Is it any wonder that "this seems to abolish logic" (*PI* par. 242). Nevertheless, this paragraph's voice of authority denies that what is on offer here is merely a causal connection.

No; I have further indicated that a person goes by a sign-post only insofar as there exists a regular use [ständigen Gebrauch] of sign-posts, a custom. (*PI* par. 198)

This passage voices a considerably improved characterization of (B). Where I have been speaking with calculated casualness simply of the hurly-burly of language, here we read of "regular use" [Gebrauch] and of custom. These two differences differentiate Wittgenstein's writing about "going-by-a-sign" from mere empirical description. Let's look a little closer.

What we have failed to find is a superfact. A fact that would be what our understanding consisted in when we suddenly understood a word or knew how to continue a series. The more than merely causal connection between the meaning of a word and its correct use would be constituted by this superfact. What is especially relevant here is that the hunt for this superfact was a hunt for something that could exist—all at once—in one present moment. But customs—regular uses of words, institutions, practices—cannot exist in one moment (*PI* par. 199, 202). So if the grammatical essence of "obeying a rule" clusters it with practices, then we were wrong even to begin looking for something that could be fully present in the present.[35]

Case 1. Consider the Smith and Jones Dismount. Suppose this is a standard gymnastic maneuver. Now, suppose I—no gymnast—am playing on the bar holding up the playground swings, and suppose I lose my grip and, for once, fall off rather gracefully in what is a fair rendition of a Smith and Jones Dismount. Was this a Smith and Jones?

Case 2. Suppose a strapping example of *Homo sapiens neanderthalis* gets up from a prone position by extending his elbows while supporting himself with his hands and toes. Was this a pushup? We might describe it that way, but such a description would be tinged with humor. (The constitutionally sober cannot do philosophy.) (See *PI* par. 200.)

Case 3. When a three year old (or the wind) puts the $10.00 on the counter, has she (or the wind) paid for the farm-fresh, road-side vegetables?[36] We might say that the wind paid for the vegetables, but such a description would also be tinged with humor.

What must I or the neanderthal or the child know in order to pull off a Smith and Jones or a pushup or pay for the vegetables (see *PI* par. 30)?

> Just as a move in chess doesn't consist simply in [darin besteht] moving a piece in such and such a way on the board—nor yet in one's thoughts and feelings as one makes the move: but in the circumstances [Umständen] that we call "playing a game of chess," "solving a chess problem" and so on. (*PI* par. 33)

This can look unpromising. Is the story to be that in order to do a Smith and Jones I must know that it is called a Smith and Jones? Suddenly that makes it sound too easy. Surely it takes more than that. Are we to say that our daughter will be able to pay for the vegetables if she can simply produce a three year old's incantation of "I'm paying" while she puts the green back on the counter?

But this only looks unpromising because we have fallen back into the Augustinian picture of meaning. We suppose that if I know *that* is a Smith and Jones, then I will know what a Smith and Jones is. But what if the meaning of "Smith and Jones Dismount" were less like the object for which it stood and more like the regular use (*PI* par. 198) of that expression. Then knowing what it was called would require knowing how to use that word in many (don't ask how many) of the circumstances in which it can appear. To have mastered the use of "Smith and Jones Dismount" requires much more of us than simply knowing that *that* is one of them.

The neanderthal case—unlike the gymnastics one—is more complicated because we are assuming that there is no ongoing practice of pushups. Yet if meaning to do a pushup consisted in some superfact, which might exist all at once in the present, then if—fortuitously—that superfact was afoot, there is no reason our neanderthal could not do a pushup. Once, and never again. But something is fishy.

> Is what we call "obeying a rule" something that it would be possible for only *one* man to do, and only *once* in his life?—This is of course a note on the grammar of the expression "to obey a rule." (*PI* par. 199)

And here, for once, Wittgenstein helpfully supplies an answer to this grammatical question in the very next sentences:

> It is not possible that there should have been only one occasion on which someone obeyed a rule. It is not possible that there should have been only one occasion on which a report was made, an order given or understood; and so on.—To obey a rule, to make a report, to give an order, to play a game of chess, are *customs* (uses, institutions). (*PI* par. 199)

The grammatical remark is a remark about the use of the expression "obeying a rule." Until there is a practice of doing pushups, no one can do a pushup. Don't say, well someone must have done the first pushup. Customs do not enter into time the way—for us—the four-minute mile did. The momentary superfact could not have answered our prayers, it isn't the *kind of thing* that meaning could consist in, even if meaning consisted in something, like a rule.

Of course one might discover rules that describe any given behavior. Perhaps they will be complicated and ungainly, but like the rules for describing the moon or the tides, they might in principle be discovered. But neither the tides nor the moon follow rules. The question is, what is it about us that makes us able to follow rules and the sea not?[37] Wittgenstein asks himself this very question: "How am I able to obey a rule?" (*PI* par. 217). But his answer, which was cited at the beginning of the last chapter, is not initially satisfying:

> —If this is not a question about causes, then it is about the justifica-
> tion [Rechtfertigung] for my doing *this* in response to the rule [das
> ich *so* nach ihr handle].
>
> If I have exhausted my justifications [Begründungen], I have
> reached bedrock, and my spade is turned. Then I am inclined to say:
> "This is simply what I do" [So handle ich eben]. (*PI* par. 217)

Then what makes it possible for us to obey a rule isn't anything fancy. It
is nothing a philosopher would expect to find. Not the Good. Not God.
Not the transcendental unity of apperception. Not the Ur-Eine of the
world. We are able to obey rules because we can be trained to obey rules.
No doubt, this seems pretty measly stuff. Explanations must come to an
end somewhere or they would not be explanations—but here? (See *PI*
par. 485.)

(4) Pragmatism, Naturalism, and Transcendentalism

Tracking the attempt to make linguistic meaning consist in something,
like a picture, like a rule, we have run into contingency. I promised this
was the first moment of our investigation of Wittgenstein's mature
account of language. But before we can look at the moment of wonder,
we must look at the moment of "contingency" to set aside three tempting interpretations: pragmatism, naturalism, and the one that tempts
Wittgenstein, transcendentalism. The moment of wonder awaits the
running out of understanding, so we must make sure it has run out. I
will look at a few paragraphs where Wittgenstein is writing about being
initiated into a rule-governed practice. Here we will see contingency
and wonder back to back.

One person, A, is trying to teach another person, B, to write down
the natural numbers in decimal notation. And the question is, how does
B learn to understand this system of numbers? Or, how is it possible for
B to learn to understand the formation rule [Bildungsgesetz] of this system? (*PI* par. 143.) By now we are not prepared for very much of a (tra-
ditionally) philosophical nature to account for this possibility. Here is
the story:

> First of all series of numbers will be written down for him and he will
> be required to copy them. . . . And here already there is a normal and
> an abnormal learner's reaction. At first perhaps we guide his hand in
> writing out the series 0 to 9; but then the *possibility of getting him to*

understand [*Möglichkeit der Verständigung*] will depend on his going on to write them down independently. (*PI* par. 143; Wittgenstein's emphasis)

A will fail in communicating the series to B, if B reacts abnormally. In particular, if B is unable to write down the series of numbers even when his hand is held, then he may be unable ever to understand the natural numbers. Wittgenstein continues:

—And here we can imagine, e.g., that he does copy the figures independently, but not in the right order: he writes sometimes one sometimes another at random. And then communication stops at *that* point. (*PI* par. 143)

So the exposure of the possibility of communication to contingency continues. The mistakes may or may not be systematic, or they may be somewhere in the middle. The paragraph concludes:

Perhaps it is possible to wean him from a systematic mistake (as from a bad habit). Or perhaps one accepts his way of copying and tries to teach him ours as an offshoot, a variant of his.—And here too our pupil's capacity to learn may come to an end. (*PI* par. 143)

The wonder is that—exposed thus to contingency—we can learn to communicate at all.

But it is not simply the normal and abnormal reactions of the pupil—the very system of natural numbers itself rests on the normal behavior of nature, without, however, being about nature (*RFM*3 p. 355: 1941–44). If we found no natural distinction between the normal and the abnormal, then many of our concepts would not exist—at least not as we know them. The previous paragraph had this:

And if things were quite different from what they actually are—if there were for instance no characteristic expression of pain, of fear, of joy; if rule became exception and exception rule; or if both became phenomena of equal frequency—this would make our normal language-games lose there point [Witz].—The procedure of putting a lump of cheese on a balance and fixing the price by the turn of the scales would lose its point [Witz] if it frequently happened for such lumps to grow or shrink for no obvious reason [Ursache]. (*PI* par. 142)

It is apparent that just as Wittgenstein is eager to reveal the dependency of linguistic meaning on the ways people just happen to react, so too he is eager to reveal a similar dependency on the ways that the world just happens to behave. But the word *point* [Witz] requires interpretation. Is Wittgenstein simply saying (pragmatically) that it would no longer *pay* to weigh cheese? Well he is, at least, saying that if cheese were prone to such growing and shrinking our practice of weighing would no longer discriminate lumps of cheese by weight for longer than a moment. It is a further question whether Wittgenstein might also be understood as suggesting that in those circumstances it would no longer *make sense* to speak of weighing the cheese, that in those circumstances to place the cheese on the scale and carefully measure its weight only to find that seconds later it was twice the size, would be, speaking quickly, lunatic.

Bringing this contingency more closely to the problem of teaching natural numbers we can read:

> But you can also say: "If you don't have any little sticks, stones, etc. at hand, then you can't teach a person how to calculate." Just as you can say "if you have neither writing surface nor writing material at hand, then you can't teach him the differential calculus" (or: then you can't work out the division $76570 \div 319$). (*RPP* II par. 192)

The *Investigations* includes:

> Disputes do not break out (among mathematicians, say) over the question whether a rule has been obeyed or not. People don't come to blows over it, for example. That is part of the scaffolding [Gerüst] on which the working of our language is based. (*PI* par. 240)

If humans couldn't hold in their heads a proof of longer than ten steps, if chalk and ink always changed shape when we weren't looking, if mathematicians couldn't agree, then mathematics would surely have a different shape. And here again, it is a further question whether Wittgenstein is suggesting that in those circumstances, the very concept of "mathematical certainty" would have changed (*PI* p. 225e).

Wittgenstein repeatedly reminds us of "extremely general facts of nature" that are usually overlooked (*PI* p. 56e). But it is not clear what these references to facts we had overlooked are meant to accomplish. It is not even clear to Wittgenstein (*PI* par. 144).

(a) Limits of Pragmatism

The repeated assertion that if cheese behaved differently, then our practice of weighing cheese would lose its *point* [Witz] tempts us to pragmatism (*PI* par. 142), tempts us to say that we understand the concepts we do because those are the ones that have proved to pay; they serve our needs and desires better than other concepts. But the temptation should be resisted. We forget the use of "point" to mean something like sense. To get a joke [Witz] is to understand what was said as a joke, and this can be described as seeing its point. But this is hardly its purpose: not why it was cracked, but why it was a crack.

Of course, we may invent a turn of phrase or a traffic sign to do some job or other just as we might invent a recipe for chocolate mousse; and if the job can't be done, or if the mousse is too sweet, then we will adjust our inventions to serve their purposes better. But language can't be like that *all the way down*. Here is Wittgenstein:

> Why don't I call cookery rules arbitrary, and why am I tempted to call the rules of grammar arbitrary? Because "cookery" is defined by its end, whereas "speaking" is not. That is why the use of language is in a certain sense autonomous, as cooking and washing are not. You cook badly if you are guided in your cooking by rules other than the right ones; but if you follow rules other than those of chess you are playing *an other game*; and if you follow rules other than such-and-such ones, that does not mean you say something wrong, no, you are speaking of something else. (*Z* par. 320; see *PI* par. 496–97)

Wittgenstein is not attending to the relatively superficial level, for example, the quantum mechanical level. He is not concerned with the search for the best conceptual system for understanding the bizarre results of the double slit experiment or some more up to date microphysical mystery. To suppose that the concepts that prove useful to physics are fundamental to understanding what it is to possess a concept, at all, is simply one more instance of our culture's general intoxication with science—especially the science of the very large and the very small. But the best conceptual system to use to understand these physical results might indeed be determined pragmatically. "Determined pragmatically"—that means we might learn from experience which system served our current interests best.

In another realm, as Dennett reminds us, the attribution of beliefs to others permits us to predict and control the behavior of others.[38] It might even be true that the causal explanation of our going in for belief-talk is that, through evolution, it has proved to pay. (Everyone else proved progeny poor.) But the justification of our attribution of beliefs to others is not that it serves our interest in prediction. We do not learn from experience, pragmatically, that we should think and judge as we do. Or better: that cannot be the deepest account of our thinking, but only of thinking at its superficial levels, like quantum mechanics. *On Certainty* has this:

> 130. But isn't it experience that teaches us to judge like *this*, that is to say, that it is correct [richtig] to judge like this? But how does experience *teach* us, then? *We* may derive it from experience, but experience does not direct us to derive anything from experience. If it is the *ground* of our judging like this (and not just the cause), still we have no further ground for seeing this as a ground.

> 131. No, experience is not the ground of our game of judging. Nor is its outstanding success. (*OC* par. 130–31: c.1951)

So what is the ground of our game of judging? The fact that, with training of *this* sort, persons like *this*, will judge like *this* (see *Z* par. 309). To say that this experience makes this way of judging worthwhile seems to get beneath our practice of judging to its roots in experience, but it doesn't. For is there any ground for taking this experience as a ground, at all?

- A good ground [Grund] is one that looks like *this* [*so*]. (*PI* par. 483)

- We expect *this* [*dies*], and are surprised at *that* [*dem*]; but the chain of reasons [Gründe] has an end. (*PI* par. 326)

- If I have exhausted my justifications [Begründungen] I have reached bedrock, and my spade is turned. Then I am inclined to say: "This [So] is simply what I do." (*PI* par. 217)

Naked contingency, dumb luck, brute fact. Pragmatism cannot go all the way down, because pragmatic reasoning remains reasoning. But reason is not self-supporting, reason's rules are not self-applying: even pragmatists are meant to believe that. It may pay to speak, but we do not speak because it pays.

(b) The Limits of Naturalism (and Supernaturalism)

Some will be tempted to understand Wittgenstein's appeal to facts as a sketch of a naturalistic (possibly evolutionary) explanation for why we speak the way we do, why we have the concepts that we do have. Simply as a matter of exegesis, we should hesitate before attributing this naturalistic proposal to Wittgenstein. At one point—in a passage Rhees calls "the most important short statement for an understanding of the [*Investigations*]"[39]—Wittgenstein explicitly rejected the suggestion that his philosophy was meant to contribute to natural science: "we are not doing natural science; nor yet natural history.... I am not saying: if such and such facts of nature were different people would have different concepts (in the sense of a hypothesis)" (*PI* p. 230: 1949). An earlier version of this passage appears in a 1947 typescript: "But I am not saying: if the facts of nature were different we should have different concepts. That is an hypothesis. I have no use for it and it does not interest me" (*RPP* I par. 48). But if his appeal to different facts of nature is not to incite empirical hypotheses about concept formation, what is it meant to do? It is meant to incite amazement, wonder.

Our question is, in what way is it contingent, a matter of chance or luck, that our conceptual space is what it is and not something else? The naturalistic proposal is that the exposure of our conceptual space to luck is revealed in a naturalistic (possibly evolutionary) explanation of how we have come to be able to think as we do, and not some other way. When this approach is directed at the *whole* of our conceptual space it is self-refuting: if this empirical hypothesis is true then it is false.

To explain something is, at least in part, to account for why *it* occurred and not some other thing. So we can explain why people in deserts don't employ the concept of "snow" or "ice" by appeal to their natural surroundings. We point to the concept of snow—which we understand—and say, "they don't have this because...." No problem. In general, to offer a natural (or supernatural, this difference makes no difference here) explanation of the fact that our conceptual space is what it is, we should have to consider what *we* find to be conceivable as just one among a number of other conceivable *spaces of conceivability*, all but one of which had been closed off by natural (or supernatural) facts. What's the problem?

The problem is that the fact being explained is that there are limits to what we can conceive: surrounding the space of conceivability is the darkness of the inconceivable. The proposed explanation attempts to explain why the darkness sets in where it does, but the explanation itself will have to see into that darkness and determine how the scaffolding of facts does its work. The naturalistic (or supernaturalistic) proposal can't have it both ways: that the darkness both starts where it does—which is to be explained—and that it doesn't—which is part of what does the explaining. Either the explanation would make sense and the limits of conceivability would be different from what we had supposed, or the limits of conceivability would be as we had supposed but the explanation would not make sense.[40]

The problem is that the limits of conceivability must be transcended by any (natural or supernatural) explanation of those very limits. To speak unguardedly of what makes our concepts possible presupposes that we can make sense of a different space of concepts, but by hypothesis we are addressing a level of inquiry where this is not possible. Hence when one of Wittgenstein's voices suggests that "'If humans were not in general agreed about the colors of things, if disagreements were not exceptional, then our concept of color *could* not exist'" (*RPP* II par. 393, my emphasis; see *Z* par. 351). A more authoritative voice says bluntly, "No:—our concept *would* not exist" (*RPP* II par. 393; see *Z* par. 351). The "could" would make sense only if we could understand what, by hypothesis, we can't understand (see *PI* par. 497). Naturalistic interpretations of Wittgenstein's appeal to unusual natural facts must fail.

(c) Limits of Transcendentalism

In this section we have been trying to determine how to understand Wittgenstein's appeal to the role of normal and abnormal reactions to training. His painting of a scene of instruction has driven home the point that the possibility of communication between two persons depends on certain very obvious natural facts, such as that each person respond in similar ways to similar suggestions; that they can be made to see similarities between this pair but not that pair of objects; that they react in similar ways to a pointed finger, to a slap, a tap, a caress, a kiss.[41] The transcendental temptation is therefore this: maybe the ground of the possibility of our concepts is the presence of just these natural facts. Here is Wittgenstein in 1948:

> It seems therefore, that our concepts, the use of our words are con- strained by a scaffolding of facts [Gerüst von Tatsächlichem]. But how *can* that be?! (*RPP* II par. 190)

And here he is on April 23, 1951:

> Indeed, doesn't it seem obvious that the possibility of a language- game is conditioned by certain facts. In that case it would seem as if the language-game must "*show*" ["*zeigen*"] the facts that make it pos- sible. (But that is not how it is.) (*OC* par. 617–18)

The use of show [zeigen] indicates that Wittgenstein is running along tracks laid out by the *Tractatus*. In the *Tractatus*, the possibility of sense was sup- ported by a scaffolding of logic whose nonsensical [unsinnig] presence was shown in the workings of language, most perspicuously in the senseless [sinnlos] bits of language (*TLP* 4.461–4.4611). The suggestion here seems to be that what gets shown in the workings of language are the unutterable (?) natural facts without which there could be no language at all. But as cer- tain as it is that Wittgenstein is tempted by this new transcendental scaf- folding, it is more certain that he intends to turn away from it.

In the typescript of 1948, Wittgenstein's immediate reaction is the incredulity manifest in the citation above. It continues:

> But how *can* that be?! How could we describe the framework if we did not allow the possibility of something else? (*RPP* II par. 190)

What is the point? You must think through what the transcendental temptation is. What we are to explain is the fact that we find this to be possible, that to be impossible, these others to be necessary, and so on. And the explanation is that there is a scaffolding of natural facts (or supernatural, again, it makes no difference). But then could we describe this scaffolding? To describe it is to be able to conceive of it otherwise. But we should *not be able* to conceive of it otherwise, for the scaffolding is meant to fix what we can and cannot conceive. So if we can describe the scaffolding of facts, then it cannot be the ground of the possibility of our finding this possible, that impossible, and that other thing necessary. *Copyrighted Material*

We were here already, for I have already cited the following passage that appears during a discussion of the "'scaffolding of facts'" (*RPP* II par. 392, citing *RPP* II par. 190):

"If humans were not in general agreed about the colors of things, if disagreements were not exceptional, then our concept of color could not exist." No:—our concept *would* not exist. (*RPP* II par. 393)

Wittgenstein is trying hard not to explain. "We must do away with all *explanation*, and description alone must take its place" (*PI* par. 109). We must do away with explanation because what we cannot understand, we cannot understand. It is not that what we cannot understand has some peculiar feature that we might explain pragmatically, naturalistically, supernaturalistically, or transcendentally. What we cannot understand we cannot understand. Or: "When a sentence is called senseless [sinnlos], it is not, as it were, its sense that is senseless" (*PI* par. 500). So, were others to react differently, we may be tempted to say that our understanding stops because the scaffolding of facts has given way, while what we should say is simply, I can no longer communicate with these people (*RPP* II par. 397).

The discussion of these matters in the 1948 typescript reaches a sort of conclusion when we read:

401. But what this really amounts to is that *consistently* following a series can only be shown by *example*.

402. And here one is tempted again and again to talk more than still makes sense. To continue talking when one should stop.

403. I can tell someone: "*This* number is the right continuation of this sequence"; and in doing this I can bring it about that for the future he calls the "right continuation" the same thing I do.

404. He must go on like this *without a reason* [*ohne grund*]. Not, however, because he cannot yet grasp the reason but because—in *this* system—there is no reason. (The chain of reasons comes to an end.) (*RPP* II par. 401–4; citing *PI* par. 326)

And we are back to where we started. There is no (A) that can be grasped in a moment that will guarantee that the pupil will pick up the practice (B) as we had intended. We can't justify our linguistic practice, but only exemplify it (see *PI* par. 201: "exhibited"). And the transcendental temptation is to treat this fact as *showing* the transcendental structure of thought. But when our justifications are exhausted, and our spade turns, then there is nothing transcendental to say or to show: this is simply what I do (*PI* par. 217).

This "I" ought to be sign enough that Wittgenstein is *not* saying that the criterion for which continuation of the series is correct is that most of us do it that way. This would abolish logic: mutilate its modality. Wittgenstein is clear:

> 413. I cannot describe how (in general) to employ rules, except by *teaching* you, *training* you to employ [verwenden] rules.

> 414. I may now, e.g., make a talkie [Sprechfilm] of such instruction. The teacher will sometimes say "That's right." If the pupil should ask him "Why?"—he will answer nothing, or at any rate nothing relevant, not even: "Well, because we all do it like that"; that will not be the reason [Grund]. (*RPP* II par. 413–14 = *Z* par. 318–19)

But if none of these are Wittgenstein's position, if he is doing none of these things by pointing to the dependence of our linguistic life on normal and abnormal reactions of pupils, then what is he doing? Inciting amazement, wonder.

(5) The Wonder of Communication

I find Wittgenstein inciting wonder in just the passages about how to apply a picture and how to continue a series that we have been discussing. But those places also reveal Wittgenstein himself of two minds about the point of his appeal to natural reactions. Recall that our pupil is being trained to write out the series of natural numbers, and Wittgenstein has just said that if the pupil reacts in an abnormal way then her capacity to learn, her capacity to communicate, will at that point have come to an end. Then citing himself, he asks:

> What do I mean when I say "the pupil's capacity to learn *may* come to an end here"? (*PI* par. 144)

This is the key question: what are we to make of Wittgenstein's appeal to natural facts? The first response:

> Do I say this from my own experience? Of course not. (Even if I have
> had such an experience.) (*PI* par. 144)

Wittgenstein is not reporting the empirical fact that at that point some
particular pupil's capacity to learn has indeed come to an end. Wittgenstein is not using one experience to falsify some theory that no pupil's
capacity to learn could possibly come to an end here. That is not his
game. He continues:

> Then what am I doing with this proposition? Well I should like you
> to say: "Yes, it's true, you can imagine that too, that might happen
> too!" (*PI* par. 144)

Exclamation point? Why? Wittgenstein would like us to exclaim, as if we
suddenly realized something. But what? There's more.

> —But was I trying to draw someone's attention to the fact that he is
> capable of imagining that? (*PI* par. 144)

Wittgenstein might have been involved in an investigation of what we
can or cannot imagine, but the discussion on these pages is not an investigation of that sort, at all. So what is he up to? A long dash introduces
Wittgenstein's answer, and concludes this paragraph:

> —I wanted to put that picture before him, and his *acceptance*
> [*Anerkennung*] of the picture consists in his now being inclined to
> regard a given case differently; namely to compare it with *this* set of
> pictures. I have changed his *way of looking at things* [*Anschauungs-
> weise*]. (Indian mathematicians: "Look at this!") (*PI* par. 144)

Suddenly changing our way of looking at all things, our attitude to the
world, *that* merits an exclamation point. So Wittgenstein's hope is not
to teach us any new facts, whether about when the pupil stopped being
able to learn or about what we find easy or difficult to imagine. "It was
true [richtig] to say that our considerations could not be scientific considerations" (*PI* par. 109). Wittgenstein is trying to change our attitude
to the things of our world, perhaps we could say his aim is to change
our mood. My hypothesis is that he would like to turn us from thinking it a flat and obvious [selbstverständlich] fact that we can communicate to feeling that it is a mystery. "Man has to awaken to wonder"
(*CV* p. 53: 1930).

This is puzzling stuff, but even more puzzling is the role being played by the defiantly obscure parenthesis about Indian mathematicians. What is that doing here? Baker and Hacker tell us that the longer version of this parenthetical remark (in *Z* par. 460) derives from an early version of the *Investigations*. It reads:

> (I once read somewhere[42] that a geometrical figure, with the words "Look at this!" serves as a proof for certain Indian mathematicians. This looking, too, effects an alteration in one's way of seeing [Anschauungsweise]). (*Z* par. 460: from "Proto-Philosophical Investigations" par. 126, Typescript 226: 1937 or 1938)

As it turns out, Wittgenstein once gave a proof of just this form:

A rectangle can be made of two parallelograms and two triangles. Proof:

RFM3, p. 57: 1937–1938

How might this change your way of looking at things? It is surprising. Wittgenstein even imagines that a child might think that it was accomplished by a trick, or something like magic, because how on earth could two such slanty shapes as the parallelograms turn into anything rectangular without magic (*RFM*3 p. 57: 1937–38). "What surprises [überrascht] me is the way straight and skew go together. It makes me, as it were, dizzy" [schwindlich] (*RFM*3 p. 60: 1937–38).

> You say you are astonished [erstaunt] at what the proof shows you. But are you astonished at its having been possible to draw these lines? No. You are only astonished when you tell yourself that two bits like this *yield* this shape. When, that is, you think yourself into the situation of seeing the result after having expected something different. (*RFM*3 p. 60: 1937–38; see *WVC* p. 68: 12–30–29)

Wittgenstein's proof that you can make a rectangle from two triangles and two parallelograms does change our way of looking at things

[Anschauungsweise]. The proof might change the way we consider the skew and the straight, rectangles and parallelograms. When our expectations about the behavior of the skew and the straight are adjusted, then this proof *may* cease to surprise and to astonish. But again, like jokes that, even though repeated, can still break us open, we might still be able to savor some of the original astonishment.

Return now to the nature of the change that Wittgenstein's appeal to abnormal and normal natural reactions was meant to induce in our way of seeing things [Anschauungsweise]. I must weigh my hypothesis that he would incite us to wonder, to the wonder that we can communicate, at all. The best way into this topic is to look at the terms in which Wittgenstein voices—and then opposes—an opposition to wonder. After closing the obscure parenthesis about Indian mathematicians, the *Investigation* continues:

> Suppose the pupil now writes the series 0 to 9 to our satisfaction.— And this will only be the case when he is often successful, not if he does it right once in a hundred attempts. Now I continue the series and draw his attention to the recurrence of the first series in the units; and then to its recurrence in the tens. (Which only means that I use particular emphases, underline figures, write them one under another in such-and-such ways, and similar things.)—And now at some point he continues the series independently—or he does not. (*PI* par. 145)

". . . *or he does not*"—that can be our emblem for the overlooked natural facts that Wittgenstein is here turning to our attention. And what does the other voice say? "But why do you say that, *that* is obvious!" [selbstverständlich!] (*PI* par. 145). The more authoritative voice replies: "Of course, I only wished to say: the effect of any further explanation depends on his *reaction*" [hänge von seiner *Reaktion* ab] (*PI* par. 145). My concern here is with the force of the objection that Wittgenstein is wasting our time with trivial platitudes: But why do you say that, *that* is obvious [selbstverständlich]! (*PI* par. 145.) Get serious; you call yourself a philosopher? Grow up.

In the *Investigations* "selbstverständlich" and "selbstverständlichkeit" are—between them—used seventeen times. Three times to indicate that Wittgenstein thinks something obvious (*PI* par. 95, 146, and 352). But each of the other occurrences of these words is either (as in *PI* par. 145) in the mouth of one of Wittgenstein's other voices or in his own mouth distancing his own position from those others.[43] This amounts to a pretty serious opposition to taking things as obvious, hence to finding them *not* selbstverständlich but difficult to understand, dark, mysterious. Consider what he says about writing:

> Don't consider it a matter of course [Sieh's nicht als selbstverständlich an] that a person is making a note of something when he makes a mark—say in a calendar. (*PI* par. 260)

Consider what he says about speaking:

> I should like to say: you regard it much to much as a matter of course [du siehst es für viel zu selbstverständlich an] that one can tell [mitteilen] anything to anyone. (*PI* par. 363)

Consider what he says about reading fiction and looking at pictures:

> Don't take it as a matter of course [Sieh es nicht als selbstverständlich an], but as a remarkable fact, that pictures and fictitious narratives give us pleasure, occupy our minds. (*PI* par. 524)

Writing, speaking, reading, and looking. Wittgenstein does write about other matters, but these four pretty much cover those areas on which his fame as a philosopher rests, and about each of these areas he warns: don't take it as a matter of course, don't take it as obvious. My suggestion is that that is what his ". . . *or he does not*"was meant to incite (*PI* par. 145). His demand that we find things surprising is put in the same words in each of these passages: Sieh es nicht als selbstverständlich an. So we can be thankful that (parenthetically) he says what this expression means:

> ("Sieh es nicht als selbstverständlich an"—that means: find it surprising [Wundere dich daruber] as you do other things that trouble [beunruhigt] you. Then the puzzling aspect will disappear, by your accepting [hinnimmst] this fact as you do the others.) (*PI* par. 524)

His other voice would find the dependence of communication on the normal reactions of the pupil to be an obvious fact. Stop! Don't! Find it surprising, troubling our quest for understanding, disquieting our thirst for peace, our need for rest.

But we can—yes—communicate. That is the wonder. The wonder is that we can communicate at all. What does it take to move us from disquiet to wonder? Simply to accept our natural reactions. What must be accepted [hinnehmen] is the form of our lives with language, with each other (*PI* p. 226). The difficulty of this task is the difficulty of discovering your natural reactions, for often our first reactions, the words first to our lips are there first for the wrong reasons (*PI* p. 201). But like discovering where reason lies, discovering which of your reactions are natural and which conventional, which conform to others and which to your self alone: the strongest illusion is that this task is easy. Quite the opposite—like Emerson's self-reliance—this can be the most difficult. Something in us refuses to swallow.[44]

> Philosophical problems can be compared to locks on safes, which can be opened by dialing a certain word or number, so that no force can open the door until just this word has been hit upon, and once it is hit upon any child can open it. (*BigT* p. 175)

In Wittgenstein's mature philosophy our real needs (*PI* par. 108) are not to be altered but to be acknowledged. The lucky surprise is that the absence of what we thought to be our salvation can itself—the absence we had feared—be our salvation: satisfy us [befriedigen], calm our cares [Sorge], bring us peace [Ruhe], for a spell. Coming face to face with the dumb fact that some things do and some things do not make sense can incite the feeling that, as Wittgenstein remarked, you are "'walking on a mountain of wonders.'"[45] The wonder of our being in a world at all.

Remember our plan: first to bring us face to face with the abyssal contingency, the beyond comprehension, of our life with language, and then to show how acceptance of that life, as it is, wanting nothing different—Nietzsche's *amor fati*—can be our salvation: "Oh, those Greeks! They knew how to live. What is required for that is to stop courageously at the surface. . . . Those Greeks were superficial—*out of profundity*" (*GS* P par. 4).

Now we can begin to end.

(6) "Good Luck"

The second letter Wittgenstein sent to Norman Malcolm was dated May 29, 1940. Wittgenstein signed it:

> Good Luck!!
>   Affectionately
>   Ludwig Wittgenstein (NM.2)

This was not his usual way of signing letters.[46] I have not found any (published) letters written by Wittgenstein, before this one to Malcolm, that wish anyone good luck.

He had written Eccles eleven letters between 1912 and 1939, not one of them wishes good luck.[47] He had written von Ficker twenty-nine letters between 1914 and 1920 and wishes no one good luck.[48] He wrote Keynes thirty-one letters between 1913 and 1939 and, although there is a "good wishes" on February 3, 1939, "good luck" is wished on no one.[49] The architect Paul Engelmann, from whom (in 1926) Wittgenstein wrested the responsibility for designing his sister's house, received fifty-four[50] letters from 1916 to 1937. Although the last letter wishes that "things go well with you [Engelmann] somehow or other!!!" good luck was never invoked. Russell received at least sixty letters and cards from Wittgenstein,[51] the first dating from 1912 and the last from (probably) 1935. Wittgenstein invoked luck in letter R.22 (November 1913) when he reminded Russell of a difficulty with his resolution of the logical paradoxes by means of the theory of types:

> ... the feeling one always had about the infin[ity] ax[iom] and the axiom of reducibility, the feeling that if they were true they would be so only by a lucky accident. (*L* R.22: 1913)

But the letters to Russell wish no one good luck.

On the other hand, of the thirty-five letters (1939–1951) Wittgenstein sent to von Wright, roughly 20 percent of them wish someone good luck. Of the fifty-seven letters he wrote to Malcolm, roughly 33 percent wish someone good luck. Of the surviving fifty-eight letters and cards to Moore,[52] only about 5 percent wish someone good luck; but although Wittgenstein's correspondence with Moore starts in 1913, the "good luck" letters start in 1941 (B.255).

I have made an effort to be thorough, but this survey of Wittgenstein's correspondence has been restricted to those of his letters and cards already published. There are certainly more, he undoubtedly wrote to other people, and even these correspondents may have lost or destroyed or otherwise held back certain of his letters to them. But this incomplete survey is fully consistent with this striking hypothesis: *all* the occasions when a letter of Wittgenstein wishes anyone good luck can be dated from 1940 on; before 1940 Wittgenstein's letters *never ever* wish anyone good luck. The thought is inescapable, that this change in his signature testifies to a deep change in Wittgenstein's view of things [Anschauungsweise].

The Wonder of Existential Meaning: Wittgenstein's Daybreak

There is a crack—a crack—in everything; that's how the light gets in.

—Leonard Cohen, "Anthem"

A being that isn't cracked isn't possible. But we go from enduring the cracks (from decline) to glory (we seek out the cracks).

—Georges Bataille, *Guilty*, p. 23

(1) Wittgenstein's Existential Investigations

One of the threads in the history of the philosophical reception of the *Tractatus* is the gradual acceptance of the importance of the mystical conclusion of that book. In the second chapter, I approached these concluding sections with an eye on the problem of the value or significance of existence, the riddle of life: *The Riddle* (*TLP* 6.4312, 6.5). It is not now unusual to emphasize this dimension of the *Tractatus*. It remains unusual to emphasize the same existential dimension of the *Philosophical Investigations*.

In one way, this imbalance is not surprising. The *Tractatus* does, while the *Investigations* does not, explicitly address the problem of the value of existence, and the latter does not mention the "riddle of life." Moreover, the *Investigations* gives a narrowly philosophical first impression. The sequence of topics discussed circle round and round the manner in which humans possess and are possessed by the language they speak. But if you ask this book why it is concerned with language in this way, you will not receive a narrowly philosophical answer. G. E. Moore, remembering Wittgenstein's lectures from the early thirties, recalls:

> I think he certainly thought that some philosophers nowadays have
> been mislead into dealing with linguistic points which . . . [form] no
> part of the proper business of the philosopher.[1]

Wittgenstein was not concerned with language as with some intrinsically interesting intellectual puzzle. From the *Tractatus* to the *Investigations*, his interests did not become intellectual. They continued to be
existential.

The existential nerve of Wittgenstein's investigations appears,
among other places, in the very first words of the *Investigations*. Wittgenstein selected a motto for the book that directs his readers precisely
to its existential dimension. For some time he had been planning to use
a line from Hertz's last work, *Principles of Mechanics* (1894), as a motto.[2]
But in 1947, Wittgenstein began to settle on his final choice, a line from
Nestroy's play *Der Schützling* (1847). I quote the motto in context, ital-
icizing the motto itself:

> There are so many means of extirpating and eradicating, and never-
> theless so little evil has been extirpated, so little wickedness eradicated
> from this world, that one clearly sees that people invent a lot of things,
> but not the right one. And yet we live in the era of progress, don't we?
> I s'pose progress is like a newly discovered land; a flourishing colonial
> system on the coast, the interior still wilderness, steppe, prairie. *The
> main point about progress [Fortschritt] is that it always seems greater
> than it really is.* (my emphasis)[3]

The progress that "always seems greater than it really is" is progress in
overcoming wickedness and evil. What kind of progress fails in that
way? Well, what is it that makes ours appear to be an "era of progress"?
I am inclined to reply: scientific and technological advances. And I
think I would be inclined to reply in that way even if I did not know
that in a preface to an earlier typescript Wittgenstein had linked the
notion of progress to that of science, and even if I did not know that he
had little affection for those who trust that science will solve their
deepest problems.

Sketching a foreword to work he had done since returning to philosophy in the late twenties (work now known as *Philosophical
Remarks*), Wittgenstein wrote of his own work and its relation to
progress:

> It is all one to me whether or not the typical western scientist under-
> stands or appreciates my work, since he will not in any case under-
> stand the spirit in which I write. Our civilization is characterized by
> the word "progress" ["Fortschritt"]. Progress is its form rather than
> progress being one of its features. (*CV* 7e: 1930)

I suspect that by placing Nestroy's line as a motto for the *Philosophical
Investigations*, Wittgenstein was again—seventeen years later—distinguishing the spirit of his work from the progressive spirit of science.[4] In
Wittgenstein's eyes, progress is only the form (not the substance) of our
scientific civilization because that civilization is not characterized by
real progress. It is characterized by the lying appearance of progress:
precisely Nestroy's thought that "progress always seems greater than it
really is." The earlier sketch continues:

> Typically it [i.e., our civilization] constructs. It is occupied with
> building an ever more complicated structure.[5] And even clarity is
> sought only as a means to this end, not as an end in itself. For me, on
> the contrary, clarity and perspicuity [die Klarheit, die Durchsich-
> tigkeit][6] are valuable in themselves.
>   I am not interested in constructing a building, so much as in hav-
> ing a perspicuous view of the foundations of possible buildings.
>   So I am not aiming at the same target as the scientists and my way
> of thinking is different from theirs. (*CV* 7e: 1930)

To avoid disputes over the true nature of scientists, let us suppose Wittgenstein to be stipulating that he means by "scientist" anyone who seeks
clarity only to make their theoretical and three-dimensional constructions better. As he tells the story, even if these constructions are successful
in their own terms, our "real needs" will be left raw (*PI* par. 108).

Nestroy again: "people invent a lot of things, but not the right one."[7]
We are convinced that each new gadget, each new political alliance, each
new epicycle of our professionalized philosophical theory will solve all
our problems, but at the top of each glassy new building, sticking out
from behind piles of "rigorously" defined concepts, we can still glimpse
the same old cares, the same deep disquietudes [tiefe Beunruhigungen]
(*PI* par. 111). With cruel irony, what we mistake for the means of our
salvation actually makes matters worse. In Wittgenstein's figure from
the 1930s, it is "as in certain states of indigestion we feel a kind of hunger
which cannot be removed by eating" (*BLB* p. 27: 1934). In Nietzsche's

from the 1880s: "What one ought to shun is found attractive. One puts to one's lips what drives one faster into the abyss."[8]

Perhaps his own sense of this irony explains why Wittgenstein speaks of science in such negative, even vicious, terms. Writing in 1946, he reflected on his being tempted to conclude that even the atomic bomb must be a good thing since it was being opposed by the "*scum of the intellectuals*"; nevertheless, realizing the fallaciousness of that inference, he remarked:

> Really all I can mean is that the bomb offers a prospect of the end, the destruction, of an evil,—*our disgusting soapy water science.* And certainly that's not an unpleasant thought; but who can say what would come *after* this destruction? (*CV* 49e: 1946; my emphases)

The problem with soapy water is that it is disgusting [ekelhaften], nauseating. It is a commonplace to represent our real needs (*PI* par. 108) as a deep hunger or thirst.[9] And in our time, it is difficult not to expect science to satisfy every thirst. But if science is soapy water, it will never slake our deepest thirst. We retch.

Wittgenstein knows his dispute is not with the detailed construction of this or that philosophical theory. It is not simply a question of correcting a mistake (*PI* par. 110). His dispute is with the spirit "which informs the vast stream of European and American civilization in which all of us stand" (*PR* foreword: 1930). And he has little hope that his writings will change this spirit:

> Nothing seems to me less likely than that a scientist or mathematician who reads me should be seriously influenced in the way he works. . . . What is needed here is artillery of a completely different kind from anything I am in a position to muster. (*CV* 62e: 1947)

The needed artillery would be capable of changing our civilization, of inciting a recognition that science is—after all—disgusting soapy water. Wittgenstein almost says that Nietzsche alone possessed the artillery he felt he lacked.[10] But he certainly believed that the spirit of our times could only be changed by a change in our mode of life,[11] not by the invention of a new philosophical technique. In the unlikely context of a discussion of Cantor's diagonal proof that there are "more" real numbers than there are integers, Wittgenstein reflected:

The sickness of a time is cured by an alteration in the mode of life of human beings [eine Veränderung in der Lebensweise der Menschen], and it was possible for the sickness of philosophical problems to get cured only through a changed mode of thought and life [Denkweise und Lebensweise], not through a medicine invented by an individual.

Think of the use of the motor-car producing or encouraging certain sicknesses, and mankind being plagued by such sickness until, from some cause or other, as the result of some development or other it abandons the habit of driving. (*RFM*3 p. 132: 1938)

There is no silver bullet. As Wittgenstein sees it, we will not be free of the sickness of our present devotion to science until we transform the manner of our living and thinking; and sometimes, when this realization strikes him, he wonders whether he cares more about that change in our manner of living than in the preservation of his philosophical ideas:

I am by no means sure that I should prefer a continuation of my work by others to a change in the way people live [eine Veränderung der Lebensweise] which would make all these questions superfluous. (*CV* 61e: 1947)[12]

No less than in the *Tractatus*, the mature Wittgenstein was concerned with how we live, and what makes our lives painful. In the motto to the *Investigations* and in the passages I have culled from his notes, it is clear that Wittgenstein thought of his philosophy as being able to play a role in a general critique of contemporary culture. That culture has turned aside from the true necessaries of human life, and the real concern of the *Investigations*, no less than the *Tractatus*,[13] was to return to the problem of satisfying our real needs. It is in this way that the mature work manifests a concern with the *Riddle:* the riddle of life.

Although it is true that the existential dimension of the *Investigations* remains to be widely accepted, it is not true that it has gone wholly unrecognized. This existential reading of the mature Wittgenstein has been a minority view for some time. Recent intellectual biographies of Wittgenstein have already increased the audibility of this approach in conversation, and I suspect we can look forward to its more regular appearance in print.

In his 1977 reading of the Wittgenstein miscellany called *Culture and Value*, von Wright Wittgenstein's sense that the spirit of his thinking was wholly different from the scientific spirit of his (our) times, and he notes that Wittgenstein did not separate his bleak picture of the "darkness of this time" (*PI* preface) from his apparently more narrowly philosophical concerns.[14] Von Wright observed that since Wittgenstein felt "philosophical problems [were] . . . disquietudes of the mind caused by some malfunctioning in the language-games and therewith in the way of life [Lebenweise] of the community," he was bound to believe that "a disorder in the former [would] . . . reflect a disorder in the latter."[15] Briefly:

> If philosophical problems are symptomatic of language producing malignant outgrowths which obscure our thinking, then there must be a cancer in the *Lebensweise*, the way of life itself.[16]

But beyond observing the error of conceiving Wittgenstein as a "cultural illiterate"[17] and revealing his sense of alienation from the progressive scientific spirit of our times, von Wright does not bring out the manner in which the *Investigations*, like the *Tractatus*, might be enlisted in a solution or dissolution of the riddle of life: the manner in which the texts of the mature Wittgenstein are already concerned with our way of life.

I mark the first sympathetic[18] acknowledgment of the more than merely professional concerns of the later Wittgenstein with the appearance in 1961 and 1962 of two articles, the first by O. K. Bouwsma and the second by Stanley Cavell.[19] Even today, there is no better account of the distinctiveness of Wittgenstein's later philosophy than is provided by these two independently insight-filled essays.

Puzzling as the dictated notes we call *The Blue Book* are, Bouwsma insists that they must be especially puzzling for philosophers.

> [For] . . . with what expectations will such readers [philosophers] read? Obviously they will expect what they are accustomed to getting when they read philosophy. Their disappointment and the measure of incoherence [they discover] will be determined in the same way. And what are they used to? They are used to proofs, to arguments, to theories, to evidences, [to] refutations, to infallibles, to indubitables, to foundations, to definitions, to analyses, etc.[20]

But *The Blue Book* presents nothing like this, or while it might occasionally appear, for example, to argue, these argumentative passages do not culminate in anything like a conclusion. And an argument without a conclusion—well, philosophical readers will be confused, only if they are charitable. Bouwsma describes the *Blue Book*:

> This author spends seventy and more pages lolling. He does not, of course, say he is lolling, which seems anyway obvious enough, since he does it so strenuously. . . . In any case it does strike some readers that this book is the work of a strangely articulate and irresponsible author. . . . Was Descartes right in his statement of the cogito or not? What we want is an answer: Yes or No. And what do we get? Not even a weak answer such as "Probably" or "Not at all likely." Surely a straightforward question deserves a straightforward answer. No wonder that man stomped out and slammed the door.[21]

This puts the expositor of "Wittgenstein's later philosophy" in a pickle. There is no content, intended by Wittgenstein, that an expositor might tell us and that we could remember and tell our friends. Bouwsma remarks: "That would be as though the author aimed to put something in the reader's pocket. But what he does is not like that."[22]

What does he do? Bouwsma wants us first of all to realize that Wittgenstein is rather doing something than telling us something (*OC* par. 204). For he is not trying to put anything in our pockets. *The Blue Book* is filled with tips for the students it was addressed to, tips about how to notice and how to escape grammatical confusions; rules of thumb; slogans; stories to contrast with what disturbs us; suggestions about the sources of philosophical puzzlement; and so on. Bouwsma wants us to think of Wittgenstein as teaching what he calls an art, a skill. So this book is not a textbook[23] (see *TLP* preface and 6.124).

Neither the *Blue Book* nor the *Investigations* is a book like *Advanced Immunobiology*. They are like *Learning to Draw* or *Five Steps to a Better Rumba*. Bouwsma italicizes thirteen aspects of the art, the skill, that Wittgenstein taught. They are:

> It is the art of attacking questions. . . . It is the art of disentangling. . . . It is the art of cure. . . . It is the art of finding one's way when lost. . . . It is the art of removal, riddance. . . . It is the art of discussion. . . . It is the art of exposure. . . . It is the art of helpful reminders. . . . It is the art of working puzzles. . . . It is the art of scrutinizing the grammar of a word. . . . It is the art of freeing us from illusions. . . . It is the art of the detective. . . . It is the art of clarification, of relief from the toils of confusion.[24]

Who is this art for? For all who are entangled in questions they can neither answer nor remove; for all who are lost in their thoughts not as in reverie but as in a forest with not too few but too many paths; for all who seek clarification, relief from the toils of confusion. And though these are confusions of thinking they are not merely intellectual, for they are as various as the variety of things we may think on.

Roughly ten years after this essay on *The Blue Book*, Bouwsma found these words to characterize Wittgenstein's *Investigations*:

> Wittgenstein was not thinking of what he was doing as correcting mistakes. It was not mistakes, but an urge, a bewitchment, a fascination, a deep disquietude, a captivity, a disorientation, illusions, confusions—these, the troubles of the mixed up intelligence, that Wittgenstein sought to relieve.... [His] interest was not in any particular problem but in the bothered individual, particularly in the hot and bothered. (Is this perhaps what distinguishes Wittgenstein as a European, a Viennese, a man who read Kierkegaard and Dostoevski?) He sought to bring relief, control, calm, quiet, peace, release, certain powers, the skill required to show one who is lost in the labyrinth the way to go home.[25]

Wittgenstein's investigations were existential.

(2) Linguistic and Existential Meaning in the *Tractatus*

Wittgenstein never lost the existential concerns that are the explicit frame of the *Tractatus*, but how—in detail—do these concerns surface in the *Investigations*? They don't. I will be inventing the *Investigations*' approach to the riddle of life, but not out of whole cloth. I will pick up a thread from my reading of the *Tractatus* and, with it in hand, embroider an answer to the riddle of life on the text of the *Investigations*. In other words, I will transpose the coda of the *Tractatus* into the key of the *Investigations*. Someone is sure to notice that whereas my first chapter featured an interpretation of the unwritten second edition of *The Birth of Tragedy*, this final chapter features an interpretation of the unwritten existential coda to the *Investigations*. This is not an expression of my flight from texts others have already written about. It is the central argument of this book. Nietzsche's turn from the depths of his first book illuminates Wittgenstein's turn from the depths of his first book.

Sometimes I think that more remarkable even than the remarkable Tractarian account of propositional sense is the audacity with which Wittgenstein used his reflections on propositional sense to orient his involvement with the riddle of life's meaning. Professional philosophers smile condescendingly whenever the laity react to learning that the philosopher has read a book about meaning by asking about the meaning of life. We condescend because, as little as we think about the meaning of life, we are sure that linguistic meaning and existential meaning are entirely unrelated. And so we condescend—as well—to the author of the *Tractatus*.

In chapter 2, I interpreted the *Tractatus*'s account of a meaningful life in terms derived from that book's account of the truth-conditions of propositions. Let's return for a moment to that interpretation. In that book we are told that "A proposition is a picture of reality" (*TLP* 4.01). The sense of a proposition is its manifest pictorial content.

> 4.022   A Proposition *shows* its sense.
>   A proposition *shows* how things stand *if* it is true. And it *says that* they do so stand.

And to understand the sense of a proposition is to know what would be the case if it were true, its truth-conditions (*TLP* 4.024).

> 4.2   The sense of a proposition is its agreement and disagreement with possibilities of existence and nonexistence of states of affairs.

The sense of a proposition is the way its truth or falsity is determined by every possible combination of states of affairs. The sense of a proposition just is its truth assignment in every possible state of the world. A proposition's sense is like the point of an arrow (*TLP* 3.144). The proposition restricts reality—in whatever shape—to two alternatives: true or false (*TLP* 4.023a). For any spot, the arrow is either pointing in that direction or not.

Wittgenstein observes that among the possible truth-conditions there are two that stand out as "extreme cases" (*TLP* 4.46). These are the tautologies that are true in all possible states of the world and the contradictions that are false in all possible states of the world. Neither kind of proposition has a sense, and so neither is really a proposition at all.

"Limiting cases" of the combination of signs, they are the boundary between sense and nonsense [der Unsinn] (*TLP* 4.466).

> 4.461   Propositions show what they say [i.e., their sense, 4.022]; tautologies and contradictions show that they say nothing.
>
>   A tautology has no truth-conditions, since it is unconditionally true: and a contradiction is true on no condition.
>
>   Tautologies and contradictions lack sense [sind *sinnlos*].
>
>   (Like a point from which two arrows go out in opposite directions from one another.)
>
> 4.4611   Tautologies and contradictions are not, however, non-sensical [sind aber nicht *unsinnig*]. They are part of the symbolism, much as "0" is part of the symbolism of arithmetic. (my emphases)

The line dividing sense from nonsense (Sinn from Unsinn) is marked by the senseless (Sinnlos), senseless tautologies and contradictions.

These disintegrating combinations of signs say nothing (*TLP* 4.461, 6.11). I am tempted to say that, unlike nonsense [Unsinn], which doesn't say anything at all, the senseless [sinnlos] propositions of logic do say something: nothing. But this paradoxical way of putting it is not the *Tractatus*'s: "The fact that the propositions of logic are tautologies *shows* the formal—logical—properties of language and the world" (*TLP* 6.12). The "logic of the world" (*TLP* 6.22), the "logical scaffolding" (*TLP* 4.23) without which we could form no sensible propositions at all, these are made manifest by the determinate limits of sense. "The fact that a tautology is yielded by *this particular way* of connecting [i.e., disintegrating] its constituents characterizes the logic of its constituents" (*TLP* 6.12b).

In the *Tractatus*, propositions were pictures of reality. If we may speak of their goal, we might say that the goal of a proposition was to be true, to speak the truth. Then there would be two ways one might attain this goal. When the world happens to be as a proposition represents it to be, then the proposition will have attained its goal, as a matter of accident, for "outside logic everything is accidental" (*TLP* 6.3). But within logic, it might be possible to attain this goal nonaccidentally.

6.1   The propositions of logic are tautologies.

6.11   Therefore the propositions of logic say nothing. (They are the analytic propositions.)

Our task was to apply this account of the sense of propositions to life: the riddle of the meaning of life.

If the goal of a proposition is to be true, what is the goal of life? To be satisfied. The *Tractatus* provided an account of the sense of propositions in terms of *truth-conditions* and of the sense of life in terms of *satisfaction-conditions*. The key ingredient here is the will. The content of a desire might be captured in a set of satisfaction-conditions: states of the world in which the will would be satisfied. So when I want to go to a certain movie, the content of that desire might be given by all those states of the world in which I would find myself at that movie. Naturally I would not like to find myself at the movie, blindfolded and blind drunk; so a complete account of desires in terms of satisfaction-conditions would have to account for the simultaneous satisfaction of a variety of desires.

Satisfaction of a given desire would provide satisfaction, but it would be an accidental satisfaction—your life would have sense, but accidentally. But there are serious difficulties with any attempt to solve the riddle of existence accidentally. (a) Before your desires are satisfied, there can be no guarantee that they will ever actually be satisfied. This is because, in the *Tractatus*:

6.373   The world is independent of my will.

6.374   Even if all that we were to wish for were to happen, still this would only be a favor granted by fate, so to speak: for there is no *logical* connection between the will and the world, which would guarantee it, and the supposed physical connection itself is surely to something that we could will.

Discovering our desire for something, we can never be sure we will satisfy that desire. (b) And even when our desire is satisfied, we can never be sure that it will continue to be. This is another consequence of the fact that whether or not a given desire is satisfied, it will always only be satisfied by accident. Since satisfied by accident, it may soon be dissatisfied by accident. This pessimistic view of the possibility of satisfaction is consistent with the early influence on Wittgenstein of Schopenhauer.[26]

The only fully satisfactory goal of human life would be a life that had no satisfaction-conditions since it was unconditionally satisfied (see *TLP* 4.461). In his "Lecture on Ethics" delivered in 1929, some time after the *Tractatus* was published, Wittgenstein described an experience that appears to be one of living a life that is unconditionally satisfied:

> It is what one might call the experience of feeling *absolutely* safe. I mean the state of mind in which one is inclined to say "I am safe, nothing can injure me whatever happens." ("LE," p. 41)

Wittgenstein's discovery of the importance and attractiveness of this thought was very important to him. Malcolm reports:

> He told me that in his youth he had been contemptuous of it [religion], but that at about the age of twenty-one something had caused a change in him. In Vienna he saw a play that was a mediocre drama, but in it one of the characters expressed the thought that no matter what happened in the world nothing bad could happen to *him—he* was independent of fate and circumstances.[27]

Biographers of Wittgenstein agree that Wittgenstein was referring to a performance of Ludwig Anzengruber's *Die Kreuzelschreiber*, which he may have seen during his Easter vacation in 1912.[28] Being absolutely safe is a description of a life that would be unconditionally satisfied. Such a life would have satisfaction-conditions analogous to the truth-conditions of a tautology, that is it would be *unconditionally* satisfied (*TLP* 4.461).

Wittgenstein never explicitly draws this analogy between a life that would be absolutely safe and a tautology that is unconditionally true. In his notebooks his first approach to the riddle of life is to suggest that perhaps the key would be to stop willing altogether: "Or is only he happy who does *not* will? . . . And yet in a certain sense it seems that not wanting is the only good. Here I am still making crude mistakes! No doubt about that!" (*NB* 77–78: 1916). If no particular desire could be satisfied in such a way as to make us absolutely safe, then perhaps the solution would be to give up willing. This—of course—is more or less Schopenhauer's solution. But Wittgenstein rejects it. I suspect his reasons for rejecting it are that not to will—just as much as willing—is simply an empirical fact about the world, and as such is unable to provide a footing for value.

> The sense of the world must lie outside the world. In the world every-
> thing is as it is, and everything happens as it does happen; *in* it no
> value exists—and if it did exist it would have no value. (*TLP* 6.41a)

The crude mistake was to think that the riddle was to discover what particular things to will or not to will. The problem is deeper and the solution is more difficult even than that. (This he never gives up.)

It is to correct this mistake that the *Tractatus* talks of the "will in so
far as it is the subject of ethical attributes" (*TLP* 6.423). In this sense the
will is "an attitude to the world" (*NB*, pp. 86–87: 1916). In the *Tractatus*
this attitude is described as living in the present: "If we take eternity to
mean not infinite temporal duration but timelessness, then eternal life
belongs to those who live in the present" (*TLP* 6.4311b). Take the traditional picture straight up: living in the present is not living in the future
or the past.[29] What would it be to live in the future? Perhaps it would be
to live a life not satisfied with the present, hoping for something different. Who doesn't live their life this way? With luck next week will be different, we will get what we want. The *Notebooks* have this: "Whoever
lives in the present lives without hope and fear" [ohne Furcht und Hoff-
nung] (*NB* p. 76: 1916). Both of these seem to face the future, but to live
in the present is also not to live in the past. What would it be to live in
the past? Perhaps it would be to live a life brooding on the past, stuck in
the stew of past mistakes. And who doesn't live their life that way? Why
did I, why did he, if only she hadn't or I hadn't, if only I had. To live in
the present is to live in neither of these ways.

To live in the past or the future is to be dissatisfied with the present.
To live in the present is to live a life of acceptance, a life of satisfaction.
Wanting nothing different. To live in the present. A familiar thought.
Fernando Pessoa's pseudonym Ricardo Reis put this familiar thought in
a poem roughly contemporaneous with the *Tractatus*, "I the roses love
in the gardens of Adonis" (c. 1914).

I the roses love in the gardens of Adonis,
Lydia, I love those fast fleeting roses
    That on the day they are born,
    On that same day they die.
Light for them is everlasting: born
After the sun comes up, they die
    Before Apollo rounds
    His visible track.

> So let us make our life *a single day,*
> And willingly ignore the night to come,
>> The night already past,
>> The little while we last.[30]

What satisfies the one who lives happily (*NB* p. 75: 1916) is not the satisfaction of this or that desire. That would take place in the future, and it would last—if at all—only as a matter of accident. So it could provide no feeling of absolute safety ("LE" p. 41). In these early writings, the feeling of absolute safety requires living in accord with the world, but not living in accord with this or that accidental fact about the world. Neither to will something in particular nor not to will something in particular, neither strategy would work. To live happily is to make one's life a great mirror of the logical form of the world (see *TLP* 5.511 and 6.13).

The sense of a proposition is its truth-conditions. The truth or falsity of propositions is always conditional; however there are some disintegrating, liminal propositions that are unconditionally true (and some are unconditionally false). These degenerate propositions are our window into the unified, ununderstandable transcendental realm that is the primordial but unutterable ground of sense, of the world, of life. The Ur-Eine of the world. It is in this terrain that Wittgenstein addresses himself to the riddle of the meaning of life. Linguistic meaning depends on this ununderstandable ground. And the propositions closest to it are the tautologies: unconditionally true. Existential meaning also depends on this primordial ground. And those who live their lives closest to the Ur-Eine of the world are those who live happily: "a man who is happy must have no fear. Not even in the face of death" (*NB* p. 74: 1916). Those who are happy are "*absolutely* safe" ("LE" p. 41: 1929). Thanks to the Ur-Eine, they are safe, absolutely.

(3) Linguistic and Existential Meaning in the *Investigations*

Destruction: The First Phase

I charted Wittgenstein's turn from sublime to superficial essentialism in chapter 3. He turned from the Tractarian discovery of the ununderstandable ground of the meaningfulness of language, of the world, of life. He turned from what *The Birth of Tragedy* (1872) calls the Ur-Eine. Figuring sublime essences as simplicities hidden beneath the surface irregularities of our language, it was natural to speak of Wittgenstein's turn as a return to the surfaces of language, a return to what we had never noticed because it was always right before our eyes (*PI* par. 129). (The proximity of romanticism.)[31]

In chapter 4, my concern was with linguistic meaning, and in particular with the manner in which the *Investigations'* account of linguistic meaning manifests Wittgenstein's conviction that "the mistake is to say: meaning consists in something" (*Z* par. 16). My discussion proceeded in two phases. *First* confronting us with the fact that there is nothing in which meaning consists. (This is the (A)—*GAP*—(B) argument.) Confronting us with the dumb contingency of our ability to speak with one another. This takes some work, some rather negative work. But what is destroyed are only houses of cards, only castles in air [Luftgebäude], only false cornices [Scheingesims] (*PI* par. 118, 217). At the end of this phase of Wittgenstein's investigations, we find ourselves face to face with the abyssal contingency of our life with language, a contingency intimated by puns. In the *second* phase of these investigations the ache of discovering that there is nothing in which meaning consists is healed by our acceptance [hinnehmen][32] of our life with language. But this is difficult. As difficult as it is to decide that this relationship, though in many ways only good, is ending. There are no criteria. Our cares cannot be fully and finally ended. We may find peace, but not once and for all, only when and for as long as we are able to accept the language we speak, the life we lead. Only for a spell.

In this chapter I will develop an appropriately analogous account of existential meaning. Let us start with the first phase: Destruction. By analogy with our consideration of propositional sense in the last chapter, we must determine whether it would also be a mistake to suggest that existential sense, the meaning of life, consisted in something (see *Z* par. 16). So we will be trying to find some (B), which seems to be a pretty acceptable account of the hurly-burly of a significant life, a life that has meaning. In the linguistic case this was the actual, ragged use of the word whose meaning we were tracking. And then we will be asking what such a life might consist in: we'll be looking for a suitable (A). In the linguistic case, this was the (mental) picture or the rule in which—whilst succumbing to the subliming impulse—we suspected the meaning of the word in question to consist.

The hope is to reach agreement on a sketch of (B), a life with meaning. And one worry is that our sketch will be trite. Off the shelf tumble all the familiar examples. The religious devotee—who might be monk or nun or Tolstoy—living a life devoted to embodying the holy. "Wedded to God, how could I take another spouse?" is how I have heard celibacy defended. So perhaps a good marriage—of two humans—would provide another uncontentious example of the hurly-burly of a meaningful life. And then, if it comes to that, perhaps we should follow Kierkegaard by taking marriage itself as a figure for the other kinds of activities around which people center their lives: making music, riding bikes, long-distance running.[33] Lift from the notion of a marriage the idea of devotion beyond passing enjoyments: the "through thick and thin" ingredient. Then to my cello I may also devote myself, or rather to the music I make with it. Or to my collection of vintage Mustangs. Or to the family firm, the family farm.

Suitably fleshed out, these suggestions might provide a budget of examples of (B), of lives worth living. So our picture looks like this:

(A)   What the meaning of life consists in.

————(*GAP*)————

(B)   The hurly-burly of a particular life worth living, a meaningful life.

We have but to assemble some suggestions for (A), for what this or that meaningful existence might consist in. And the again usual suspects rumble off the shelf. (i) There are first of all various appeals to pleasure. Personal pleasure. Giving pleasure to those individuals we care most about. Maximizing the amount of pleasure, overall, in the world. Eternal pleasure. (ii) Then there are various appeals to authority. So it was written, in a—or *the*—book. Or my psychotherapist says. Or I had a teacher who always said. Or my father used to say.[34] Or this is how we always did it. Or these are the rules. (iii) Perhaps there is a third class of candidates: the "feels right" class. It just feels right. Of Luther: I can no other.

Wittgenstein's strategy in the *Investigations* was to remind his other voices of the existence of the gap between (A) and (B)—for example, between the picture or rule and our reaction to the picture or rule. We need a concrete example of (A), a stalking horse. What happens if in order to avoid dull generalities we divulge the particulars of our lives? (Immediately we risk appearing self-indulgent, so we hold back, hesitate.) For instance I could list the following events of the last months of 1993 about which I might have thought: "Yes, this is what is important."

Dragging my two daughters Cary and Alice (seven and four) around the yard and down a hillock of dead leaves on a big blue plastic sheet. Burying and being buried in those leaves. Sherry at night, by the creek. Cooking up for breakfast a recipe out of *Like Water for Chocolate*, and watching it discovered delicious by my family at the table. Savoring the taste of shrimp in a red curry, just hot enough. Watching Alice walk, or rather march, off to school feeling as big as her big sister at her side.

Wittgenstein's first destructive move would be to ask how this odd assortment of actions, tastes, sights could possibly be, that in which the meaningfulness of a life might consist.

(Enter: Café Nihilist, in black.)[35]

"Let's see. You say your life is meaningful because you dragged your children down a hill on a piece of plastic? Because you drank sherry and ate spicy shrimp? *That*? That is what makes your life meaningful?" . . . "Oh, you *enjoyed*[a] yourself, did you? You felt good about yourself. I see. Like the Marquis de Sade enjoyed himself? Like a torturer feels after an especially productive day?" . . . "Different from that? Okay. How?" . . . "What you saw mattered, counted for something? What does dragging two girls on plastic count for?" . . . "*No!* Not Mother Theresa! Always Mother Theresa. So she spends her time with the hopelessly poor, the hopelessly diseased? THIS matters? Why? So some diseased persons are fed. Warmed. They die—as they would have anyway—but with fewer maggots in their sores. Like execution by dismemberment, agony prolonged by the administration of opium.[36] And for this we should praise her? This gives her life meaning?" . . . "Right on schedule, here comes Nobodaddy.[b] It comes down to 'God says.' 'God's will.' 'God's call.' But how does that change anything, let alone everything?" . . . "Oh yeah, so this never seen creator of those very disease-riven bodies on whose backs Mother Theresa saves her soul. Some fellow." . . . "Well now you got me: eternal happiness,[c] that'd do it. So tell me is this like some crack high that you never come down from?" . . . "Whooooah. Cool down. I'm sorry. So I guess it's not anything like a drug?" . . . "Okay. What do you *do* in heaven?" . . . "What? That's it? Just hanging out on heaven's stoop, and you don't think you'll need drugs?" . . . "Yea, but the more it's like earthly life the more it'll inherit the emptiness of our existence. If you

---

a. Pleasure.
b. Authority.
c. Pleasure, again.

ran up to heaven to *escape* the hollow of this world, you can't very well return to the world to account for how great heaven is." ... "I thought so. No reason.[d] Belief. And I suppose you believe in Santa Claus too."

(Exit: Café Nihilist, fumbling for a match.)

That is why we pause and hesitate. Escalate, inflate the metaphysical presuppositions as much as you like; the nihilist always wins. It would have been safer not to divulge the personal particulars but simply to recite insipid generalities: being good, doing good, respecting others. As Kierkegaard asserted against Hegel, our lives are in each case particular. And the particulars of our lives are never safe. If we give any particularity to what it is that we care about, the nihilist can represent it flat and without value. Is it living life in a convent? Then what's the good of singing songs in big stone buildings? Is it standing on the sea wall in a December storm? Then what's the good of getting so cold and so wet? Is it being a hermit or a monk? Then what's the good of tending turnips? Paintings? Stained canvases. Your grandmother's ring? A hunk of metal. Caressing her, caressing him? Rubbing. The nihilist always wins. And you will have guessed the way it works. The nihilist simply describes the cold facts of what his interlocutor asserts as (A), as that in which the meaning of their life consists, and the meaning disappears. Whatever the sciences touch returns to us with the cadaverous perfume of formaldehyde (Nietzsche, *EH* III; *BT* 1 p. 270). No wonder we hesitate. There is no answer to the nihilist. At least no answer in his terms. This is the end of the destructive, first phase of this construction of Wittgenstein on the meaning of life.

Where, it will be asked, is there justification for attributing the nihilist's voice to the *Investigations*, even if only to one phase of their pursuit? We have already seen what Wittgenstein thought of "our disgusting soapy water science" (*CV* p. 49e: 1946). He is also aware of the nihilistic dimension of his writings.

> Where does our investigation get its importance from, since it seems only to destroy everything interesting, that is, all that is great and important. (As it were all the buildings, leaving behind only bits of stone and rubble.) (*PI* par. 118)

A parenthesis in the *Big Typescript* announces: "(All that philosophy can do is to destroy idols)"[37] (*BigT* p. 171). So philosophy is destruction,

---

d. Feels right.

only destruction. What it destroys are idols, and in the *Investigations* these idols are interpreted as the products of the tendency to sublime the objects of our cares, the tendency to find one simple essence under the surface extravagance of our lives, our cares. So one form of this tendency would be to sublime the absence of idols, hence the parenthesis in the *Big Typescript* concludes: "(And that means not creating a new one—for instance as in 'absence of an idol')" (*BigT* p. 171). Creating a new idol out of the absence of idols is both to sublime the destructibility of idols and to arrive at nihilism. The nihilist sublimes the failure of the tendency to sublime.

In Nietzsche's mature writing, the destruction of idols is figured as the death of God, and nihilism is one reaction to this. Since the value, the significance, the meaning of life dangled from one supernatural point, God, the loss of that one point was the loss of all meaning. Nietzsche's notebooks for 1887 have this: "One interpretation has collapsed; but because it was considered *the* interpretation it now seems as if there were no meaning at all in existence, as if everything were in vain." (*WP* par. 55: 1887). A madman, announcing the death of God, cries:

> How could we drink up the sea? Who gave us the sponge to wipe away the entire horizon? What were we doing when we unchained this earth from its sun? Where is it moving now? Where are we moving? Away from all suns? Are we not plunging continually? Backward, sideward, forward, in all directions? Is there still any up or down? Are we not straying as through an infinite nothing? Do we not feel the breath of empty space? Has it not become colder? Is not night, and again more night, continuously closing in? Do we not need lanterns in the morning? Do we hear nothing of the noise of the grave diggers who are burying God? Do we smell nothing as yet of the divine decomposition? Gods, too, decompose! God is dead! God remains dead! And we have killed him! (*GS* par. 125: 1882)

But this nihilistic result, shared by Wittgenstein and Nietzsche, should not be confused with skepticism. Skepticism, if it needs doubt, is relatively unterrifying. Some cares are deeper than doubt.

(4) Interlude: A Dread Deeper Than Doubt

It has been a philosophical commonplace since the publication of Wittgenstein's *On Certainty* that doubt needs grounds, that without grounds there can be no doubt (*OC* par. 4). This might have been learned from Peirce, or even Descartes.[38] Skeptical worries are supported by doubt, and so skeptical worries are domesticated worries. Blanchot caught it crisply: "Bereft of certitude, he does not doubt; he hasn't that support."[39] We need an example. "The mud on his car made me doubt his story." That is doubt. "He said he didn't drive in this morning from the old cabin by the lake. He said that he had stayed at his parents apartment in town; so he couldn't have been at the lake when it happened. But you don't cover your tires with mud driving across town. And there was something in his speech, it came so fast, was so peppered with jokes, like someone lying off his cuff, or surprised in the act." Doubting is a domestic worry, because so much of the world of what we believe must be accepted for there even to be doubt.[40]

But, it will be remarked, these doubts can escalate until the whole of the world can be lost. This is what happened to Descartes himself. He describes the result in terms of a lucid dream, a dream one knows to be a dream.[41]

> I am like a prisoner who is enjoying an imaginary freedom while asleep; as he begins to suspect that he is asleep, he dreads being woken up, and goes along with the pleasant illusion as long as he can. In the same way, I happily slide back into my old opinions and dread being shaken out of them, for fear that my peaceful sleep may be followed by hard labor when I wake, and that I shall have to toil not in the light, but amid the inextricable darkness of the problems I have now raised.[42]

These are the closing words of the first *Meditation*. The second continues in this bleak mode:

> So serious are the doubts into which I have been thrown as a result of yesterday's meditation that I can neither put them out of my mind nor see any way of resolving them. It feels as if I have fallen unexpectedly into a deep whirlpool which tumbles me around so that I can neither stand on the bottom nor swim to the top.[43]

How, it will be asked, can these deep, dark, and dreadful thoughts be shallow? How can Descartes's doubt possibly be shallow? The answer is simple. Although—at this stage of his meditating—there are no particular empirical or mathematical beliefs left to Descartes, the faculty to be used in evaluating the dubitability of any particular belief has never been questioned: reason and Descartes's own rationality. This does not beg the question by guaranteeing that Descartes's reconstructive hopes will be satisfied, for his foundational project might still fail.[44] The awkwardness of Descartes's reliance on the authority of reason is rather that he has guaranteed that it might succeed. It could never work if he gave up his confidence in judgments such as that THIS is a good reason for doubting or believing THAT. If he didn't trust his judgments of relevance and irrelevance there would be no project at all, for in that case his mind would be, as the Cartesian scholar H. G. Frankfurt puts it, "empty" and any so-called doubts simply "mindless."[45]

What I think of as the shallowness of Cartesian skepticism comes out not only in the comfortable life of the mind so easily found in the second Meditation, but already in Descartes's confrontation with madness in the first. The first Meditation expends almost all its energy finding reasons to doubt large classes of belief. Descartes's eagerness to avoid any suggestion that his doubts are ungrounded (and therefore mindless) is italicized by his exclusion of being mad (mindless) as a possible ground of doubt. (And it thus becomes significant that it was a "madman" who announced the death of God in *The Gay Science,* par. 125.) Descartes is quick to exclude this as a possible ground for doubt, but not by appeal to a domain of truth that survives within the domain of the insane.[46] Descartes excludes the possibility that he is mad by what Foucault calls "a strange act of force."[47] Thus Descartes preserves reason's peace and harmony with violence.

The procedure of the first Meditation is to eliminate whole classes of belief by appeal to somewhat general grounds of doubt. So the fact that we've been mistaken about distant and tiny objects gives us our first reason for rejecting many of our beliefs, but there is a domain of truth that survives this initial ground of doubt.[48] For instance, Descartes's beliefs about medium-sized objects near at hand, like his hands, his body, his stove. The possibility of being mad is not treated in the same way. Descartes writes:

> Again, how could it be denied that these hands or this whole body are mine? Unless perhaps I were to liken myself to madmen, whose brains are so damaged by the persistent vapors of melancholia that they firmly maintain they are kings when they are paupers, or say they are dressed in purple when they are naked, or that their heads are made of earthenware, or that they are pumpkins, or made of glass.

But such people are insane, and I would be thought equally mad if I
took anything from them as a model for myself.[49]

At first it looks as if Descartes does indeed have a reason for excluding
the possibility that he is mad: perhaps his mind is not damaged by the
vapors of melancholia. But it hardly seems likely that empirical beliefs
about the relatively esoteric—the vapors—would be able to survive the
first round of grounds for doubt. So if that were Descartes's reason, it
would not be a *good* reason for excluding the possibility that he was
mad. But in fact Descartes doesn't seem to rest his case against being
mad on black bile, or on anything else for that matter: "But such people
are insane, and I would be thought equally mad if I took anything from
them as a model for myself."[50] Descartes simply asserts: They are mad. I
am not. No grounds are given. This is the "strange act of force" that preserves reason's peace and harmony.

It is usual to assert—as does Derrida in his reply to Foucault on this
point—that once the possibility of dreaming has been entered then all
the beliefs that would have fallen before the possibility of being mad, fall
anyway.[51] So it looks as if Foucault and those who follow his lead in finding violence in the rejection of madness have not been careful enough.

This misses the point. The issue is not one of detail: does he or does
he not find a reason for doubting the belief that he is not a pumpkin?
The possibility of dreaming gives him just such a reason. The issue is
rather one of the manner in which this belief, for example, is excluded.
If Descartes admitted the possibility that he was outside of reason—
mindless, mad—then there would be no rational, nonarbitrary way to
stop the doubt. Exiting from reason, there is no rational way back. But
then it becomes *imperative* to silence the possibility that he is mad. And
this is just what Descartes does. The domain of reason is secured, by a
strange act of force.

Wittgenstein's destructive practices were even more destructive
than the skeptical considerations of Descartes's first Meditation.[52] Wittgenstein does not police the precinct of reason, he shakes it down. And
quite apart from violently excluding madness from his writing, Wittgenstein occasionally writes as if it is his aim to bring the terrifying proximity of madness permanently into view.

The philosopher is the man who has to cure himself of many sicknesses of the understanding before he can arrive at the notions of a
healthy human understanding.

> If in life we are surrounded by death, so too in the health of our
> understanding we are surrounded by madness. (*CV* p. 44e: 1944)

I enjoy the way this passage turns away from the strange act of violence
in the *Meditations*, but I do not think it would be best to interpret Wittgenstein as suggesting that there is always a possibility that we are insane.
"Insanity," and "madness," name psychological domains with more or
less determinate criteria. This is still too tame. They remain within the
domain of the rational: "the language of psychiatry is a monologue of
reason *about* madness."[53] Even in a book as apparently sober as the *Investigations* we can find ourselves confronting not worry or anxiety about
this or that recognizable something nor yet about this or that unrecog-
nizable something, but simply anxiety about nothing, nothing in particular, at all.[54] Wittgenstein's destructive moments attempt just what
Descartes refused to do: to shake our trust in our sense that THIS is relevant to THAT, our sense that THIS is a good reason for THAT, and so
on. Remember: these are *not* rational doubts about whether these rele-
vances are trustworthy or not. Again that would be too tame.

> 482. We are misled by this way of putting it: "This is a good ground
> for it makes the occurrence of the event probable." That is as if we had
> asserted something further about the ground, which justified it as a
> ground; whereas to say that this ground makes the occurrence prob-
> able is to say nothing except that this ground comes up to a pa

rticular standard of good grounds—but the standard has no grounds.

> 483. A good ground is one that looks *like this* [der *so* aussieht]. (*PI*
> par. 482–83)

In a distrustful mood, this can seem arbitrary, can induce an anxiety not
supported by grounds, a dread beyond grounding's grasp.

Wittgenstein's difficulty is to express the groundlessness of our lives
without resting that expression on any grounds. Sometimes this is done
with questions:

> 477. "Why do you believe that you will burn yourself on the hot-
> plate?"—Have you grounds [Gründe] for this belief; and do you need
> grounds?

> 478. What kind of ground have I to assume that my finger will feel
> resistance when it touches the table? What kind of ground, to believe
> that it will hurt if this pencil pierces my hand?—When I ask this, a

hundred grounds present themselves, each drowning the voice of the others [die einander kaum zu Wort kommen lassen wollen]. "But I have experienced it myself innumerable times, and as often heard of similar experiences, if it were not so, it would . . . ; etc." (*PI* 477–78)

"If it were not so, it would . . ."—this is the domesticated voice of grounds and of doubts. But in the case Wittgenstein introduces, each of these reasons drowns out the others. All rushing to be first, nobody gets out at all. Cavell comments:

> The point of this passage is not that what are being called "reasons" are not true enough statements; nor that if they weren't true, we shouldn't believe what we believe, know what we know; nor even that, in *certain* circumstances, they might not be good and real reasons for what we claim we know. It is rather that, in the context in which these "reasons" are proffered, they are inoperative *as reasons.*[55]

These hundred "reasons" that rush in are not reasons for the particular claim they are meant to support, any more than they are reasons for any other mundane claim. That means they cannot ground any particular claim at all. Cavell again:

> Those hundred reasons are, roughly, the same reasons we would give to the questions, "How does he know his name?" "How does he know he has five fingers?" "How does he know the jar will fall if he releases it from his grasp?" "How does he know the sun will rise tomorrow?" Offering such "reasons" is not offering grounds for certifying belief in a particular claim I have made, but protestations of knowledge, entreaties that I be credible. No one of them, in their rootlessness, would remove a doubt; they are signs to ward off doubt.[56]

Wittgenstein's concern here is *not* to raise skeptical doubts but to confront us with grounding's groundlessness. "The difficulty is to realize the groundlessness of our believing." (*OC* par. 166)

There is nothing sophisticated in the *Investigations*. Touching a table is all it needs. Nothing turns on sophisticated constructions. There are few arguments.[57] Sometimes just a question. But that is how worlds collapse. Tolstoy reports:

> An intelligent and honest man by the name of S. told me the story of how he lost his faith. At the age of twenty-six, while resting overnight on a hunting expedition, he followed an old childhood custom of kneeling down to pray in the evening. His elder brother, who was

with him on the expedition lay on some straw watching him. When S. had finished and was preparing to lie down his brother said to him: "Do you still do that?" Nothing more was said between them. But from that day on S. stopped saying his prayers and going to church. . . . This comment of his brother's was like a finger being pushed against a wall that was on the verge of collapsing from its own weight. These words indicated that the place where he had thought faith to be had long been empty and that the words he spoke, the signs of the cross and the genuflections he made in prayer, were essentially meaningless actions. Having recognized their meaninglessness he could no longer continue doing them.[58]

"Do you still do that?" and the world collapses. Since there is nothing sophisticated in Wittgenstein's considerations, when they do their work, there is nothing more mundane to fall back on. S. could fall back on the mundane world, but Wittgenstein never leaves the mundane, so when his questions do their work, there is nothing left to fall back on. Nothing. Nothing at all.

The destructive moment of the *Investigations* threatens the fabric of our daily lives so it is more destructive than textbook skepticism. In the textbooks you are provided with some domain of knowledge and asked how you can justify an extension of it to a second domain, so even if you can't justify the extension you are always free to say, knowledge stops in the first domain. This is not Wittgenstein's game. In terms of this picture, his goal is to change our attitude to the first domain. In discussing the meaning of words, Wittgenstein's effort was to drive the grounds of meaning outside philosophy to a place where meaning was no longer any more safe than our natural reactions. Our sense that THIS is like THAT and not otherwise. And this is no longer a philosophical issue (*PI* par. 85).

We were looking for enlightenment. We wanted to know what the meaning of words and of our lives consisted in, and all we get is darkness. "When I obey a rule, I do not choose. I obey the rule blindly" (*PI* par. 219). The dark night of nothing. Breaking the spell of our involvement with the world delivers us to nothing.[59] Consider these two passages from *On Certainty*:

369. If I wanted to doubt whether this was my hand, how could I avoid doubting whether the word "hand" has any meaning? So that is something I seem to know after all.

> 370. But more correctly: the fact that I use the word "hand" and all the other words in my sentence without a second thought, indeed that I should stand before the nothing [vor dem Nichts stünde], if I wanted so much as to try doubting their meanings—shows that the absence of doubt belongs to the essence of the language-game, that the question, How do I know? drags out the language-game or does away with it.

To try to doubt the meaning of the word *hand* stands us before the nothing. Doubt can't get a grip here. Terror can. Dread can. The result of the first destructive phase of Wittgenstein's investigations is a dread deeper than doubt, beyond grounding's grasp.

(5) Linguistic and Existential Meaning in the *Investigations*

Acceptance: The Second Phase

There could hardly be a more striking difference than that between the groundless dread just indicated and the arrogant confidence of the café nihilist. Nihilism—like skepticism—is tame. Shocking to others, not one-self. And neither Wittgenstein nor Nietzsche thought that the destructive phase of their work was anything but "transitional" (*WP* par. 13: 1887). Nietzsche's suggestion is that nihilism still rests on the faith that *IF* life did have meaning, then it would have a theologically grounded or sus-pended meaning. Nihilism is the last form of religious belief: "the faith in the categories of reason is the cause of nihilism" (*WP* par. 12 B: 1887–88). Wittgenstein's immediate response to the thought of philosophy's destructive tendencies is similar. We have—he wrote—got to see that what is being destroyed is not worth anything: "What we are destroying is nothing but houses of cards [Luftgebäude][60] and we are clearing up the ground of language on which they stand" (*PI* par. 118). Wittgenstein attempts to show us that what he destroys are only idols.

In the last chapter, two ways of bridging the gap between (A) and (B) failed. The problem was that anything short of our actual use of a word would need to be interpreted in order to account for our use, and that interpretation would then face the same problem. Following an uncanny logic, the further we went the more we found ourselves back where we had begun. "But this is where we were before" (*PI* par. 146). And "what this shows is that there is a way of grasping a rule [or a pic-ture] that is *not* an *interpretation* but that is exhibited in what we call 'obeying a rule' or 'going against it' in actual cases" (*PI* par. 201). Our grasping a rule consists in nothing deeper than the fact that we call THIS "obeying the rule" and THAT "going against it." The mistake is to sublime our linguistic life and say that meaning consists in something, something sublime (*Z* par. 16).

The destructive phase of Wittgenstein's investigations received more attention in the previous chapter, so I will linger briefly over the role of acceptance: *The Second Phase*. Forms of the verb *hinnehmen* appear only four times in the *Investigations*.[61] I have already cited (at the opening and at the closing of chap. 4) its appearance in Wittgenstein's attempt to make the fact of human communication less obvious [selbstverständlich] (*PI* par. 524). Not to sublime the logic of our language but to accept it, that is his new approach to philosophical problems. Hence, in part II (1949) he writes:

> Look at what can be meant by "description of what is seen." But this [tangled tale] is just what is called description of what is seen. There is not *one genuine* proper case of such a description—the rest being just vague [unklar], something which awaits clarification [Klärung], or which must just be swept aside as rubbish.
>
> Here we are in enormous danger of wanting to make fine distinctions. It is the same when one tries to define [erklären] the concept of a material object in terms of "what is really seen." What we have rather to do is *to accept* [hinzunehmen] the everyday language, and to note *false* accounts of the matter as false.[62] The primitive language-game which children are taught needs no justification; attempts at justification need to be rejected. (*PI* p. 200; Wittgenstein's emphases)

We are in enormous danger of wanting to sublime the logic of our language, enormous danger of trying to force the completely ragged surface patterns of our use of an expression into one simple, sublime essence. Something about the use of the expression unsettles us, but seeking the sublime won't calm our cares. The impulse to sublime delivers us not to peace [Ruhe] but to hell (*CV* p. 30: 1937). What we need is a perspicuous description [übersichtliche Darstellung] of the unruly surfaces of our language (*PI* par. 122). Such descriptions can save us from the surprising irregularities of our language, or rather, not from the irregularities themselves but from their being surprising. Such perspicuous descriptions can help us learn our way about our language. Acceptance brings peace. The tendency to sublime expresses ressentiment. Acceptance, saying yes, brings peace. But how?

"How am I able to obey a rule?" (*PI* par. 217). This may be a demand for causes, in which case we are doing empirical science. How can I obey the rule that all candidates for citizenship must present themselves at such and such a time in such and such a place? I can obey it by taking a bus, or hailing a cab, or (praying for a parking space) driving. That is how. But the question might also be a demand for a philosophical explanation, a demand for what following a rule consists in; hence a demand for a "justification for my following the rule in the way I do [handle]" (*PI* par. 217). Hence, a demand for my doing THIS in response to the rule. The result of the last chapter is that there can be no satisfying answer to this demand for a justification of my doing THIS.

> If I have exhausted the justifications [Begründungen] I have reached bedrock, and my spade is turned. Then I am inclined to say: "This is simply what I do [handle]." (*PI* par. 217)

"This is simply what I do" is not an answer to the demand for a ground. It is a rejection of that demand and an expression of acceptance of what I (not we) do. It is an expression of complete security.

> 211. How can he *know* how he is to continue a pattern by himself—whatever instruction you give him?—Well, how do I know?—If that means "Have I grounds?" the answer is: my grounds will soon give out. And then, without grounds, I will act [handeln]. (*PI* par. 211)

> 212. When someone whom I am afraid of orders me to continue the series, I act [handeln] quickly, with perfect security [völliger Sicherheit], and the lack of grounds does not trouble me. (*PI* par. 212)

Perfect security, peace, will be ours when we can act with security, without grounds and without cares.

The *Investigations* uses "security" [Sicherheit] in what appear to be two incompatible ways.[63] Wittgenstein can be found writing:

> When, for example, I am given an algebraic function, I am SURE [SICHER] that I shall be able to work out its values for the arguments 1, 2, 3, . . . up to 10. This security [Sicherheit] will be called "well-founded," for I have learned to compute such functions, and so on. In other cases no reasons will be given for it—but it will be justified by success. (*PI* par. 320, W's emphasis; also see *PI* par. 679)

Here, in both kinds of case, it will make sense to speak of the security being supported by evidence. So sometimes the *Investigations* uses "security" in what we could call an evidential sense. But we can also discern another use of security, a nonevidential use, and at this point we can begin to discern a difference between certainty [Gewissheit] and security [Sicherheit].

Begin with this discussion of "certainty":

> What does this mean?—"The certainty [Gewissheit] that the fire will burn me is based on induction." Does that mean that I argue to myself: "Fire has always burned me, so it will happen now too?" Or is the previous experience the *cause* of my certainty, not its ground? Whether the earlier experience is the cause of the certainty depends on the system of hypotheses, of natural laws, in which we are looking at the phenomenon of certainty.
>
> Is our confidence justified?—What people accept as a justification—is shown by how they think and live.
>
> We expect *this*, and are surprised at *that*. But the chain of reasons [Gründe] has an end. (*PI* par. 325–26; W's emphases)

Wittgenstein begins by mocking the thought that our acceptance that fire can burn us is an inductive certainty [Gewissheit]. His point is that the inductive account gets the distance between us and the power of fire to burn wrong. It distances that power. It holds it at reason's length. It would be *better* to suggest that our past experience causes our acceptance than to suggest that it grounds our inductive certainty. But there is an illusion even here. The illusion is that we have gone outside the space of reasons to support it from the space of causes. We succumb to the temptations of naturalistic explanation because we overlook the fact that whether or not we take X to be the cause of Y presupposes the space of reasons, the system of hypotheses, with which we look at X. So the naturalistic turn will not do what we want it to do. It will not support our reasons from the outside. What we accept as a justification can in some instances be justified, but this cannot go on forever. "A good ground [Grund] looks *like this*" (*PI* par. 483). The chain of reasons has an end. It ends in how people think and act.

There is a connection between these passages concerning certainty [Gewissheit] and security [Sicherheit]. The connection is made by the example we have been discussing, for Wittgenstein uses our acceptance of this proposition (to which we have seen evidence not to be relevant) as the paradigm of security.

> 474. I shall get burnt if I put my hand in the fire: that is security [das ist Sicherheit].
>
> That is to say: here we see what security means [bedeutet]. (Not only what the word "security" ["Sicherheit"] means, but also what it amounts to.) (*PI* par. 474)

Security can be supported by evidence, but there is also a deeper sense of security that respects its etymological relation to being without care. In its nonevidential sense, security is not a matter of evidence, it is an affair of the heart.

In the *Investigations*, when we find that "the chain of reasons [Gründe] has an end" (*PI* par. 326), we find ourselves not with what is certainly true, but with what is (peacefully) secure (*PI* par. 474). So also in *On Certainty*:

> 196. Sure [Sicher] evidence is what we *accept* [*annehmen*] unconditionally sure [unbedingt sicher], it is evidence we go by in *acting* [*handeln*] surely, acting without any doubt.

> 204. Giving grounds, however, justifying the evidence, comes to an end;—but the end is not certain propositions' striking us immediately as true, i.e., it is not a kind of *seeing* on our part; it is our *acting* [*handeln*], which lies at the bottom of the language-game. (*OC* par. 196, 204; cf. 307)

It is not certainty [Gewissheit] that lies at the bottom of our linguistic practice, it is *secure [sicher] action*. But we would be regressing to pragmatism if we thought of this as action in service of a purpose that we might or might not attain. The secure action with which reason ends is a natural[64] action, a reaction. We find it natural to continue the series in this way not in that: "We expect *this* and are surprised at *that*. But the chain of reasons [Gründe] has an end" (*PI* par. 326).

When we discover that Wittgenstein is suspending our epistemic practices from the security of our natural reactions, one easy response is the one Wittgenstein had asked himself in part 2 of the *Investigations*. "But if you are secure [sicher], isn't it that you are shutting your eyes in the face of doubt?" and Wittgenstein answered: "They are shut" [Sie sind mir geschlossen] (*PI* p. 224e). Of course I may have willfully chosen to shut my eyes, but here Wittgenstein tells us this has not happened. His eyes are simply shut; almost as if his security consisted in his discovering himself naturally blind to doubt. ("When I obey a rule I do not choose, I obey the rule blindly" [*PI* par. 219].) Describing an example of this peaceful security [beruhigt Sicherheit] (*OC* par. 357), he writes:

> Why do I not satisfy myself that I have two feet when I want to get up from the chair? There is no why. I simply don't. This is how I act [So handle ich]. (*OC* par. 148; see *PI* par. 217)

According to Wittgenstein, I accept my having two feet as I accept the power of fire to burn, without willfulness, without anxiety, and (recalling the mystic Angelus Silesius)[65] without why. They are shut.

It is a simple matter to extend this account of linguistic sense to existential sense. In the face of the Café Nihilist's embalming of our dearest concerns, the aim is to be able to say: This is how I act. They are shut. I love sledding (seasons change) with my children, but what in this activity is the source of that meaning? What does existential sense consist in? Scraping over the snow with children? The importance of family? Does it matter that these are my biological children? Why wouldn't any children do just as well? It must matter that these are children I care about? But why do I care about them? What is so special about these children? Well, I care about them. And the circle has closed.

> If I have exhausted my groundings I have reached bedrock, and my spade is turned. Then I am inclined to say: "This is simply what I do." (*PI* par. 217)

I just do. That's all. The task is to come to find that this almost nothing is enough.[66] The question is how does this strategy work? How does it escape the groundless dread before nothing in particular at all? How can this be an answer to the question of the meaning of life? How can the absence of a ground deliver what we had always thought only a ground could deliver? How can the absence of a God deliver what we had always thought only a God could deliver? What is the power of finitude? There is a crack in everything. That's how the light of wonder gets in.

(6) Wonder: A Delight More Delicate Than Knowledge

The goal of Wittgenstein's account of existential sense cannot persist unchanged from the *Tractatus*. There can no longer be any hope of making oneself "*absolutely* safe" ("LE," p. 41: 1929). "It makes no sense at all to speak of the 'absolutely simple parts of a chair'" (*PI* par. 47).[67] And if this is so, then neither will it make any sense to speak of becoming absolutely safe. But why does it *not* make sense to speak of the absolutely simple parts of a chair? Wittgenstein's sober voice, the voice of what is "obvious," appears unnerved when it asks, somewhat mournfully:

> But isn't a chessboard for instance, obviously [offenbar], and absolutely, composite? (*PI* par. 47)

Here is the reply:

> —You are probably thinking of the composition out of thirty-two white and thirty-two black squares. But could we not also say, for instance, that it was composed of the colors black and white and the schema of squares? And there are quite different ways of looking at it, do you still want to say that the chessboard is absolutely "composite"?—Asking "Is this object composite?" *outside* a particular game [*Ausserhalb* eines bestimmten Spiels] is like what a boy once did, who had to say whether verbs in certain sentences were in the active or passive voice, and who racked his brains over whether the verb "to sleep" was active or passive. (*PI* par. 47)

In the last chapter, when we saw Wittgenstein reminding his other voice that a picture of a cube might also represent a triangular prism we were at a similar point. The obviousness of something was the result of our forgetting more unusual possibilities. Here too, the sense of absoluteness is a function of forgetting. Philosophy is assembling reminders.

Let's be more accurate: "The work of a philosopher is assembling reminders for a particular purpose" (*PI* par. 127). If feeling safe is the goal, if the goal is to live in peace and security [mit Ruhe und Sicherheit] (*PI* par. 607), then this feeling is not something absolute but particular. Disquiet incited by particular circumstances is silenced by particular reminders, not once and for all but again and again. This is familiar from our consideration of linguistic meaning. I suggested that Wittgenstein would change our attitude to the world, our way of looking at things [Anschauungsweise] (*PI* par. 145). His hope was not to find our life with language obvious [selbstverständlich], but to find it striking, a groundless wonder. But Wittgenstein also insisted that the task of working ourselves into the position of finding our eyes shut, enjoying a peaceful security, is a never completed task. He did not think that the attractions of sublimity could ever be completely silenced. Or he thought that *if* they could be finally silenced, there would have to be a change in the way people live [Lebensweise], perhaps even, in Nietzsche's terms, an overcoming (*CV* p. 61: 1947).

So the absence of a ground will never supply a permanently peaceful security, there is no perpetual peace. That makes my defense of this view somewhat easier, but it can still seem incredible that absence can do what presence could not. But it is true. The tightrope walker who turns out to be walking on a glass platform no longer amazes, and we begin to puzzle out "how it was done."

> I could imagine somebody might admire not only real trees, but also the shadows or reflections that they cast, taking them too for trees. But once he has told himself that these are not really trees after all and has come to be puzzled at what they are, or at how they are related to trees, his admiration will have suffered a rupture that will need healing. (*CV* p. 57e: 1947)

When we understand something or are actually trying to figure something out, wonder gets little grip. So too God's support sublimes our wonder, or worse, anesthetizes wonder itself.

Think about something wonderful. These are pat, but they will do: The hairs on the underside of a leaf. Leaves on the forest floor, decayed into lace. There is something amazing about the lace skeleton that remains after the leaf has rotted away. But imagine someone thinking about how it happens, what makes the veins less prone to decay than the bits between. Now the wonder of the leafy lace retreats into the wonder that two such similar substances should decay at such different rates. And we could anesthetize even that wonder by retreating further into chemistry or physics. Or theology. There is no difference here between naturalistic and supernaturalistic anesthetics. If this seems puzzling, replace God with a very clever person. Suppose this person goes all over the world lacing leaves on the forest floor. Where is the amazement? Not in the lace but in how she gets all around the world so fast? So too with the deity. The amazement or wonder strikes no longer at the level of the lacy leaves, but at the level of the nature of the deity. How does the deity accomplish this? Why does the deity bother with this? And the more there are theological answers to these questions the more wonder will be anesthetized. In theological terms, we are quite close to the concept of grace. In that case, the multiple wonders of the world would have sublimed, and there would be only one wonder left: God's grace. Theology and science are here in the same business: putting wonder to sleep. The *Investigations* are an attempt to wake us up.

Wonder is the mirror image of the dread deeper than doubt that appeared in the interlude above. If the dread is dread of nothing in particular, then if that dread subsides, it could not be for a reason. Since it is not a grounded dread, it won't listen to reason. Hence if it subsides, our release will be beyond grounding, too. There is a familiar worry about whether wonder is a function of ignorance, so that the more knowledge we acquire the less room there is for wonder.[68] But on my account, wonder is not under threat from knowledge, it is under threat from a certain way of looking at things [Anschauungswiese], a pun-deaf way of looking at things. The enemy here is the voice of common sense, the defender of the obvious [Selbstverständlichkeit]. The enemy of wonder is a certain attitude to our epistemic practices, and wonder is made possible by a change in our attitude to those practices rather than by any failure of those epistemic practices in their own terms.

Turn this to the problem of answering the Café Nihilist. What are we to say in the face of his embalming our cares? Nothing he would accept as an answer. In his own terms, we lose. What we need is to recognize the groundlessness of our commitment to our loves—human, mechanical, musical, or whatever—while yet being able to say, this is what I care about. *So* sorge ich eben (see *PI* par. 217; *OC* par. 148). But it doesn't matter so much *what* you care about as *that* you care about something.

> If anyone should think he has solved the problem of life and feel like telling himself that everything is quite easy now, he can see that he is wrong just by recalling that there was a time when this "solution" had not been discovered; but it must have been possible to live *then* too and the solution which has now been discovered seems fortuitous in relation to how things were then. And it is the same in the study of logic. If there were a "solution" to the problems of logic (philosophy) we should only need to caution ourselves that there was a time when they had not been solved (and even at that time people must have known how to live and think). (*CV* p. 4e: 1930)

If life's meaning depended on something that could be discovered or lost—like a particular person or a particular skill or a particular distribution of goods—well then *life* would not have meaning. The skill or the person or the distribution of goods would. Neither in the *Tractatus* nor in the *Investigations* is the meaning of life something that can be discovered. But in the earlier work, there was a solution to the riddle of life: make your life a tautology. In the later work, if there is a solution it is to accept your life, repeatedly.

The account of existential meaning intimated between the lines of the *Investigations* is that in the face of the nihilist's destructive attack on what we find important or significant, we can find ourselves on the verge of saying, I have no reply to make to your attack; I have said all I can say to justify my life to you; I have no more justifications to give; you have shaken my reasons, but not me: this is what I care about. But finding ourselves able to say, and mean, these words is not easy. There are cracks everywhere. It is the groundlessness of our lives that makes it possible to find our lives wonderful, significant. But that very groundlessness also makes the wonder of our lives impermanent, fragile. This wonder is doubled—cracked—for simultaneously we would recognize the abyss and accept the surface: *superficial, out of profundity* (*GS* preface par. 4: 1886). In 1930 Wittgenstein described a situation that would be uncanny and wonderful [unheimlich und wunderbar] at the same time.[69]

> Let us imagine a theater; the curtain goes up and we see a man alone in a room, walking up and down, lighting a cigarette, sitting down, etc., so that suddenly we are observing a human being from outside in a way that ordinarily we can never observe ourselves; it would be like watching a chapter of biography with your own eyes,—surely this would be uncanny and wonderful at the same time. We should be observing something more wonderful than anything a playwright could arrange to be acted or spoken on the stage: life itself.—But then we do see this every day without its making the slightest impression on us! True enough, but we do not see it from *that* point of view. (*CV* p. 4e: 1930)

"Superficial—out of profundity," to see your life from within and from without at the same time. An impossible simultaneity, which we can yet taste for a spell. Wittgenstein's romanticism consists in his not turning from this impossibility. Peaceful security can be ours, but only for a spell. "The solution of philosophical problems can be compared with a gift in a fairy tale: in the magic castle it appears enchanted and if you take it outside in the daylight it is nothing but an ordinary bit of iron (or something of the sort)" (*CV* p. 11e: 1931). A momentary wonder can be ours, but it must be won—again, and again again.

(7) Linguistic and Existential Meaning

Michael Dummett is responsible for the recent currency of the opinion that what is distinctive about analytic philosophy is this: for analytic philosophers, first philosophy is the philosophy of language.[70] And there is some truth to this. But given the privilege accorded Saussure's account of language in the foundation both of what is called structuralism and what is called poststructuralism, the foundation of a philosophy in the philosophy of language could at best be a necessary condition for being analytic. It should be possible to tighten up the criteria for being a part of the culture of analytic philosophy, but I am rather more inclined to understand what draws the philosophers of our century together than to understand what drives them apart.

It is clear enough that many of the significant philosophers of our century have been centrally concerned with language, from Husserl to Heidegger to Derrida, from Russell to Wittgenstein to Davidson. And it is clear enough that any general characterization of a century of philosophizing will be partial and personal. Thus hedged, I continue. Some of Heidegger's work, notably *Being and Time*, though it addresses language and even offers an account of linguistic meaning that resonates in some ways with that of the *Investigations*, does not begin from language.[71] What that book claims to be about is meaning, in the first instance the meaning of being, and by way of authenticity, with something recognizable as the meaning of life. And this projects the hypothesis that the unifying philosophical theme of the twentieth century is not the true, nor the good, nor the beautiful; the unifying theme is meaning: linguistic and existential meaning.[72]

Looked at this way you would not expect to find the dominant philosophers of our century contributing to the advancement of something called epistemology, or aesthetics, or moral and political theory. And, difficult as this can be for us to admit, one does not think of the importance of the six philosophers I have just listed as resting on their contributions to these areas of professional specialization. However, they have all produced distinguished accounts of linguistic or existential meaning, or both. By focusing on meaning rather than language, we have a theme tying otherwise separate philosophers together: linguistic and existential meaning.

Supposing this to be an adequate description of much of twentieth-century philosophy, we will be looking around for an explanation. The particular concern with meaning in this century can be put in Kantian terms as the question of how linguistic or existential meaning is possible, at all. So if we could find an explanation for why philosophers might have felt a threat to the very possibility of linguistic or existential significance, we would have found one possible explanation for this turn in twentieth-century philosophy. One candidate explanation would appeal to the prestige of the empirical sciences. It is a commonplace to recognize the threat posed to the meaning of life by the flat factual world of the empirical sciences. But those same sciences pose a threat also to the possibility of linguistic meaning. Frege, Husserl, Wittgenstein, and Heidegger were each of them positive that linguistic meaning could not be reduced to the terms of empirical science. The efforts of the friends of behavioral or cognitive science to provide naturalistic reductions of meaning would fall into the same tradition, it is simply that rather than fleeing the challenge of science, they were trying to answer it, in scientific terms. So we might be able to explain the fact that twentieth-century philosophy has focused on the possibility of linguistic and existential meaning as a combative or conciliatory response to the rising intellectual power and prestige of the empirical sciences.

I recognize that this picture of the century may seem to be an ad hoc construction designed to place Wittgenstein, as here interpreted, at its center. I hope this picture of our century is more valuable than that, but there is no denying that Wittgenstein's *Tractatus* and his *Investigations* are each concerned with showing how linguistic and existential meaning are possible. And each of them is concerned with showing how the possibility of meaning in either of these senses is not to be accounted for scientifically. On the other hand, it is also true that in the English-speaking world (at least) philosophy has professionalized itself out of any concern with the meaning of life. And there is in the end no getting around the fact that neither Wittgenstein nor Nietzsche had much respect for professional philosophers. They both resigned their professorships. The passion of their interest in philosophy is out of all proportion to the importance of the professionalized institution of philosophy. They might even have thought of the professionalization of philosophy as philosophy's aping the sciences, veiling from professionals the reasons for philosophical passion. It is clear, in any case, that Wittgenstein thought there was not much point to studying philosophy if it only turned you into a professional philosopher. In November 1944 he wrote to Norman Malcolm:

> What is the use of studying philosophy if all that it does for you is to enable you to talk with some plausibility about some abstruse questions of logic, etc., & if it does not improve your thinking about the important questions of everyday life.[73]

And he feared: "The seed I am most likely to sow is a certain jargon" (*LFM* p. 293). Neither Wittgenstein nor Nietzsche appears very interested either in sounding professional or in receiving the respect of professional philosophers. And sometimes the profession has returned the compliment.

But in Wittgenstein's case there could be no question of leaving the profession entirely behind. This is because, early and late, Wittgenstein used his account of how linguistic meaning is possible to understand how existential meaning might be possible. So he could not leave behind the abstruse questions of "logic, etc.," for it was precisely in these questions that he found the answer to his logical and also existential cares. It was precisely there that he developed the two phases of his mature approach to meaning. A first phase of destruction, ruining the prospects for presenting what the meaning of a word or a life might consist in. And a second phase of acceptance, when intellectually or existentially beaten down, empty-handed, our engines of declaration put aside, we accept our reactions for what they are, confronting ourselves almost as we would an other object. This is simply what I do; this is simply what I care about. Wittgenstein turned the results of his confrontation with the question of how linguistic meaning was possible against the question of how existential meaning was possible. This explains the otherwise surprising passion of Wittgenstein's concern with the question, But how many kinds of sentence are there? (*PI* par. 23.)[74]

We might have noticed the passionate existential thread of Wittgenstein's mature philosophical investigations of language by looking at his account of the nature of a philosophical problem. "A philosophical problem has the form: 'I don't know my way about'" (*PI* par. 123). This is already to read philosophical problems as existential problems, for on this account, philosophy begins with the feeling of being lost, not at home, in an unfamiliar place, anxious and afraid. And if this is how Wittgenstein conceived philosophical problems, then philosophical solutions would have to resolve the anxiety, restore the peace, lead us home again. Wittgenstein's existential investigations aim to convince us that the way to find our way back home is to follow the trail of our language. Not to force on "knowledge," "belief," "love," "responsibility," "action," some sublime—probably scientific—model of explanation, discovering essences hidden beneath the surface. The trail back home is difficult to find. The birds have eaten the bread crumbs. We are in the wild—bewildered—and bewildered, we find ourselves bewitched by science (*PI* par. 109). But there is a way home (*PI* par. 116).

Wittgenstein's writing gets its passion from these forms of disquiet, unrest, anxiety. His concern with words gets its passion from questions about the meaning of life: The Riddle (*TLP* 6.4312 and 6.5). We academics pretend not to understand, but we all know what the problem of existential meaning is. You grow up on your mother's knee, warming yourself at the family hearth, centering yourself on your family's tastes, prejudices, religion. For some this is a far as it goes. For others, college, or a friend, or a neighbor, or *Thus Spoke Zarathustra* can cause what seems like a sudden break. A loss. And then a sense of recovery: alcohol, kinkier drugs, skankier clothes, money, influence. Hansel and Gretel have been walking in the woods for three days, they are hungry, afraid, lost, and then a hopeful sign, a dove, guides them to a house they hadn't thought possible: built neither of stone nor brick, but of bread, roofed with pancakes, glazed with candy. The kind old lady gives them a hot meal, tucks them in, and the boy and the girl agree, this must be heaven.

And for some, this is as far as it goes. But for others, this heaven can lose its charm. One morning, your blouse untucked, pants stained, glasses broken, you find yourself walking down Sixth Avenue in the morning, the suits in sneakers are off to work, and there is something sticky in your hair. That is the problem. Your recovery has proved illusory, the nice old lady in the heavenly house was not feeding you, she was fattening you up. In such a nihilistic position, where can we turn to recover the sense that our life is worth something?

On the sublime picture of (linguistic and existential) meaning, meanings are hidden. The essence of a table is the one thing that all tables share, but it can't be seen; it is hidden in the table. So we might think that the significance of life was outside life or was the thing that all lives shared—food, shelter, sex. Don't think, look! (*PI* par. 66). Look at a meaningful life. The life of satisfied monks. They wake up. Spend some time alone. Sweep. Clean the stone walks. Rake the garden. Spend some time alone. Stroll. Drink. Laugh. Sleep. There is nothing to it. The subliming voice says: there must be something else, something we can't see, which is giving these ordinary things significance. Turn away.

On Wittgenstein's superficial picture of (linguistic and existential) meaning, essences are not hidden deep beneath our life with words and with others. Significances lie in the surfaces. The trick is to say "yes," to accept your life with others, your life with language, your life. In the light of this acceptance we can discover that it may be enough simply to rest on our reactions—our reactions to others, to their words, to the world—finding our affections simultaneously uncanny and wonderful (*CV* p. 4: 1930).

But nothing is really safe. Wonder is as precarious as it is precious. There is no absolute safety. And it can be terrifying to look into the dark groundlessness not only of the meaning of our words, but also the significance of our lives. But then, looked at from the other side, turning our whole investigation around the fixed point of our *real need*, coming back up from the depths to the surfaces, we can discover the earth itself, filled with wonder. Daybreak. Wonder: the small, delicate, precious. These hairs along the stem of a plant. This downy fuzz on your lover's lip, on your child's ear. This mole on his shoulder. This. This is what I do. This. This is what I love. This is what I care about. This. And the whole thing seems like magic. It may not last. It is precious. Wonderful.

Afterword

The Plain Sense of Things

At last we are here. Where we began. Heller's thesis that the turn in Wittgenstein's work is properly viewed in terms of the turn in Nietzsche's work has now been sympathetically defended. The existential discovery of the *Investigations* is the same one Nietzsche described in 1886:

> Oh, those Greeks! They knew how to live. What is required for that is to stop courageously at the surface, the fold, the skin, to adore appearance, to believe in forms, tones, words, the whole Olympus of appearance. Those Greeks were superficial—*out of profundity.* And is not this precisely what we are again coming back to, we daredevils of the spirit who have climbed the highest and most dangerous peak of present thought and looked around from up there—we who have looked *down* from there? Are we not, precisely in this respect, Greeks? Adorers of forms, of tones, of words? And therefore—*artists*? (*GS*, P par. 4)

Wittgenstein's philosophy begins with deep disquietudes and ends with the acceptance of the exuberant variety of forms and tones that articulate our life with language. Waking to wonder is saying "yes" to the groundless surfaces of our lives.

Wonder is fragile. Again and again it vanishes before the tendency to sublime the logic of our language and life. That is why wonder is so precious. Again and again it must be drawn from the ordinary. Is it not in this respect that we are Greeks? Adorers of forms, of tones, of words? And therefore artists? Artists?

One of the forces of Nietzsche's invocation of the concept of art is that art can be associated with the surfaces of things, for example, the visual arts with the visual surfaces of things. Thus to be—in any sense—an advocate of superficiality is to be an advocate of an artistic attitude. But the concept of art has another aspect with which I would like to close. Drawing wonder from the ordinary, finding wonder in the mira-

203

cle of ordinary life, this takes work. It requires artistry. It is an art, a theatrical art.

Consider Wittgenstein's attempt to write his readers first into their disquietudes and then to the peace he sets as his goal. Each of these writing tasks is theatrical. Wittgenstein could not simply have said:

> Look! There is no explanation for how we are able to follow a rule, no ground for the judgment that $2+2=4$. Accept it. Give up Realism and Antirealism. There is no point to constructing a Theory of Knowledge, a good reason is one that looks like *this*. This is simply what I do.

If his readers are to follow his writing, Wittgenstein must stage his encounter with his readers so that they will experience the wonder. The purpose of his book would be achieved if it brought one person to feel that they were walking on a mountain of wonders. But in the darkness of our times, it is not likely that this will happen. So Wittgenstein develops the theatrical art of his writing.

The simplicity of simply "doing what I do" is something we must be brought to see. Wittgenstein shows us this. Asks us to consider that. Reminds us of something else. Gives his other voices free rein to follow their subliming tendencies as far as they would like, as far as failure. Likely as not we will have become the other voices, so when the flight of their lines of thought is over, we are tired. But what is *he* saying? What kind of theory is *he* defending? We start all over again. Differently detailed, our subliming tendencies find themselves frustrated, again. Don't we see what we have been doing? Look. Look at the various forms, tones, and words we have been tossing aside in our earnest search for something deep and essential. Their variety was frustrating our subliming tendencies. Stop saying "No." This is what I do. Yes. This is what I care about. Yes. Yes.

It is theater. And its vision of language is theatrical. A word has a role [Rolle] it plays [spielt] in the language-game [Sprachspiel] (*PI* par. 21). Language-games take place on a stage [Schauplatz] constituted by all the circumstances that surround the language-games (*PI* par. 179). And I am not sure what to do with the fact that *PI* paragraph 66 tells its readers repeatedly to look [Schau] at what we call "games" ["Spiele"], thus bringing "Schau" and "spiel" near enough to produce "Schauspiel" the theatrical word for a play or performance. But once one is thinking about theatricality, the very idea of a game can incorporate theater. Stylized moves, following a script or play book, emotional reactions incited by pieces of wood. To figure language as a game is already to figure it theatrically. And if peace will be ours when we accept the language we speak, the life we lead, then Wittgenstein is asking us to accept the naturalness of a move in a game, the naturalness of the unnatural.

I cannot help feeling that this brings the peaceful wonder that was Wittgenstein's goal into the orbit of Wallace Stevens's description of the plain sense of things. The peace Wittgenstein reaches, the wonder he enjoys, were they perfect, would last. But they do not last. They are not perfect. The plain sense of things is not fully plain. The plain sense of things is staged. Nietzsche, Wittgenstein, and Stevens aim to turn from "No" to "Yes."[1] They would say "Yes" to the things nearest. But this "Yes" is not pure, it is staged, theatrical.

The Plain Sense of Things

After the leaves have fallen, we return
To a plain sense of things. It is as if
We had come to the end of the imagination,
Inanimate in an inert savoir.

It is difficult even to choose the adjective
For this blank cold, this sadness without cause.
The great structure has become a minor house.
No turban walks across the lessened floors.

The greenhouse never so badly needed paint.
The chimney is fifty years old and slants to one side.
A fantastic effort has failed, a repetition
In a repetitiousness of men and flies.

Yet the absence of the imagination had
Itself to be imagined. The great pond,
The plain sense of it, without reflections, leaves,
Mud, water like dirty glass, expressing silence

Of a sort, silence of a rat come out to see,
The great pond and its waste of the lilies, all this
Had to be imagined as an inevitable knowledge,
Required, as a necessity requires.[2]

It is only "as if" we had come to the end of the imagination. The great structures of the imagination are falling apart. A fantastic effort has failed. The leaves have fallen and we think we have returned from things as we wished them to be, to things as they are. To the plain sense of things. And we think that we have returned to the simply real. To Moore's hands. But the simply real isn't simple. It had to be imagined simple. Moore needed fifteen pages and centuries of philosophy if his little performance was to have any persuasive power at all. The redemptive power of the rough ground, the smell of earth, is inaccessible unless staged correctly. Improperly staged the redemptive power of the earth is simply dirt.

Wonder, a new intimacy with the things nearest, must be mediated, staged. And so Wittgenstein's peaceful wonder is as fragile as the spell cast by theater, or movies; it can be broken by something as simple as a cough or a question. It makes no sense to speak of the absolutely simple parts of a chair (*PI* par. 47). So too there is nothing absolutely simple, nothing absolutely plain. And the things nearest, however wonderful, are not absolutely near, absolutely wonderful. Although, for a spell, they can be enough. The spell cannot last. Wonder is precarious. That is what makes it so precious. And perhaps that is also what tinges Wittgenstein's redemptive voice with melancholy, making Wittgenstein, no less than Nietzsche, a philosopher of tragic knowledge.

Notes

Preface

1. *Relativism and Realism: The Nature and Limits of Epistemological Relativity* (Doctoral Dissertation, Yale University, 1985). The central result of this dissertation was published as "Relativism as *Reductio,*" in *Mind* 95.375 (July 1985): 389–408.

2. I was, in addition, quite eager to reconfigure the passage from Wittgenstein's *Tractatus Logico-Philosophicus,* which makes an analogous move in defense of solipsism: "For what the solipsist *means* is quite correct; only it cannot be *said,* but makes itself manifest" (*TLP* 5.62).

3. L. Wittgenstein, *On Certainty* (New York: Harper Torchbooks, 1969), p. 166.

4. M. Foucault, "Preface," 1966, to *The Order of Things* (New York: Vintage, 1973), p. xv.

5. See R. J. Anobile, ed., *Who's on First? Verbal and Visual Gems from the Films of Abbott and Costello* (Avon Books, 1972), pp. 220–33. In *Wittgenstein: From Mysticism to Ordinary Language* (Albany: State University of New York Press, 1987), R. Nieli links this scene to the confrontation with nothing. This does not strike me as correct. The lines "One morning I shot an elephant in my pajamas. How he got in my pajamas, I don't know," are spoken by Groucho Marx in *Animal Crackers* (1930); see P. D. Zimmerman and B. Goldblatt, *The Marx Brothers at the Movies* (New York: G. P. Putnam's Sons, 1968), p. 39.

6. S. Cavell, *The Claim of Reason* (New York: Oxford University Press, 1979), 140.

7. See for example, Barry Stroud, "Understanding Human Knowledge in General," in M. Clay and K. Lehrer, eds. *Knowledge and Skepticism* (Boulder: Colo. Westview Press, 1989).

8. S. Cavell, "The Politics of Interpretation," 1982, in *Themes out of School* (San Francisco: North Point Press, 1984), p. 34.

9. S. Cavell, "Emerson, Coleridge, Kant," 1983, in *In Quest of the Ordinary* (University of Chicago Press, 1988), p. 48.

10. Ibid., p. 40.

11. S. Cavell, "The Availability of Wittgenstein's Later Philosophy" (1962), reprinted in G. Pitcher, ed., *Wittgenstein: The "Philosophical Investigations"* (Notre Dame, Ind.: University of Notre Dame Press, 1968), pp. 160–61.

12. S. Cavell, *The Claim of Reason* (New York: Oxford University Press, 1979), p. 178.

13. A. Schopenhauer, "On The Vanity and Suffering of Life," 1844, in *The World as Will and Representation* (New York: Dover, 1969), vol. 2, p. 574.

14. F. Nietzsche, *The Birth of Tragedy* (1872) (New York: Vintage 1967), p. 3.

15. See D. Hume, *A Treatise of Human Nature* (1776), Book I, part iv, sect. vii. Two recent philosophers who take the instability of skeptical argument seriously are Cavell and Williams. See S. Cavell, *The Claim of Reason*, pp. 129, 159, 199, 202; and the final chapter of M. Williams, *Unnatural Doubts: Epistemological Realism and the Basis of Scepticism* (Cambridge Mass.: Blackwell, 1991).

16. Erich Heller, "Wittgenstein and Nietzsche," *Encounter* 13 (Sept 1959): 40–48, reprinted as "Wittgenstein: Unphilosophical Notes," in K. T. Fann, ed., *Ludwig Wittgenstein: The Man and His Philosophy* (New Jersey: Humanities Press, 1967), pp. 89–106.

17. Erich Heller, "Wittgenstein and Nietzsche," 1959, in K. T. Fann, ed., *Ludwig Wittgenstein*, p. 98.

18. Ibid., p. 94.

19. Ibid., p. 106.

20. A. Schopenhauer, "On The Vanity and Suffering of Life," 1844, in *The World as Will and Representation* (New York: Dover, 1969), vol. 2, p. 574.

21. F. Nietzsche, *The Gay Science*, 2d ed. 1887 (New York: Vintage, 1974), preface, par. 4.

22. The groundlessness of what we care about makes this wonder possible, but it also makes it impossible to realize this wonder perfectly. In Derridean terms, we could say that the groundlessness of what we care about broaches and breaches our wonder. (Note the appearance of the words *entamer* and *fonds sans fond* from behind the English of Derrida's *Dissemination* (Chicago: University of Chicago Press, 1981), pp. 25, 127).

23. Wittgenstein, in conversation with G. E. M. Anscombe, reported in her "Opening Address [of the 6th International Ludwig Wittgenstein Sympo-

sium, Kirchberg am Wechsel, August 1981]," in *Language and Ontology*, W. Leinfellner et al., eds. (Vienna: Hölder-Pichler-Tempsky, 1982), p. 28.

Chapter 1. Superficial—Out of Profundity

1. Nietzsche, Letter to Fritzsch, August 29, 1886. The complete letter is translated by W. Kaufmann and appears in *Nietzsche: Philosopher, Psychologist, Antichrist*, 4th ed. (Princeton, N.J.: Princeton University Press, 1974), pp. 466–67 (a facsimile appears on pp. 476ff.).

2. M. A. Gillespie notes that *BT* would have distinguished the tragic from the philosophical instead of linking them with the expression "the philosopher Dionysus," and Gillespie resolves this issue by suggesting that in *TI* Nietzsche now thought of himself as the Socrates who practices music imagined at *BT* par. 14 and 15 (M. A. Gillespie, "Nietzsche's Musical Politics," *Nietzsche's New Seas*, M. A. Gillespie and T. B. Strong, eds. (Chicago: University of Chicago Press, 1988), pp. 117–49.)

This is consistent with the familiar view, originally due to Kaufmann, that in his maturity, Nietzsche used "Dionysus" to refer to what *BT* meant when speaking of the union of Apollo and Dionysus. See W. Kaufmann, *Nietzsche: Philosopher, Psychologist, Antichrist* (Princeton, N.J.: Princeton University Press, 1950, 1974), pp. 281–82.

3. A. Nehamas, *Nietzsche: Life as Literature* (Cambridge, Mass.: Harvard University Press, 1985), pp. 42–43.

4. The first substantial review of *BT* was by Nietzsche's near contemporary—and fellow alumnus of Schule Pforta—Ulrich Wilamowitz-Möllendorff. It was viciously critical of Nietzsche's scholarship. Nietzsche fed Erwin Rhode information to use in a reply to this attack, but Wilamowitz-Möllendorff's criticism of this reply was equally acidic. Even in 1950, scholars were citing these criticisms with respect—adding only that, from *BT*, "it is but a step to Hitler's *Mein Kampf*" [J. H. Groth, "Wilamowitz-Möllendorff on Nietzsche's *Birth*," *J. Hist. Ideas*, 11 (April 1950): 179–90]. Wilamowitz-Möllendorff wrote these pamphlets when he was a young man, but he was to become "the most celebrated Greek scholar of his time." H. Lloyd-Jones, *Blood for the Ghosts* (Baltimore: Johns Hopkins University Press, 1982), p. 172. My biographical information is from R. Hayman, *Nietzsche* (Oxford University Press, 1980).

A very concise discussion of these philological concerns is provided by W. Geoffrey Arnott, "Nietzsche's View of Tragedy," *Arethusa* 17 (1984): 135–49. A short summary of the exchanges between Wilamowitz-Möllendorff and Rhode is in W. Kaufmann's introduction (1967) to *BT*. All these reviews and replies—including an open letter Wagner wrote—are conveniently reprinted in

Karlfried Gründer, ed., *Der Streit Um Nietzsches "Geburt Der Tragödie"* (Hildesheim: Georg Olms Verlagsbuchhandlung, 1969).

A terrifically thorough discussion—of all but recent French interpretations of *BT*—is provided by M. S. Silk and J. P. Stern, *Nietzsche on Tragedy* (Cambridge, Mass.: Cambridge University Press, 1981). A helpful collection of essays is J. C. O'Flaherty, et al., eds., *Studies in Nietzsche and the Classical Tradition* (Chapel Hill: University of North Carolina Press, 1976).

5. This group reads *BT* in roughly the spirit that Heidegger approaches Nietzsche's entire oeuvre: G. Deleuze, *Nietzsche and Philosophy* (1962) (New York: Columbia University Press, 1983), esp. pp. 10–14; S. Kofman, "Metaphor Symbol and Metamorphosis," in D. Allison, ed., *The New Nietzsche* (New York: Dell Publishing, 1977), e.g., p. 202; A. Nehamas, *Nietzsche: Life as Literature* (Cambridge, Mass.: Cambridge University Press, 1985), e.g, pp. 42–43; H. Staten, *Nietzsche's Voice* (Ithaca, N.Y.: Cornell University Press, 1990), "Appendix: *The Birth of Tragedy* Reconstructed"; I. Soll, "Pessimism and the Tragic View of Life: Reconsiderations of Nietzsche's *Birth of Tragedy*," in R. C. Solomon and K. M. Higgins, eds., *Reading Nietzsche* (Oxford: Oxford University Press, 1988), e.g., p. 109.

6. This group of antimetaphysical interpreters of *BT* includes:

P. de Man, "Genesis and Genealogy (Nietzsche)," (1972) in *Allegories of Reading* (New Haven, Conn.: Yale University Press, 1979), esp. pp. 93–102. Also see de Man's "Rhetoric of Tropes (Nietzsche)" (1974), in *Allegories of Reading*, esp. pp. 116–18. There is an interesting exchange between W. Kaufmann and de Man in the discussion of the essay on Rhetoric in *Symposium* 28.1 (spring 1974): 45–51.

J. Hillis Miller, "Stevens' Rock and Criticism as Cure" (1976), in *Aesthetics Today*, rev. ed., M. Philipson and P. J. Gudel, eds. (New York: New American Library, 1980), pp. 497–536.

J. Sallis, "Dionysus—In Excess of Metaphysics," in *Exceedingly Nietzsche*, D. F. Krell and D. Wood, eds. (New York: Routledge, 1988), pp. 3–12. Also see his extended discussion in *Crossings: Nietzsche and the Space of Tragedy* (Chicago: University of Chicago Press, 1991).

R. Schacht, *Nietzsche* (London: Routledge and Kegan Paul, 1983), e.g., pp. 485–86.

7. Nietzsche's "Attempt at a Self-Criticism" (August 1886) was published with the 1886 edition of *BT*. What appears to be an earlier attempt at writing this self-criticism was published as *WP* par. 853.

8. Nietzsche, Letter to Franz Overbeck, July 2, 1885. Cited in Ronald Hayman *Nietzsche: A Critical Life* (Oxford: Oxford University Press, 1980), p. 286. "Ingrown": his mature thoughts have grown back into his first immature production.

9. When I was his student, James Ogilvy emphasized this dimension of *Ecce Homo* and drew my attention to this passage of *WP*. Also see his *Many Dimensional Man* (Oxford: Oxford University Press, 1978).

10. L. Wittgenstein, *Philosophical Investigations* (Oxford: Blackwell, 1976), par. 124, also see par. 126 and 129.

11. See, for example, Meredith Williams, "Transcendence and Return: The Overcoming of Philosophy in Nietzsche and Wittgenstein," *International Philosophical Quarterly* 28.4 (December 1988): 403–19. Most of what Williams says about Wittgenstein in this article does not, on my interpretation, separate his work from Nietzsche. von Wright shares Meredith Williams's approach to the comparison of Nietzsche and Wittgenstein in "Wittgenstein in Relation to His Times"(1977), in *Wittgenstein* (Minneapolis: University of Minnesota Press, n.d.), p. 211.

12. Fritzsch had been Nietzsche's publisher for the original edition of *BT*, but most of his succeeding works were published with Schmeitzner, so the turn to Fritzsch was in fact a return. Schmeitzner was going bankrupt and attempting to raise money by selling the rights to Nietzsche's publications. See R. Hayman, *Nietzsche*, pp. 277, 297.

13. According to *KSA* 12.123, the seven publications were to be (1) *The Birth of Tragedy* (2) *Untimely Meditations* (3) *Human, All-Too-Human* (4) *Assorted Opinions and Maxims* (5) *The Wanderer and His Shadow* (6) *Dawn* (7) *The Gay Science*. Only five were written, because the second volume of *Human, All-Too-Human* includes two books from the original seven, and because Nietzsche decided not to republish the *Untimely Meditations*. See Nietzsche to Fritzsch, August 26, 1886; and *HH* II, P par. 1.

14. F. Nietzsche, Letter to Fritzsch, August 29, 1886, as translated by W. Kaufmann in *Nietzsche: Philosopher, Psychologist, Antichrist*, 4th ed. (Princeton, N.J.: Princeton University Press, 1974), p. 466.

15. Nietzsche to Fritzsch, August 26, 1886.

16. Beethoven, Quartet in A minor, Op. 132, third movement. At the start of this movement, Beethoven wrote: "Heiliger Dankgesang eines Genesenen an die Gottheit, in der lydischen Tonart" and then, some measures later in the same movement, "Neue Kraft fühlend." *GS* P par. 1 also speaks of a returning strength [Kraft]. This reference to Beethoven in the first paragraph of the preface to the new 1887 edition of *GS* nicely balances the reference (indicated by Kaufmann in his translation) to Beethoven's Ninth Symphony in the epilogue to that new edition (*GS* par. 383:1887)

17. Nietzsche goes into these genealogical details in this preface because he wants to explain the stage at which *Human, All-Too-Human* was written. His imagery implies that it was written at the first phase of convalescence.

The first phase of convalescence is described in terms of flying to a "cool," "bird-like altitude" [Vogel-Umblick] where one can see "tremendous numbers of things *beneath*" oneself (*HH* I, P par. 4). And in another preface, *HH* (vol. I) is described as "a book 'for free spirits,' there reposes upon it something of the almost cheerful and inquisitive coldness of a psychologist who takes a host of painful things that lie *beneath* and *behind*" (*HH* II, P par. 1). The stage of sickness, like the first phase of convalescence, is also described as cold (*HH* I, P par. 3), but the match with the altitude from which so many things are seen beneath one overpowers this particular ground of doubt.

18. It is in this familiar way that Plato's forms seem to be required to be outside of time. There are epistemological reasons for their position outside of time: the slipperiness of the modal operator in the truth of (Nec: $Kp \longrightarrow p$) seems—falsely—to require a timeless object for knowledge. There are also metaphysical reasons for forms being outside of time: if the ONE table all the many tables participate in was in time, then that ONE table would change from moment to moment. But if it changed from moment to moment there would now be a problem about what made all those many moments moments of ONE table. And this seems to incite the invention of a new TIMELESS table for all the moments to participate in. It is just such reflections as these that Nietzsche was attempting to abbreviate in his assertion that the fundamental faith of metaphysicians was a faith in opposite values.

19. Hegel, in *Hegel's Introduction to "Aesthetics,"* trans. T. M. Knox, with an interpretive essay by C. Karelis (Oxford: Clarendon Press, 1979), par. 3, p. 5.

20. This suspicion of any simple reversal also appears in *BGE* par. 2 during Nietzsche's discussion of the two "dangerous maybes." It is reminiscent also of what Derrida refers to as the "double gesture," or the "double writing," or the "double science" of deconstruction. See J. Derrida, in an interview published in *Positions* (1972), trans, A. Bass (Chicago: University of Chicago Press, 1981), p. 41; but also note the anxiety Derrida expresses about this interview in J. Derrida, "Deconstruction in America: An Interview with Jacques Derrida," *Critical Exchange*, no. 17 (winter 1985): 7.

21. In a certain sense, this means that nothing is small—because everything is the same. Nietzsche 1872: "For science there is nothing great and nothing small" (*P* par. 34).

22. Apart from his suggestion (at *Being and Time*, p. 173) that this mood reveals being as a burden, Heidegger has described a mood that we may think of as the mood of this cooler phase of convalescence:

> Furthermore, the pallid lack of mood [die fahle Ungestimmtheit]—indifference—which is addicted to nothing and has no urge for anything, and which abandons itself to whatever the day may bring, yet in so doing takes every-

thing along with it in a certain manner, demonstrates *most penetratingly* the power of forgetting in the every day mode [alltäglichen Stimmungen] of that concern which is closest [nächsten] to us. Just living along [Das Dahinleben] in a way that "lets" everything "be" as it is ["sein lässt," wie es ist] is based on a forgetting and abandoning oneself to one's thrownness.

M. Heidegger, *Being and Time* (1927) (New York: Harper and Row, 1962), p. 396, also see p. 173.

Sartre's characters Annie and Antoine in *Nausea* just as much as Camus's stranger might be characterized—at some moments—as living in this pallid lack of mood.

23. In "On the Afterworldly" (*Z* I par. 3), Zarathustra tells his listeners to give up "'that world',," which is only a heavenly nothing [ein himmlisches Nichts], and try to discover the meaning of the earth [Sinn der Erde]." This is the task Nietzsche sets himself in virtually all of his publications.

24. I discussed Nietzsche's defusing nihilism in the context of relativism in my "Nietzsche, Feyerabend, and the Voices of Relativism," *Metaphilosophy* 17 (1986): 135–52.

25. I owe this observation to André Jacq. In 1972, he asked or told his French class: "Are you still pissing on the altar?—Then you still believe!"

26. Today we are more familiar with this as a paradox of relativism. There are those who argue that since we cannot attain a transcendent perspective, since "it is impossible to step outside our skins," we must conclude that all views on a given—or on any—subject are equally acceptable. Cousin to the flat earth view of the colder phase of convalescence, this relativism only survives because such relativists persist in believing that the only way to judge the acceptability of an opinion is from a transcendent position they believe to be unattainable. But if on the relativist's own account, we cannot leave the earth, then neither can we flatten the earth from the vantage point of the birds. These are forms of nihilism and relativism that only a God could attain, but—inconsistently—these nihilists and relativists are sure god is dead.

27. This is Kaufmann's translation of the motto of *The Gay Science* (1882), from "History," the first essay of Emerson's *Essays: First Series* (1841). R. W. Emerson, *Essays and Lectures*, (New York: Library of America, 1983), p. 242.

28. Nietzsche was not unaware that truth has often been figured as a woman.

(1) In *BT* (1872) par. 15, p. 95, Nietzsche remarks that if truth—"that one nude goddess"—were the only goal of science, then there would be no science, because science cannot strip that goddess bare.

(2) In *BGE* P (June 1885), Nietzsche remarks that if truth is a woman, then she has certainly not let herself be won by the clumsy hands of dogmatic metaphysicians. So if truth is a woman she cannot be what metaphysicians have thought she was.

(3) In *GS* P par. 4 (fall 1886), we can read: "Perhaps truth is a woman who has reasons for not letting us see her reasons? Perhaps her name is—to speak Greek—*Baubo*." Nietzsche seemed to think of Baubo's story as an allegory of his approach to tragedy.

29. Perhaps we can think of these natural objects as members of one of David Lewis's "elite classes." See David Lewis, "Putnam's Paradox," *Australasian Journal of Philosophy*, 62, 3 (September 1984): 227–29.

30. See M. Nussbaum, *The Fragility of Goodness* (Cambridge: Cambridge University Press, 1986), pp. 341–42, and throughout.

31. The wanderer is associated with blindness at *GS* par. 287. In *Oedipus at Colonus*, Oedipus was a blind wanderer who travelled with what must have been to him a voice, the voice of his sister/daughter Antigone. So I sometimes think that the wanderer and his shadow are blind Oedipus and Antigone. If this is right, then *The Wanderer and His Shadow* elaborates *P* par. 87: "Oedipus: Soliloquy of the Last Philosopher." This is by way of saying that the sentiments I cite from *HH* II WS are not foreign to the sentiments of the opening scene of *Oedipus at Colonus*.

32. Heidegger's late essay "The Thing" (1950) describes one of the significant effects of this technological age as the loss of the things near: "the frantic abolition of all distances brings no nearness; for nearness does not consist in shortness of distance" (*Poetry, Language, Thought* [New York: Harper, 1971], p. 165). I have persistently retranslated *nahe* and *nächst* as "near" and "nearest" in order to reach out to this aspect of Heidegger's thought and also to the link between being near and being a neighbor that appears in Thoreau's *Walden*, about which Cavell has written:

> What is next [nächst] to us is what we neighbor. The writer has spoken of finding himself suddenly neighbor to the birds; and he speaks of the pond in neighborly terms. . . . Our relation to nature, at its best, would be that of neighboring it. . . . You may call this mysticism, but it is a very particular view of the subject; it is not what the inexperienced may imagine as a claim to union, or absorption in nature.

S. Cavell, *The Senses of Walden*, expanded edition (San Francisco: North Point Press, 1972, 1981), pp. 105–6. Cavell appends a long footnote to these words articulating the world's "externality" as its "nextness to me." The notion of neighboring is helpfully thought through with A. R. Ammons's "Neighbors" in *A Coast of Trees* (New York: Norton, 1981): "I can't regain the lost idyllic at all, but the woods are here with us."

33. This is where to situate Nietzsche's so-called perspectivism. The perspective of metaphysics shrinks the value of the little things nearest to us. Nietzsche incites us to turn the telescope back around again.

34. R. W. Emerson, *Essays and Lectures*, pp. 261–62.

35. Ibid., p. 262.

36. Unlike Kant, Nietzsche thinks that the autonomous self is not a purely rational being, but involves many impure drives and inclinations. The pigtail paragraph (*BGE* par. 214) is followed by one in which Nietzsche suggests that "we modern men" should be construed as planets illuminated not by the one (Platonic/Rational) sun but by many different suns of various colors (*BGE* par. 215).

37. This brief interpretation of Emerson on "Whim" is very close to Cavell's in "An Emerson Mood," in *The Senses of Walden*, expanded ed. (San Francisco: North Point Press, 1981), pp. 152–60, esp. p. 154: "The call of one's genius presents itself with no deeper authority than whim."

38. A third change was the elimination of the frontispiece, a depiction of Prometheus at a moment between being bound and being unbound. See Reinhard Brandt, "Die Titelvignette von Nietzsche's *Geburt der Tragödie aus dem Geiste der Musik*" *Nietzsche-Studien* 20 (1991): 314–28.

39. A. Schopenhauer, *The World as Will and Representation* (1819), trans. E. F. J. Payne (New York: Dover, 1969), v. I, par. 56, p. 310. (Hereafter referred to as Schopenhauer, *WWR*.)

40. Schopenhauer, *WWR* I, par. 51, p. 252.

41. Ibid., p. 253.

42. Ibid.

43. Nietzsche thinks that *BT* makes an advance in the "science of aesthetics" (*BT* par. 1). The aesthetic problem is that "From the nature of art as it is usually conceived according to the single category of appearance and beauty, the tragic cannot be honestly deduced at all, it is only through the spirit of music that we can understand the joy involved in the annihilation of the individual" (*BT* par. 16, pp. 103–4). So, like the "Self-Criticism," the text of *BT* suggests that Nietzsche is out to defend the ugly, the painful, the violent, the delight Burke called "sublime." Nietzsche does work the notion of the sublime, in opposition to the beautiful, but it is surprising that he does not do so more systematically.

John Sallis draws attention to the sometimes casual uses of the term *sublime* in Nietzsche's book. See J. Sallis, *Crossings: Nietzsche and the Space of Tragedy* (University of Chicago Press, 1991), pp. 93–94.

44. See F. Love, *Young Nietzsche and the Wagnerian Experience* (Chapel Hill: University of North Carolina Press, 1963). Love believes that as early as 1866 Nietzsche's reading of Lange helped liberate him from Schopenhauer's metaphysics of the will (ibid., p. 41). And he notes that

> Seen in retrospect, the relationship with Wagner decidedly fostered Nietzsche's development as a cultural psychologist, but in the period at hand the prolonged dealings with the philosopher of Wagner's choice merely contributed to the rank confusion, in *Die Geburt der Tragödie* of Schopenhauerian and specifically Nietzschean concepts. (ibid., p. 62)

For an extended investigation of the impact of Lange on Nietzsche's work, see G. Stack, *Lange and Nietzsche* (Berlin: de Gruyter, 1983). John T. Wilcox wrote an appreciative review in *Man and World*, v. 20 (1987), 232–40. A symposium on Stack's book with discussion by Wilcox, Breazeale, and Siegfied, and a reply to these discussions by Stack appeared in *International Studies in Philosophy* 21, 2 (1989): 81–124. In the harsh light of Breazeale's critique of Stack's book, it is worth observing that Love's use of Lange's influence on Nietzsche would not be open to the specific criticisms Breazeale directs at Stack's book.

45. See I. Soll, "Pessimism and the Tragic View of Life: Reconsiderations of Nietzsche's *Birth of Tragedy*," in K. Higgins and R. Solomon, eds., *Reading Nietzsche* (Oxford: Oxford University Press, 1988), pp. 104–31.

46. Nietzsche speaks at a number of places about question marks; see, e.g., *GS* par. 346 (1887): "our question mark."

47. P. de Man, *Allegories of Reading* (New Haven, Conn.: Yale University Press, 1979), p. 93.

Richard Schacht, a rather different interpreter of Nietzsche, also describes what he calls Nietzsche's "dubious purported role as one of the sources of existentialism." R. Schacht, "Routledge Nietzsche Studies," in L. H. Hunt, *Nietzsche and the Origin of Virtue* (New York: Routledge, 1991), p. ii.

48. Nietzsche's letter to E. Rhode, November 20, 1868, translated in W. Arrowsmith, "Nietzsche on Classics and Classicists," pt. 2, *Arion*, 2, 2 (summer 1963): 7. E. Rhode defended (with Nietzsche's help) the first edition of *The Birth of Tragedy*, and then produced *Psyche* (1893), which included an interpretation of the cult of Dionysus with no reference to Nietzsche's work at all.

49. As Kaufmann's notes observe, Nietzsche's Silenus is quoting from Sophocles's *Oedipus at Colonus*, lines 1224 ff.

50. John Sallis emphasizes the excessive dimension of Dionysus in *Crossings: Nietzsche and the Space of Tragedy* (Chicago: University of Chicago Press, 1991).

51. Grausen... *BT* par. 1, p. 36. Entsetzliche... *BT* par. 7, p. 60. Schrecken... *BT* par. 15, p. 98.

52. Verzückung . . . *BT* par. 1, p. 36. Entzückung . . . *BT* par. 17, 105.

53. We might still rely on reason, but once reason has been revealed to be without grounds, afloat, we will persist in our reliance on reason—if at all—with an added anxiety.

54. In a conversation in the fall of 1992, Alexander Nehamas suggested to me that Dionysian ecstasy, which is a doctrine about the individuality of the self, might reappear in the mature Nietzsche as his new doctrine of the creation of the self.

55. H. Staten, *Nietzsche's Voice* (Ithaca: Cornell University Press, 1990), pp. 213–14.

56. Not only the imperative to live for oneself, but even this last concession that Nietzsche will help others echoes Emerson. Emerson spurned "miscellaneous popular charities," but conceded that "there is a class of persons to whom by all spiritual affinity I am bought and sold." "Self-Reliance" (1841), in *Emerson: Essays and Lectures* (New York: Library of America, 1983), p. 262.

57. I completely ignore the question of historical accuracy both in these portraits of Euripides and Socrates and also in Nietzsche's explanation of death of tragedy. My concern is exclusively with the opposition between these two types: the Dionysian and the Socratic. If it turns out that (in Nietzsche's terms) Euripides and Socrates were *really* Dionysian that is—supposing the Socratic type is really exemplified in other thinkers—a secondary, merely historical point.

58. Nietzsche scorns "poetic justice" (*BT* par. 14, p. 91; par. 21, p. 126; par. 22, p. 133). He suggests that for the completely unartistic, poetic justice might be all they could hope to receive from tragedy, and he sends them off to G. G. Gervinus, *Shakespeare Commentaries* (English trans. 1863). Nietzsche adverts (*BT* par. 22, p. 132) to a debate about the significance of Aristotelian catharsis. The debate was between those who understood catharsis in *moral* terms and those who, like Bernays, understood it in *medical* terms (Jacob Bernays "Aristotle on the Effect of Tragedy" (1857), in J. Barnes et al., eds., *Articles on Aristotle*, v. 4 (New York: St. Martin's Press, 1978), pp. 154–65). Nietzsche thought that neither interpretation made contact with the aesthetic effects of tragedy, effects attendant on experiencing "the highest artistic primal joy [Urfreude], in the bosom of the primordially one [Ur-Eine] . . . this return to the primal home" [Urheimat] (*BT* par. 22, p. 132).

59. Heidegger's most famous attack on the pretensions of science is his inaugural lecture at Freiburg University: "What is Metaphysics?" (July 24, 1929), in *Basic Writings*, D. F. Krell, ed. (New York: Harper and Row, 1977).

Predictably, Carnap took offense at this lecture, and used it to show how metaphysics could be overcome through an analysis of language. "Overcoming Metaphysics Through Logical Analysis of Language" (1932), in *Logical Positivism*, A. J. Ayer, ed. (New York: Free Press, 1959), pp. 60–81. (Note however Carnap's soft spot for Nietzsche: p. 80.)

Wittgenstein's "Apropos of Heidegger" is fully sympathetic to Heidegger. It survives in Waismann's notes of a conversation at Schlick's on December 30, 1929, and it seems to have been addressed to Heidegger's lecture of the previous summer. F. Waismann, *Wittgenstein and the Vienna Circle*, B. McGuinness, ed. (New York: Barnes and Noble, 1979), pp. 68–69. Also see Murray's discussion of these remarks in *Heidegger and Modern Philosophy*, M. Murray, ed. (New Haven, Conn.: Yale University Press, 1978), pp. 81–83.

60. Wittgenstein's belief that the most important matters were inaccessible to science was the driving force behind the *Tractatus*. The *Philosophical Investigations*, par. 109, has: "It was true to say that our considerations could not be scientific ones." This is equally true of the grammatical investigations of the *Investigations*.

One of the first persons to emphasize the nonempirical dimension of Wittgenstein's later philosophy was Stanley Cavell in his debate with Benson Mates (December 19, 1957). Both contributions are accessible in *Ordinary Language*, V. C. Chappell, ed. (Englewood Cliffs, N.J.: Prentice Hall, 1964). Cavell recalls the violence of this episode in *This New Yet Unapproachable America* (Albuquerque, N.M.: Living Batch Press, 1989), p. 80.

61. This example is equally familiar to readers of Nietzsche and to readers of Donald Campbell. I like to think of my use of it as commemorating the philosophical presence of Donald Campbell at Lehigh University.

62. Of these two "brothers," it is Dionysus who is described as the "primordial mother" [Urmutter] of Attic tragedy (*BT* par. 16, p. 104). Hence Dionysus—who is an effeminate character in Euripides' *Bacchae*—is the mother and Apollo the father of Attic tragedy.

63. To the extent that Apollo names the beautiful and Dionysus names the sublime, Attic tragedy, which is both, would fall in the category Kant once called "splendid" [Prächtige], in his (precritical) *Observations on the Feeling of the Beautiful and Sublime* (1764), J. T. Goldthwaite, trans. (Berkeley: University of California Press, 1960, 1980), p. 48. Also see Burke, *A Philosophical Enquiry into the Origin of Our Ideas of the Sublime and Beautiful* (1757) (University of Notre Dame Press, 1968), pp. 120 and 156, where the fine is almost said to unite the sublime and the beautiful.

64. The next words in the quotation are "for it is only as an *aesthetic phenomenon* that existence and the world are eternally *justified*." Roughly these

words are repeated at *BT* SC par. 5, p. 22; par. 5, p. 52; and par. 24, p. 141. The discussion in my text is an interpretation of these famous words.

65. These are sentiments that also surfaced in protofascist literature between the wars; see Daniel T. O'Hara, "Mask Plays: Theory, Cultural Studies, and the Fascist Imagination" in *Boundary 2*, 17.2 (summer 1990): 129–54. Nietzsche discusses the importance of myth to the endurance of the modern state at *BT* par. 23, pp. 135–38, and this too has a protofascist ring.

66. Nietzsche, "The Philosopher" par. 37. The "philosopher of tragic knowledge" is closely related to "The Last Philosopher" (*P*, par. 38, par. 85) and also to the blind and wandering Oedipus (*P*, par. 87). A more speculative hypothesis would link The Wanderer—of *The Wanderer and His Shadow* (1880)—to the wandering, blind Oedipus and would link his Shadow to his daughter and half-sister Antigone who wanders with him.

67. It is hard not to understand "the fold, the skin" as a reference to the female genitals linked to this text by the name "Baubo" (*GS* P par. 4). S. Kofman suggests that for Nietzsche, Baubo and Dionysus are "multiple names for protean life."

Demeter was cured of her despair at the loss of her daughter by Baubo's dance, which displayed either her stomach with a picture of Dionysus on it or her genitals. Supposing the latter, then Irigaray provides a way of receiving Baubo as the limits of phallogocentric reason—precisely what *BT* describes as the cause of terror. But when this absence is presented as art—in a dance—it heals. Pharmaceutical medicines are poisons, and only cure when carefully presented, introduced into the diet self-consciously, theatrically. See (a) S. Kofman, "Baubo: Theological Perversion and Fetishism" (1976), in *Nietzsche's New Seas*, M. A. Gillespie and T. B. Strong, eds. (University of Chicago Press, 1988), pp. 175–202, esp. p. 198; (b) L. Irigaray, "This sex which is not one," in *This Sex Which Is Not One* (1977), C. Porter and C. Burke, trans. (Ithaca, N.Y.: Cornell University Press, 1985), pp. 23–33, esp. 29.

68. "Forms, tones, and words": these last anticipate the reading of Wittgenstein I will be presenting in later chapters. Especially *Philosophical Investigations* (Oxford: Blackwell, 1976), par. 52, which compares the linguistic facts that are of concern to Wittgenstein to "grey rags and dust."

69. "The tragedy begins" resonates with *GS* par. 342: 1882, with *TI* IV par. 6, and of course with the title of *BT*.

70. Sophocles, *Oedipus at Colonus*, R. Fitzgerald trans., ll. 1–6.

71. Wittgenstein, "peace" [Ruhe], *Philosophical Investigations*, par. 133. Also *Culture and Value*, p. 10. "Thoughts that are at peace [Friede in

den Gedanken]. That's what someone who philosophizes yearns for." Nietzsche, "peace on earth" (Friede auf Erden), *HH* II WS par. 350.

72. My thoughts about Nietzsche are inseparable from conversations I have had over the last few years with Joseph Volpe. At his suggestion I began to take the 1886 prefaces—as a group—seriously, and specific remarks of his clarified both Nietzsche's conception of metaphysics and the possible role of fragility or precariousness in understanding the great health. A previous draft of this chapter was improved by the suggestions of Russel Wiebe and Michael Raposa. Norman Melchert showed me that value—in general—is not what fragility increases; thus he prompted my emphasis in this chapter, and hence in the book as a whole, on wonder.

Chapter 2. The Sublime Scaffolding of Logic and Life

1. This note provides a brief summary of actual and hypothesized contacts between Wittgenstein and the writings of Nietzsche. I have no basis for thinking that any of these three lists is complete. Again I cite Heller's pathbreaking essay: Erich Heller, "Wittgenstein and Nietzsche," *Encounter* 13 (Sept 1959): 40–48, reprinted as "Wittgenstein: Unphilosophical Notes," in K. T. Fann, ed., *Ludwig Wittgenstein: The Man and His Philosophy* (N.J.: Humanities Press, 1967), pp. 89–106.

READING NIETZSCHE. On September 1, 1914, Wittgenstein started reading Tolstoy's *The Gospel in Brief.* Later in the fall he purchased and read the book that meant so much to Nietzsche, Emerson's *Essays.* As McGuinness tells the story:

> Within a month of reading Emerson Wittgenstein bought volume 8 of Nietzsche's works in Cracow—presumably from Naumann's Leipzig edition, where volume 8 contains . . . "Der Antichrist," . . . "Der Fall Wagner," "Götzen-Dämmerung," "Nietzsche contra Wagner," and Nietzsche's poems. Parallels and faint echoes are worth looking for in all.

B. McGuinness, *Wittgenstein: A Life,* v. 1 (Berkeley: University of California Press, 1988), pp. 220–29, esp. p. 225. At that time (Dec. 8, 1912), Wittgenstein reflected on his reading of Nietzsche in his coded diary, and these reflections were translated and reproduced in McGuinness, *Wittgenstein,* v. 1, p. 225. Also see R. Monk, *Ludwig Wittgenstein: The Duty of Genius* (New York: Free Press, 1990), pp. 122–23. Monk paradoxically thinks that Nietzsche exhibited themes that were important for Wittgenstein throughout his life, while bluntly claiming "Certainly there is no trace of Emerson's influence in the work that he [LW] wrote at this (or indeed at any other) time" (Monk, p. 121). Given the abiding influence of Emerson on Nietzsche, these two beliefs are in some tension.

WRITING ABOUT NIETZSCHE. In addition to (a) the coded diary just mentioned, there are references to Nietzsche in *The Brown Book* and in the collection of miscellaneous remarks, *Culture and Value* (University of Chicago Press, 1980). There are probably other references I do not know about.

(b) In 1931 he wrote that Nietzsche probably got as close to the "problems of the intellectual world of the west" as any philosopher ever got (*CV* p. 9).

(c) In the 1934–35 lectures, since published as *The Brown Book*, Wittgenstein referred to Nietzsche, mentioning the "idea that what can happen must have happened before" (*BrB* p. 104).

(d) In 1947 he refers to a passage from *Human, All-Too-Human*, v. 1 par. 155. Nietzsche is describing the working style of great artists and mentions Beethoven (*CV* p. 59).

HYPOTHETICAL INFLUENCE OF NIETZSCHE. Baker and Hacker, *Analytical Commentary*, v. 1, note (pp. 326n and 535n respectively).

(a) The phrase "family resemblance" [Familien-Änlichkeit] appears in Nietzsche's *Beyond Good and Evil* (1886), par. 20, as well as *PI* par. 67: "Familienähnlichkeiten." Von Wright's view is that the seed of this notion was planted by Spengler's use of "Ursymbol" (see *CV* p. 14, and von Wright's *Wittgenstein*, p. 213). Spengler, of course, read Nietzsche quite carefully.

(b) Wittgenstein regretted not having acknowledged the influence of Paul Ernst (Nachwort (1910) to Grimm's *Kinder-und Hausmärchen*) in the preface to *TLP*. Rhees remembers Wittgenstein saying that he took the phrase "mythology in our language" from Ernst, but as Baker and Hacker point out, that phrase does not appear in Ernst; although it does appear in *Human, All-Too-Human*, v. 2, part 2: *The Wanderer and His Shadow*, par. 11.

2. E. Heller, "Wittgenstein and Nietzsche" (1959) republished as "Wittgenstein: Unphilosophical Notes" in K. T. Fann, ed., *Ludwig Wittgenstein: The Man and His Philosophy* (New Jersey: Humanities Press, 1967), p. 98.

3. Wittgenstein, "peace" [Ruhe]: *Philosophical Investigations*, par. 133. Nietzsche, "peace on earth" [Friede auf Erde]: *HH* II WS, par. 350.

4. Since the middle eighties, there has been more and more research on middle Wittgenstein: the works between *TLP* and *PI*, which were mainly written in the thirties. In spite of this interest, there is no doubt that Wittgenstein's early philosophy is best represented by *Tractatus*. The question of the importance of the missing middle to the more mature works remains contested. Of course there are no superlative moments that divide Wittgenstein's development into isolated periods. I work under the hypothesis that part I of the *Investigations* (deriving from typescripts extending from c. 1938–1945) is Wittgenstein's settling old accounts and his initiating something new, which his last manuscripts pursue into various domains. This hypothesis is, itself, derived

from von Wright, *Wittgenstein*, p. 136: "I lean, myself, toward the opinion that Part I of the *Investigations* is a complete work and that Wittgenstein's writings from 1946 onwards represent in certain ways departures in *new* directions."

For examinations of the transitional writings see:

(a) A. Kenny, *Wittgenstein* (Harmondsworth: Penguin, 1973).

(b) J. Hintikka and M. Hintikka, *Investigating Wittgenstein* (New York: Blackwell, 1986).

(c) S. Stephen Hilmy, *The Later Wittgenstein* (New York: Blackwell, 1987).

5. The German title *Logische-Philosophische Abhandlung* sounds more humble than the "Spinoza title" G. E. Moore gave to the English translation. (Letter from C. K. Ogden to Russell [Nov. 5, 1921] reprinted in L. Wittgenstein, *Letters to C. K. Ogden* [Oxford: Blackwell, 1973], p. 2.) Wittgenstein wrote to Russell (March 13, 1919) that he had finished writing the *Tractatus* in August 1918 (*L* R.35). In a letter to Engelmann (August 5, 1922), Wittgenstein described the first (1921) German edition of the *Tractatus* as "a pirated edition: it is full of errors." Paul Engelmann, *Letters from Wittgenstein with a Memoir* (Oxford: Blackwell, 1967), letter E.44, p. 49. A reliable, bilingual German-English version of the *Tractatus* was published in 1922.

See G. H. von Wright, "The Origin of the *Tractatus*," in *Wittgenstein* (Minneapolis: University of Minnesota Press, 1982), pp. 63–109.

6. What we know as part I of the *Investigations* was substantially finished in 1945, although von Wright believes that Wittgenstein continued to adjust it as late as 1949 or 1950. What we know as part II of the *Investigations* is a 1949 typescript (now lost). Both parts were first published in 1953 in a bilingual German-English edition.

See G. H. von Wright, "The Origin and Composition of the *Investigations*," in *Wittgenstein*, pp. 111–36.

7. See Russell's letter to C. K. Ogden, Nov. 5, 1921, in L. Wittgenstein, *Letters to C. K. Ogden*, introduction, p. 2.

8. Wittgenstein to C. K. Ogden, April 23, 1922, in *Letters to C. K. Ogden*, p. 20.

9. I have not found the original location of this remark, it is cited by Copi and Beard in their introduction to their *Essays on Wittgenstein's "Tractatus"* (New York: Macmillan, 1966), p. x. I suspected it would be in Blanshard's *On Philosophical Style* (1954) (New York: Greenwood Press, 1969), but I have been unable to locate the passage.

10. C. I. Lewis to F. J. Woodbridge, cited in B. Dreben and J. Floyd, "Tautology: How Not To Use A Word," *Synthese* 87 (April 1991): 23.

11. G. Bergmann, *The Metaphysics of Logical Positivism* (New York: Long-mans. Green, and Co., 1954), lists these four theses on page 2:

> All Logical Positivists could still agree that they (a) hold Humean views on causality and induction; (b) insist on the tautological nature of logical and mathematical truths; (c) conceive of philosophy as logical analysis, i.e., as a clarification of the language which we all speak in everyday life; and (d) that such analysis leads to the 'rejection of metaphysics' in the sense that, e.g., the points at dispute among the *traditional* forms of idealism, realism, and phe-nomenalism could not even be stated, or, at least not stated in their original intent, in a properly clarified language.

The *Tractatus* endorses versions of these "diplomatic formulae" (Bergmann, p. 2) in these places, among others: (a) at 5.134–35.1361; (b) at 6.1 (c) at 4.112; (d) at 6.53.

12. G. Bergmann, *Metaphysics*, p. 3.

13. R. Carnap, "Autobiography," in *The Philosophy of Rudolf Carnap*, P. A. Schilpp (La Salle: Open Court, 1963), p. 24.

14. R. Carnap, "Autobiography," p. 25, writes "For me personally, Witt-genstein was perhaps the philosopher who, besides Russell and Frege, had the greatest influence on my thinking." He isolates (1) the *Tractatus*'s conception of "the truth of logical statements" and one assumes the Tractarian account of logical inference, and (2) the opposition to metaphysics as nonsense.

15. R. Carnap, "Autobiography," pp. 26–27. I have pieced together pas-sages spread widely over these two pages, so this patchwork is as much an interpretation as a citation of Carnap.

16. G. E. M. Anscombe, *An Introduction to the "Tractatus,"* 1959 (Phila-delphia: University of Pennsylvania Press, 1959), p. 82n.

17. Anscombe who helped to launch the second phase of the reception of the *Tractatus*, begins her first chapter with a long passage from Karl Popper, who was one of the philosophers in Vienna just outside the circumference of the Vienna Circle. His epistemological interpretation of the *Tractatus* is now available in Popper's *Conjectures and Refutations* (New York: Basic Books, 1962), pp. 39–40. Anscombe's vigorous criticism of Popper's interpretation in the opening pages of *An Introduction to the "Tractatus"* was responded to by Popper in *Realism and the Aim of Science* (c. 1962) (Totowa N.J.: Rowman and Littlefield, 1983), p. 194n1, also see pp. 214–16.

18. This expression signals the fact that this division between the first two phases of the reception of the *Tractatus* is shared by G. H. von Wright: see his "Modal Logic and the *Tractatus*" 1972, in *Wittgenstein*, p. 186.

19. G. E. M. Anscombe, *An Introduction to Wittgenstein's "Tractatus,"* 3d ed. (Philadelphia: University of Pennsylvania Press, n.d.), 1st ed. 1959, 2d ed. 1971. The largest changes in the later editions concern chap. 10.

20. Erik Stenius, *Wittgenstein's "Tractatus,"* 1960 (Westport: Greenwood Press, 1981).

21. M. Black, *A Companion to Wittgenstein's "Tractatus"* (Ithaca: Cornell University Press, 1964). The very title of this book marks the maturity of concern with the proper interpretation of a book, rather than with what the book could do for logical empiricism. Black's book, coming after Stenius's and Anscombe's takes issue with them.

22. Many of the responses to this new manner of interpreting the *Tractatus* and some of its first anticipations in the essays by Daitz [= O'Shaugnessy], Copi, and McGuinness, which were published in the 1950s, were helpfully reprinted in I. M. Copi and R. W. Beard, eds., *Essays on Wittgenstein's "Tractatus"* (New York: Macmillan, 1966).

Also in this generation is James Griffin, *Wittgenstein's Logical Atomism* 1964 (Seattle: University of Washington Press, 1969).

23. G. E. M. Anscombe, *An Introduction,* pp. 12–13.

24. E. Stenius, *Wittgenstein's "Tractatus,"* chap. 11: "Wittgenstein as a Kantian Philosophy," pp. 214–26.

25. This division between the first two phases of the reception of the *Tractatus* is shared by G. H. von Wright: see his "Modal Logic and the *Tractatus,*" 1972, in *Wittgenstein,* p. 186.

Somewhat earlier, this division was recognized by J. O. Urmson who, for reasons of his own, followed the interpretation of the Vienna Circle. See J. O. Urmson, *Philosophical Analysis: Its Development Between the Wars* (Oxford: Clarendon Press, 1956), esp. pp. ix–x.

26. Paul Engelmann, *Letters from Ludwig Wittgenstein with a Memoir* (Oxford: Blackwell, 1967).

27. L. Wittgenstein, *Briefe an Ludwig von Ficker,* G. H. von Wright, ed., assisted by W. Methlagl (Brenner Studien, I: Salzburg: Otto Müller, 1969). These letters have now been translated by B. Gillette: see L. Wittgenstein, "Letters to Ludwig von Ficker," in C. G. Luckhardt, ed., *Wittgenstein: Sources and Perspectives* (Hassocks, Sussex: Harvester Press, 1979), pp. 82–98. Also see A. Janik, "Wittgenstein, Ficker, and *Der Brenner,*" in Luckhardt, ed., *Wittgenstein: Sources and Perspectives,* pp.161–89.

28. Wittgenstein, "Letters to von Ficker," E 23, undated.

29. Ibid.

30. In "Wittgenstein, Ficker, and *Der Brenner*," A. Janik mentions the following three anticipations of his own work with Toulmin:

a. E. Heller, "Ludwig Wittgenstein: Unphilosophical Notes," *Encounter* 13 (1959): 40–48.

b. W. Kraft, Ludwig Wittgenstein und Karl Kraus," *Neu Rundschau* 72 (1961): 812–44.

c. G. Steiner, *Language and Silence* (New York: Atheneum, 1967).

31. A. Janik and S. Toulmin, *Wittgenstein's Vienna* (New York: Simon and Schuster, 1973).

32. See D. LaCapra's criticism of the naive contextualism of Janik and Toulmin in "Reading Exemplars: *Wittgenstein's Vienna* and Wittgenstein's *Tractatus*," in *Rethinking Intellectual History* (Ithaca, N.Y.: Cornell University Press, 1983).

33. VON WRIGHT. Georg Henrik von Wright's work is helpfully collected in *Wittgenstein*. Von Wright has done marvelous historical work on the origin of the *Tractatus* and the *Investigations*, but I am here referring principally to his three articles: "Wittgenstein on Certainty" (1972), "Modal Logic in the *Tractatus*" (1972), and "Wittgenstein in Relation to His Times" (1978).

RHEES. I cannot remember where I first heard Rhees's influence described in terms of a "Swansea School" of Wittgensteinian exegesis. Since von Wright and Rhees were both Wittgenstein's literary executors (with Anscombe) this phase of the reception of the *Tractatus* might also be called the Executive Phase. The following are helpful here:

a. R. Rhees, *Without Answers* (London: Routledge and Kegan Paul, 1969).

b. R. Rhees, *Discussions of Wittgenstein* (London: Routledge and Kegan Paul, 1970).

c. P. Winch, *Ethics and Action* (London: Routledge and Kegan Paul, 1972).

d. H. O. Mounce, *Wittgenstein's "Tractatus": An Introduction* (Chicago: University of Chicago Press, 1981).

e. P. Winch, *Trying to Make Sense* (Oxford: Blackwell, 1987).

f. D. Z. Phillips and P. Winch, eds., *Wittgenstein: Attention to Particulars, Essays in Honour of Rush Rhees (1905–1989)* (New York: St. Martin's Press, 1989).

g. J. Conant, "Must We Show What We Cannot Say?" in *The Senses of Stanley Cavell*, R. Flemming and M. Payne, eds. (Lewisburg, Penn.: Bucknell University Press, 1989), pp. 242–83.

h. R. Gaita, ed., *Value and Understanding: Essays for Peter Winch* (London: Routledge, 1990).

i. C. Diamond, *The Realistic Spirit: Wittgenstein, Philosophy, and the Mind* (Cambridge: MIT Press, 1991).

34. R. J. Fogelin, *Wittgenstein*, 2d ed. (New York: Routledge and Kegan Paul, 1976, 1987), pp. 98–99.

35. Wittgenstein as reported by Drury in M. O'C. Drury, "Conversations with Wittgenstein," in R. Rhees, ed., *Recollections of Wittgenstein* (New York: Oxford University Press, 1984), p. 159.

36. See (a) Brian F. McGuinness, *Wittgenstein: A Life*, v. 1 (Berkeley; University of California Press, 1988). (b) There is something of the same awareness of Wittgenstein's irony in James Conant's "Must We Show What We Cannot Say?" in *The Senses of Stanley Cavell* (*Bucknell Review* 32.1; Lewisburg, PA: Bucknell University Press, 1989). (c) Joachim Schulte remarks: "In the face of the objective difficulty of the text, of which even Wittgenstein was well aware, a kind of irony could be imputed to the author. But that is surely not the whole story." J. Schulte, *Wittgenstein: An Introduction* (Albany: State University of New York Press, 1992), p. 46.

37. B. McGuinness, *Wittgenstein*, v. 1, p. 301; see p. 305.

38. This observation is due to D. LaCapra, "Reading Exemplars . . .," in *Rethinking Intellectual History* (Ithaca, N.Y.: Cornell University Press, 1983), p. 111.

39. The paradoxical status of this remark is observed by Marjorie Perloff in her "Toward an Avant-Garde *Tractatus*: Russell and Wittgenstein on War," in *Common Knowledge* 2.1 (spring 1993): 34.

40. B. McGuinness, *Wittgenstein: A Life*, v. 1, p. 303.

41. I follow McGuinness in relinquishing his own and Pears's translation of proposition 7 for the more evocative, more famous, and more literal translation of C. K. Ogden.

42. See Ogden to Russell, November 5, 1921 in L. Wittgenstein, *Letters to C. K. Ogden* (Oxford: Blackwell, 1973), cited in von Wright's introduction, pp. 2–3.

43. H. Hertz, *The Principles of Mechanics* (1894) (New York: Dover 1956) Wittgenstein was especially fond of pages 7–8 of the introduction. See

    (a) Wittgenstein, *Tractatus*, 4.04 and 6.361.

    (b) Wittgenstein, *Culture and Value*, p. 9: 1931.

    (c) Wittgenstein, *Blue Book* (1933–34), p. 26.

    (d) Wittgenstein, "Big Typescript" (1933), par. 89, in *Synthese* 87 (April 1991), p. 13.

(e) Wittgenstein, *Brown Book* (1934–35), p. 169.

(f) T. Redpath, *Ludwig Wittgenstein: A Student's Memoir* (London: Duckworth, 1990), pp. 82–86, reporting on a meeting of the Moral Science Club held on February 23, 1939.

44. B. McGuinness, *Wittgenstein: A Life*, v. 1, p. 265.

45. Russell and Whitehead, *Principia Mathematica*, vol. 1 (1910) (Cambridge: Cambridge University Press, 1976), p. 91.

46. I owe the observation that proposition 2.01 ought to comment on the nonexistent proposition 2.0 to Robert Barnes. It is tempting to put the absence of 2.0 together with states of affairs being beyond the world. This would make the discussion of objects in the 2.0's a discussion of nothing. But there is a less exciting interpretation available: the .0's are definitions. And indeed 2.01 defines "state of affairs." The comments such as n.011, n.012 need not themselves be definitions, though such a prop as 2.201 ought to give a definition. When we look up that proposition in the *Tractatus* it is indeed relatively definitional. There might still be a joke here, for these definitions in the 2.0's are of objects, the signs for which are primitive and, hence, impossible to define according to the *Tractatus* itself (*TLP* 3.202 and 3.26)

The suggestion that Wittgenstein got his numbering system from Russell and Whitehead confirms Stenius' claim that whereas 2.1 and 2.2 (and their ilk) look ahead, building to a summary conclusion in 3, the 2.0's, 2.20's (and their ilk) look backward to 2 or 2.2 and articulate presuppositions or consequences of the previous proposition. E. Stenius, *Wittgenstein's "Tractatus"* (Westport: Greenwood Press, 1960, 1981), pp. 7–10.

47. In conversation, Robert Barnes observed that the *Tractatus* is thus already a hypertext.

48. The first paragraph of J. Derrida's *Dissemination* (1972) is "This (therefore) will not have been a book" (Chicago: University of Chicago Press, 1981), p. 3.

49. I suspect this would be the preference of Wittgenstein's biographer, Ray Monk.

50. Wittgenstein to Malcolm, November 16, 1944, in N. Malcolm, *Ludwig Wittgenstein: A Memoir* (Oxford: Oxford University Press, 1984), pp. 93–94.

51. Wittgenstein introduced this comma sometime between the *Prototractatus* (1918) and the *Tractatus* itself. In the *Prototractatus* there is no comma. L. Wittgenstein, *Prototractatus* (c. 1918) (Ithaca, N.Y.: Cornell University Press, 1971), ms. page 3.

Although this comma has not—as far as I know—been noticed, two previous commentators have praised Wittgenstein's semicolons. Erich Heller has this on the power of Wittgenstein's thought style:

> Its temperature is of its essence, in its passion lies its seriousness, the rhythm of the sentences that express it is as telling as is that which they tell, and sometimes a semicolon marks the frontier between a thought and a triviality. How can this be? Are we speaking of an artist or a philosopher? We are speaking of Ludwig Wittgenstein. "*Der Philosoph behandelt eine Frage; wie eine Krankheit*" [*PI* par. 255]. It is a profound semicolon, and not even a philosophically initiated translator could save the profundity: "The philosopher's treatment of a question is like the treatment of an illness" is, by comparison, a flat *aperçu.*

E. Heller, "Wittgenstein and Nietzsche" (1959) in Heller's *The Importance of Nietzsche* (Chicago: University of Chicago Press, 1988), pp. 142–43.

And more recently, J. Schulte, commenting on the same semicolon and Wittgenstein's habits of punctuation in general, has this:

> Although Wittgenstein always had problems with spelling and (above all) with punctuation, occasionally his punctuation was masterful—for example, his use of the semicolon in this quotation [*PI* Vorwort, para 8], and in the above-quoted remark on the way the philosopher "treats" a question. (*PI* par. 255)

J. Schulte, *Wittgenstein* (Albany: State University of New York Press, 1992), p. 23n27.

And Wittgenstein, himself remarked: "I really want my copious punctuation marks to slow down the speed of reading. Because I should like to be read slowly (As I myself read.)" (*CV* p. 68: 1948; see p. 57: 1947).

52. Analogous considerations prompt Searle's appeal from representations to what he calls "The Background." Searle's "background" is Wittgenstein's "scaffolding." Searle writes:

> The Background is a set of nonrepresentational mental capacities that enable all representing to take place. Intentional states only have the conditions of satisfaction that they do, and thus only are the states that they are, against a Background of abilities that are not themselves intentional states. In order that I can now have the Intentional states that I do I must have certain kinds of know-how: I must know how things are and I must know how to do things, but the kinds of "know-how" in question are not, in these cases, forms of "knowing that."

J. Searle, *Intentionality* (Cambridge: Cambridge University Press, 1983), p. 143.

It will be obvious to many that this paragraph is far closer to the later than to the early Wittgenstein. I cite it here to underline Wittgenstein's constant theme: that the domain of sense is autonomous with respect to the domain of fact. What changes as Wittgenstein gets older is that although the logical grammar of our language is exclusively truth functional in the *Tractatus*, it becomes positively exuberant in the *Investigations*.

53. This may seem to conflict with Kripke and Putnam's account of the scientific discovery of essences, e.g., S. Kripke, *Naming and Necessity* (Cambridge: Harvard University Press, 1972, 1980). The conflict is only apparent, because these essences are only available—if they are—once we accept a *practice of naming kinds*. That practice cannot be given an empirical foundation, any more than any normative practice can be reduced to facts. Thus Kripke's *Wittgenstein on Rules and Private Language* (Cambridge: Harvard University Press, 1982) raises difficulties for the confident naturalized metaphysics that some saw outlined in *Naming and Necessity*.

54. I elided 2.025 "It [substance] is form and content." This proposition, speaking as it does about *content* as well as form, is dangerously close to contradicting 2.0231: "The substance of the world *can* only determine a form, not any material properties." To bring them together we might think of the content [Inhalt] of a proposition; then just as objects are the ground of logical space, so perhaps we are to think of them as the ground of semantic space too (see E. Stenius, *Wittgenstein's "Tractatus"* pp. 79ff.).

55. The law of excluded middle asserts that there is no middle value between truth and falsity. Frege seems to use this law interchangeably with the principle *tertium non datur* (latin: third not given), which means that there is no third category between truth and falsity. Frege, *Basic Laws of Arithmetic*, v. 2 (1903), par. 56 in P. Geach and M. Black, eds., *Translations from the Philosophical Writings of Gotlob Frege*, 3d ed. (Oxford: Blackwell, 1980), p. 139.

For an attempt to systematize and differentiate these and other semantical principles from the logical laws that are their syntactical twins, see M. Dummett, *Truth and Other Enigmas* (London: Duckworth, 1978), preface, p. xix.

56. This bracketing of epistemological concerns is also present in *NB* 62.

57. G. Frege, *Basic Laws of Arithmetic*, 1903, v. 2, par. 56, in Geach and Black, 3d ed., 1980, p. 139.

58. This dispenses with the theory of types. What type theory tries to force into the penalty box, takes itself out of play. These thoughts are supported by the superb analysis of nonsense in Cora Diamond's "What Nonsense Might Be," *Philosophy* 56 (1981): 5–22.

59. Frege, *Basic Laws of Arithmetic*, 1903, v. 2, par. 62, Geach and Black, 3d ed. 1980, p. 146.

60. This is how it looked to John Hare when we first discussed the *Tractatus*.

61. M. Heidegger, "The Origin of the Work of Art" (1935–36), in M. Heidegger, *Basic Writings*, D. F. Krell, ed. (New York: Harper and Row, 1977), p. 170.

62. Russell's introduction, 1922:

> What causes hesitation is the fact that, after all, Mr. Wittgenstein manages to say a good deal about what cannot be said, thus suggesting to the sceptical reader that there may be some loophole through a hierarchy of languages, or by some other exit.

B. Russell, in *TLP*, p. xxi.

63. The apparently middle road, according to which we simply call on higher levels of the hierarchy as needed, must supply an account of this ability, and it will then find that its problems reduce to one or the other of the two just named. For a defense of this style of hierarchy less rooted in Wittgenstein than in W. Sellars, see Mark Lance, "Rules, Practices and Norms," in *Ludwig Wittgenstein: A Symposium on the Centennial of His Birth*, S. Teghrarian, A. Serafini, and E. Cook, eds. (Wakefield, N.H.: Longwood Academic, 1990), pp. 77–86.

64. Russell believed that the expression "Socrates is mortal" both *contains* Socrates [the human being] and is *about* Socrates. As Hylton points out, Russell's view in the *Principles* (1903) was that sentences including denoting phrases, unlike those including names, could be *about* an object without actually containing the object they were about. See P. Hylton, "The Significance of 'On Denoting,'" in C. Wade Savage and C. Anthony Anderson, eds., *Rereading Russell*, Minnesota Studies in the Philosophy of Science, 12 (Minneapolis: University of Minnesota Press, 1989), pp. 90–91.

65. B. F. McGuinness, "The So-Called Realism of the *Tractatus*," in *Perspectives on the Philosophy of Wittgenstein*, ed. I. Block (Cambridge: MIT Press, 1981), pp. 72–73.

66. On this point see G. Baker in *Wittgenstein, Frege, and the Vienna Circle* (Oxford: Blackwell, 1988), chap 3, esp., pp. 76–77.

67. This is the bipolarity of the proposition. See L. Wittgenstein "Notes on Logic," 1913, in *NB*. Russell tells this story about a-p-b:

> Whitehead described for me the first time that Wittgenstein came to see him. He was shown into the drawing room during afternoon tea. He appeared scarcely aware of the presence of Mrs. Whitehead, but marched up and down the room for some time in silence, and at last said explosively: "A proposition has two poles. It is *apb*." Whitehead, in telling me, said: "I naturally asked what are *a* and *b*, but I found that I had said quite the wrong thing. '*a* and *b* are indefinable,' Wittgenstein answered in a voice of thunder."

B. Russell, *The Autobiography of Bertrand Russell,* vol. II: 1914–1944 (London: George Allen and Unwin Ltd, 1968), p. 101.

68. Von Wright has a very good discussion of bipolarity and of this passage in *Wittgenstein,* pp. 185–200, esp., p. 190.

69. Gordon Baker, *Wittgenstein, Frege, and the Vienna Circle* (Oxford; Blackwell, 1988), pp. 76–77.

70. The *Tractatus* is a pharmakon. See J. Derrida, "Plato's Pharmacy," in *Dissemination* (1972) (Chicago: University of Chicago Press, 1981).

71. Wittgenstein (Dec. 30, 1929), apparently commenting on Heidegger's "the nothing noths" lecture (What Is Metaphysics?):

> To be sure, I can imagine what Heidegger means by being and anxiety. Man feels the urge to run up against the limits of language. Think for example of the astonishment that anything at all exists. This astonishment cannot be expressed in the form of a question, and there is also no answer whatsoever. Anything we might say is *a priori* bound to be mere nonsense.... But the inclination, the running up against something, *indicates something.* St Augustine knew that already when he said: "And woe to those who say nothing concerning thee just because the chatterboxes talk a lot of nonsense."

Wittgenstein as reported by Waissmann in *WVC,* pp. 68–69. I have replaced the paraphrase of St. Augustine with Wittgenstein's own rendition as recalled by Drury in Rhees, ed., *Recollections of Wittgenstein* (Oxford: Oxford University Press, 1984), p. 90.

72. This is a rejection of a Russellean view that there is acquaintance with logical forms:

> Since we desired to give the name "form" to genuine objects rather than symbolic fictions, we gave the name to the "fact" "something is somehow related to something." If there is such a thing as acquaintance with forms, as there is good reason to believe that there is, then a form must be a genuine object; on the other hand, such absolutely general "facts" as "something is somehow related to something" have no constituents, are unanalyzable, and must accordingly be called simple. They have therefore all the essential characteristics required of pure forms.

B. Russell, *Theory of Knowledge: The 1913 Manuscript, Collected Papers of Bertrand Russell,* v. 7 (London: George Allen and Unwin, 1984), p. 129. The relevance of this manuscript to the *Tractatus* was first brought to my attention in lectures (since published) of David Pears. It is by now widely recognized.

73. L. Wittgenstein, *Letters to C. K. Ogden* (Oxford: Blackwell, 1973), pp. 36–37.

74. M. Heidegger, "What is Metaphysics?" in M. Heidegger, *Basic Writings* (New York: Harper and Row, 1977), p. 111.

75. "The one with the gospels" is cited by H. Wittgenstein in B. Leitner, *The Architecture of Ludwig Wittgenstein* (Halifax, Nova Scotia: The Press of the Nova Scotia College of Art and Design, 1973), p. 19. Also see McGuinness, *Wittgenstein*, v. 1, p. 220; McGuinness cites a letter of Russell's December, 20, 1919: "He read it and reread it, and thenceforth had it always with him, under fire and at all times."

76. McGuinness, *Wittgenstein*, v. 1, p. 220. Letters to Ficker, in Luckhardt, p. 91, F.18.

77. L. Tolstoy, *The Gospel in Brief* (1883), in *A Confession, The Gospel in Brief, and What I Believe*, Aylmer Maude, trans. (London: Oxford University Press, 1961), p. 123. Hereafter cited as Tolstoy, *Gospel.*

78. P. Engelmann to F. A Hayek, April 23, 1953, cited in von Wright, *Wittgenstein*, p. 68.

79. Wittgenstein, *Prototractatus*, c. 1918 (Ithaca, N.Y.: Cornell University Press, 1971), ms p. 0.

80. The propositions on this page (ms p. 3) are: 1, 1.1, 2, 2.1, 2.2, 3, 3.1, 3.2, 4, 4.1, 4.2, 4.3, 4.4, 5, 6. The main differences from correspondingly numbered propositions in *TLP* are these: *Proto-T* 1 has no comma after "alles." *Proto-T* 2.1 reads: Facts are grasped by us in pictures. *Proto-T* 3.2 reads: A propositional sign with its mode of depiction is a proposition. There are some other differences, but these are even more minor.

81. Tolstoy, *Gospel*, p. 118.

82. Ibid.; see the slightly different versions of par. 5 and par. 6 at pp. 172 and 186.

83. Ibid., "peace" 172; "joy" 172; "secure and true life" 270.

84. G. Frege, *The Basic Laws of Arithmetic*, v. 1, 1893, trans. M. Furth (Berkeley: University of California Press, 1964), p. 15 [German: xvii].

85. Again this appeal to nonsense is supported by the analysis of nonsense in Cora Diamond's "What Nonsense Might Be," *Philosophy* 56 (1981): 5–22.

86. It does seem blind in this way to R. J. Fogelin, *Wittgenstein*, 2d ed., p. 96.

87. L. Wittgenstein, "Lecture on Ethics," *Philosophical Review* (January 1965), p. 5. The editors of the *Philosophical Review* report that this lecture "was prepared by Wittgenstein for delivery in Cambridge sometime between September 1929 and December 1930" (p. 3).

88. I do not think that this "sinnlos" is being used in the technical sense of the *Tractatus*: as the particular kind of senselessness characteristic of the propositions of logic.

89. This is McGuinness's translation as it appears in *Wittgenstein*, v. 1, p. 255.

90. L. Wittgenstein, *Prototractatus*, 3.16021: "A theme in music is a proposition."

91. The following brief interpretation of "wax and wane as a whole" is due to Norman Melchert and a nod and a smile that restored my strength when I found I couldn't shake the conviction that my Tolstoyan approach made no sense at all.

92. F. Nietzsche, *Human, All-Too-Human*, trans. R. J. Hollingdale, preface to vol. I of the 2d ed. (1886), par. 5.

93. John Hare reacted with this thought when he first heard these ideas.

94. Baker and Hacker point out that this is a rejection of Russell's view as it is expressed in *Our Knowledge of the External World*, chap. 3. See G. Baker and P. M. S. Hacker, *Analytical Commentary*, v. 1 *Wittgenstein Understanding and Meaning* (Chicago: University of Chicago Press, 1980), p. 464.

95. Goethe, *Faust*, W. Kaufmann, trans. (New York: Doubleday Anchor, 1961), pt. 2: Midnight, lines 11453–66.

96. James Conant, "Must We Show What We Cannot Say," *The Senses of Stanley Cavell*, R. Flemming and M. Payne, eds. (Lewisburg, PA: Bucknell University Press, 1989), p. 279n31.

97. Some of these thoughts on the *Tractatus* reach back to my first reading of that book with Simon Blackburn. This version of them was produced in relative isolation, but with tips provided by conversation with Evan Conyers, Mark Bickhard, and Norman Melchert. The idea that the *Tractatus* is virtually hypertextual is due to Robert Barnes, and this idea lead me to the nothing at the heart of that book. The idea that the *Tractatus* is pervasively ironic is due to Brian McGuinness. Certain essays of Peter Winch, Rush Rhees, Cora Diamond, and James Conant were very important to me in the writing of this chapter. Russel Wiebe looked over the first version of this chapter and this version is correspondingly cleaner.

Chapter 3. Superficial Essentialism

1. Erich Heller, "Wittgenstein and Nietzsche" (1959), *Encounter*, republished as "Wittgenstein: Unphilosophical Notes," in K. T. Fann, ed., *Ludwig*

Wittgenstein: The Man and His Philosophy (New Jersey: Humanities Press, 1967, 1978), p. 98.

2. Thankfulness is one face of what Nietzsche calls "Yes-saying."

3. This passage resonates with the *Tractatus*'s remark that "There must indeed be some kind of ethical reward and ethical punishment, but they must reside in the action itself" (*TLP* 6.422).

4. Wittgenstein, in conversation with G. E. M. Anscombe, reported in her "Opening Address [of the 6th International Ludwig Wittgenstein Symposium, Kirchberg am Wechsel, August 1981]" in *Language and Ontology*, W. Leinfellner et al., eds. (Vienna: Hoelder-Pichler-Tempsky, 1982), p. 28.

5. J. Derrida, *Dissemination* (1972) (Chicago: University of Chicago Press, 1981), p. 3.

6. See O. K. Bouwsma, "The Blue Book" (1961) in *Philosophical Essays* (Lincoln: University of Nebraska Press, 1965), pp. 178–79.

7. In the *Yellow Book* this landscape is referred to as language. See A. Ambrose, ed., *Wittgenstein's Lectures: Cambridge 1932–1935* (Chicago: University of Chicago Press, 1979), p. 43: "The country we are talking about is language, and the geography its grammar." This passage was brought to my attention by Norton Batkin, in 1983.

8. Ibid. p. 43.

9. G. E. Moore, "Wittgenstein's Lectures in 1930–33" (1954 and 1955), in Moore's *Philosophical Papers* (New York: Collier Books, 1966), p. 316.

10. "A difference in which everything and nothing differs is uncanny." S. Cavell, "The Uncanniness of the Ordinary," (1986) in *In Quest of the Ordinary* (University of Chicago Press, 1988), p. 166.

11. For a time, Wittgenstein considered using a passage from Hertz as motto for *PI* (Baker and Hacker, *Volume I*, pp. 16–18): "When these painful contradictions are removed, the question as to the nature [of force] will not have been answered; but our minds, no longer vexed [gequälte], will cease to ask illegitimate questions." H. Hertz, *Principles of Mechanics* (1894) (New York: Dover, 1956), pp. 7–8.

12. Walt Whitman, *Specimen Days* (1882), in J. Kaplan, ed., *Whitman: Poetry and Prose* (Library of America, 1982), p. 926.

13. R. Rorty, "The Philosophy of the Oddball," *The New Republic* (June 19, 1989): 39–40.

14. See S. Cavell, *This New Yet Unapproachable America: Lectures After Emerson After Wittgenstein* (Albuquerque: Living Batch Press, 1989), esp. pp.

56–58. At p. 58, Cavell discovers Kant's linking of excess and abyss with the mathematical sublime in Wittgenstein's linking of the hyperbolic and the groundless. I. Kant, *Critique Of Judgment* (1790), W. S. Pluhar, trans. (Indianapolis: Hackett, 1987), p. 115.

My distinction from Cavell is this. I have linked the tendency to sublime (*PI* par. 38) only to the "hyperbolic" demand for a superorder between superconcepts (*PI* par. 97). This makes more sense of the terms in which Wittgenstein discusses this tendency: "In wiefern ist die Logic etwas Sublimes? (*PI* par. 89) I would rather link the role of the aesthetic notion of the sublime (das Erhabene) to the groundlessness of our (linguistic) life. So my distinction from Cavell is *first* to disjoin the hyperbolic from the groundless. *Second* I interpret the tendency to sublime in terms not of solidified liquids but of gasifying solids. Cavell is encouraged in the former by his reading of Coleridge's *Rime of the Ancient Mariner* (Cavell, *This New*, p. 57, *In Quest*, pp. 56–65). I was encouraged in the latter by the role of the verb "sublimierung" in chemistry. But these two approaches to the sublime are not as wholly opposed as one might suspect, for one common instance of the latter is dry ice.

At least one reference to the sublime in *Zettel* (*Z* par. 444) invites a comparison with Freud's notion of sublimation. I leave this investigation to others, hoping as I do that they will discover chemical (rather than aesthetical) sources for Freud's use of sublimation. Baker and Hacker, *Volume I*, pp. 508–9 point to some paths this comparative investigation might follow.

15. H. Kaal and A. McKinnon, eds., *Concordance to Wittgenstein's "Philosophische Untersuchungen"* (Leiden: E. J. Brill, 1975). Variants of sublimieren and its relatives appear in paragraphs 38, 89, and 94.

16. Baker and Hacker refer to this as "Proto-Philosophical Investigations" (PPI) and compare its arrangement with that of *PI* itself in their *Volume I*, p. 456. PPI was the version of *PI* Wittgenstein gave to Rhees to translate before the war.

17. Cavell gives the tendency to sublime the logic of our language an existential motivation (flight from responsibility) when he describes it as the feeling that "I must empty out *my* contribution to words, so that language itself, as if beyond me, exclusively takes over the responsibility for meaning" (S. Cavell, *This New*, p. 57). Cavell's sentence puts one in mind of Thompson Clarke's description of the "siren call of philosophy." See T. Clarke, "The Legacy of Skepticism," *Journal of Philosophy* 69.20 (November 1972): 759–62.

18. G. Frege, *Basic Laws of Arithmetic*, 1903, v. 2, par. 56, in P. Geach and M. Black, eds., *Translations from the Philosophical Writings of Gotlob Frege*, 3d ed. (Oxford: Blackwell, 1980), p. 139.

19. There is an apparent contradiction between *PI* par. 28, which gives an actual example of a perfectly exact [vollkommen exakt] definition, and *PI* par. 91, which denies that the goal of Wittgenstein's investigations is a state of complete exactness [vollkommenen Exaktheit]. I suspect that the way to resolve this apparent contradiction is to observe that Wittgenstein is denying that his goal is a certain *state*, one of complete exactness, but he is not denying that— in some circumstances—a definition may actually perform its function perfectly.

20. Compare: "At the end of the line it would be just as if I had said: 'I am interested in the idiom in painting.'" J. Derrida, "Passe-Partout," in *The Truth in Painting* (1978) (Chicago: University of Chicago Press, 1987), p. 2.

21. P. Geach and M. Black, eds., *Translations from the Philosophical Writings of Gotlob Frege,* 3d ed. (Oxford: Blackwell, 1980), p. 139.

22. See for example, G. Frege, "Thoughts," 1918, in *Logical Investigations* (Oxford: Blackwell, 1977), p. 7.

23. See E. Stenius's discussion of moods in *Wittgenstein's Tractatus.*

24. M. Dummett, "Frege and Wittgenstein," in I. Block, ed., *Perspectives on the Philosophy* (Cambridge: MIT Press, 1981), pp. 40–42.

25. Dummett, "Frege and Wittgenstein," p. 41.

26. Ibid.

27. Ibid.

28. Ibid., p. 33, also see discussion of Wittgenstein in the preface to Dummett's *Logical Basis of Metaphysics* (Cambridge: Harvard University Press, 1991).

29. Dummett, "Frege and Wittgenstein," pp. 41–42.

30. S. Cavell, *The Claim of Reason* (New York: Oxford University Press, 1979), p. 208.

31. Among these friends of Austin I count two of my own teachers, Robert Fogelin and Michael Williams. I remember Fogelin saying that where Wittgenstein had "countless," Austin would rather have counted up the seventeen there actually were. On my interpretation, "countless" is closer to the truth than any determinate number.

32. Lists this long are quite difficult to continue. I find their sheer length anaesthetizes my imagination; so I can only add new cases by finding parts of life left off the list. For example, he leaves off the language associated with lovers (courting, lovemaking, breaking up, making up, and so on). The whole domain of what Austin would call "explicit performatives" is also left off his

list. In *Being and Time* (1927), Heidegger provides a related list of human activities. Heidegger presents it as an open-ended list of the multiplicity of ways of being *concerned*: "The multiplicity is indicated by the following examples: having to do with something, producing something, attending to something and looking after it, making use of something, giving something up and letting it go, undertaking, accomplishing, evincing, interrogating, considering, discussing, determining . . ." (Heidegger's ellipsis) (*BT* English, page 83).

33. Dummett, "Frege and Wittgenstein," pp. 41–42.

34. See Margaret Urban Walker, "Augustine's Pretence: Another Reading of *Philosophical Investigations* 1," *Philosophical Investigations* 13.2 (April 1990): 99–109.

35. Writing about *PI* par. 2, Cavell describes one way of taking the builders in these terms:

> But when I try to imagine adults having just these words—for example the builder and his assistant—I find that I imagine them moving sluggishly, as if dull-witted, or uncomprehending, like cave men.

S. Cavell, *Philosophical Passages: Wittgenstein, Emerson, Austin, Derrida* (Oxford: Blackwell, 1995), p. 146. This passage is from notes Cavell used in lecturing on the *Investigations* throughout the 1960s and 1970s. Some of these ideas surfaced in Warren Goldfarb's "I Want You To Bring Me A Slab: Remarks on the Opening Sections of the *Philosophical Investigations*," *Synthese* 56 (1983): 265–82.

36. The first paragraph of the *Investigations*—"explanations come to an end somewhere"—refigures the last line of the *Tractatus*—"whereof we cannot speak, thereof we must be silent." Cavell finds something comic in the precipitousness with which Wittgenstein's book reaches its end. S. Cavell, *Philosophical Passages*, p. 147.

37. F. Nietzsche, *The Case of Wagner* (1988), par. 5: "Man setzt an die Lippen, was noch schneller in den Abgrund treibt."

38. M. Dummett, "Frege and Wittgenstein," p. 41.

39. B. A. W. Russell and A. N. Whitehead, *Principia Mathematica* I (1910) (Cambridge University Press, 1976), introduction, chap. 3, p. 66. This maxim is discussed by Gareth Evans in *Varieties of Reference* (New York: Oxford University Press, 1982).

40. In a phone conversation I still remember, it didn't seem like much to Robin Dillon.

41. And we *will* find such a mental state, even if we have to invent one out of something nearly empty, like thin air. This is the power of the tendency to sublime the logic of our language.

42. See Baker and Hacker, *Volume I*, pp. 639–40.

43. I here set aside the connection between charm and the uncanny.

44. Today a conversation with Joe Volpe brought out that there might be something charming about explanations, period. That is, any elegant account of diverse phenomena in terms of a few simple principles or substances has an elegance, dignity, charm. So Wittgenstein's opposition to charm might be of a piece with his assertion in *PI* par. 109 that "We must do away with all *explanation* [Alle *Erklärung muss fort*], and description alone must take its place." It is perhaps not irrelevant that this sentence arrives in the same paragraph in which Wittgenstein speaks of the bewitchment of his understanding [die Verhexung unseres Verstandes].

45. Again:

> If you have the idea that mathematics treats of mathematical entities, then just as some members of the animal world are exotic, there would be a realm of mathematical entities that were particularly exotic—and therefore particularly charming. Transfinite numbers, for example, as Hilbert says, this realm is a paradise. (*LFM*, p. 140)

46. But Rorty does recognize the limits of this anti-essentialist reading. For example, he writes:

> Derrida's suspicion of what he calls "Heideggerian nostalgia" is the counterpart to Davidson's suspicion of the later Wittgenstein's distinction between "grammar" and "fact."

R. Rorty, "Wittgenstein, Heidegger, and Language," in *Essays on Heidegger and Others, Philosphical Papers*, v. 2 (Cambridge: Cambridge University Press, 1991), p. 59n21.

Also see Samuel C. Wheeler III, "Wittgenstein as Conservative Deconstructor," *New Literary History* 19.2 (winter 1988): 257n10.

47. I have inserted Wittgenstein's version of the words following the last full colon. This was Wittgenstein's 1939 correction of Rush Rhees's English translation of TS. 220, called "Proto-Philosophical Investigations." Rhees's translation is TS. 226. I owe this correction to Baker and Hacker *Volume I*, p. 346. Their discussion of this line is excellent, their remarks on the Moebius strip are especially enlightening; see pp. 346–47.

48. Kripke writes of Wittgenstein's "*penchant* for a certain degree of obscurity" in *Wittgenstein on Rules and Private Language* (Cambridge: Harvard University Press, 1982), p. 5.

49. Augustine is cited at *PI* par. 1, 89, 436, 618.

50. Thanks to Vera Stegman, for help in this little foray into German ordinary language philosophy.

51. Quite felicitously, my Cassell's reports that in the language of mining, *zutage liegen* can be translated "to be *or* lie on the surface," just the significance that the *Investigations* seems here to require.

52. Rhees recalled: "Years later Wittgenstein said to me: 'You know I said I can stop doing philosophy when I like. That is a lie! I *can't*.'" R. Rhees in R. Rhees, ed., *Recollections of Wittgenstein* (New York: Oxford University Press, 1984), p. 219n7. But once we see that the *Investigations* predicts the endlessness of philosophy's endings, this joke of Wittgenstein's can be assimilated for what it is.

53. I am thinking here of a conversation with Robert Hanna in which he pushed just this criticism against Wittgenstein while defending the advantages of existential phenomenology in the hands of Heidegger and Merleau-Ponty.

54. Wittgenstein's corrected translation; see Baker and Hacker, *Volume I*, p. 515.

55. I noticed the aptness of this characterization of philosophy while reading Stanley Cavell's *Pursuits of Happiness* (Cambridge: Harvard University Press, 1981), but I haven't been able to put my finger on the passage that called it to my mind.

56. I have been unable to confirm my memory that Geach makes this argument. I have also heard it from my colleague Norman Melchert, e-mail from NZ 12–3–92.

57. There is nothing in this acceptance that prohibits putting out fires. "Leaving everything as it is" is like *amor fati.*

58. L. Wittgenstein, *Culture and Value* (Chicago: University of Chicago Press, 1980), p. 43 (1944). At least once in *OC*, Friede plays a role that is cousin to that played by Ruhe: "My *life* consists in my being content to accept many things" [Mein *leben* besteht darin, dass ich mich mit manchen zufrieden geben] (*OC* par. 344).

59. L. Wittgenstein, *Culture and Value*, p. 11 (1931).

60. Kant wrote *Perpetual Peace* [*Zum ewigen Frieden*] in 1795 (Indianapolis: Hackett, 1983), pp. 107–43.

Chapter 4. The Wonder of Linguistic Meaning

1. G. E. M. Anscombe, "Opening Address [of the 6th International Ludwig Wittgenstein Symposium, Kirchberg am Wechsel, August 1981]," in *Language and Ontology*, W. Leinfellner, E. Kraemer, J. Schank, eds. (Vienna: Hoelder-Pichler-Tempsky, 1982), p. 28.

2. A. C. Jackson's notes of Wittgenstein's Lectures as published in P. Geach, ed., *Wittgenstein's Lectures on Philosophical Psychology 1946–47* (Chicago: University of Chicago Press, 1988), p. 238.

3. Wittgenstein mentions Bertrand Russell and H. G. Wells as two who suffer from such a loss of problems. By the end of the century, Rorty will come—voluntarily—to wrap himself in just such a description.

4. This quotation is Ray Monk's translation of *Big Typescript* (c. 1933) S. 421, in R. Monk, *Ludwig Wittgenstein: The Duty of Genius* (New York: Macmillan, 1990), p. 446. The quotation concludes "(Hertz)"; thus recalling one of Wittgenstein's favorite passages from Hertz.

5. This inevitably raises the question of whether we can think without language. This is a surprisingly attractive question, and one that seems—at first—to be of the utmost significance. Some of the apparent importance of this question seems to derive from the fear that if we could *only* think in language, then the powers of thought would somehow be restricted—or worse. So, typically, we will comb our minds for examples of thinking without words hoping thereby to save the power of thought. Why do we suppose so much depends on thinking without words? It helps to be in the grip of the Augustinian picture of the essence of human language: the meaning of the word *thinking* is the object for which it stands. And what is that object? Certainly not mere noises in the air or blank marks on paper. The meaning of *thinking* has to be a mental process hidden behind those noises and marks. (Remember that the absence of any reference to thought as mental process was part of what lent the feel of the living dead to the interactions described in the opening paragraph of the *Investigations*.) So if thinking requires language, then it is just as if there is no real thinking going on at all.

Wittgenstein moves against this way of thinking thinking in at least two ways (see *PI* par. 330 and p. 233e; *RPP* II par. 7 and 183). First, he notes that if thinking is a mental process we should be able to find it, but this is difficult: the mental process was not the result of investigation, it was a requirement (*PI* par. 107). Second, he provides relatively clear cases of thinking without words, which break the spell of this way of thinking. Front and center like that, thought without words reveals itself not as evidence of a queer power but simply as one of the things that people do—one of the things we rely on description to understand. But without the Augustinian picture to back it up, these examples can no longer comfort our craving for a queer medium of: thought.

6. Baker and Hacker, *Volume I*, pp. 522–23.

7. Pope, *Dunciad* cited in J. Derrida, "Proverb: 'He that would pun . . . ,'" in G. L. Ulmer and J. P. Leavey, Jr., *Glassary* (Lincoln: University of Nebraska Press, 1986), p. 18.

8. Bertrand Russell, *My Philosophical Development* (London: George Allen and Unwin Ltd, 1959), pp. 216–17. Also see B. Russell, "The Cult of 'Common Usage,'" *British Journal for the Philosophy of Science* 3.12 (February 1953): 303–7. I sometimes think that Russell's criticism of the mature Wittgenstein is that Wittgenstein has made philosophy kitsch. Compare Clement Greenberg, "Avant Garde and Kitsch" (1939), *Collected Essays* vol 1, ed. John O'Brian (Chicago: University of Chicago Press, 1986).

9. This example is taken from J. Culler, "The Call of the Phoneme," in J. Culler, ed., *On Puns: The Foundation of Letters* (Oxford: Blackwell, 1988), p. 8.

10. Baker and Hacker *Volume I*, p. 523.

11. This is where Heidegger speaks of the ontological difference and Derrida (early on) of différance. But Derrida concedes that différance remains a metaphysical name. And it was at a point such as this that the *Tractatus* turned to showing. The *Investigations* will simply describe our actions [die Handlung].

12. Baker and Hacker *Volume I*, p. 523.

13. The German text of this remark was published in *The Philosophical Review*, January 1965, p. 12. To my knowledge, this conversation is the only recorded discussion of Heidegger by Wittgenstein.

14. On May 25, 1915 Wittgenstein wrote:

The urge toward the mystical comes of the nonsatisfaction of our wishes by science. We *feel* that even if all *possible* scientific questions are answered *our problem is still not touched at all.* Of course in that case there are no questions any more; and that is the answer. [very close to *TLP* 6.52] (*NB*)

15. This distinction between "charm" and "depth" (already intimated in chap. 3, sect. 5) recalls a distinction tentatively suggested by Burke (1757) and used by Kant (1764), a distinction between the sublime feeling of looking up into the bright stars and that of looking deep into a dark abyss. Here is Burke:

Extension is either in length, height, or depth. Of these the length strikes the least; an hundred yards of even ground will never work such an effect as a tower an hundred yards high, or a rock or mountain of that altitude. I am apt to imagine likewise, that height is less grand than depth; and that we are more struck at looking down from a precipice, than at looking up at an object of equal height, but of that I am not very positive. A perpendicular has more force in forming the sublime, than an inclined plane; and the effects of a rugged and broken surface seem stronger than where it is smooth and polished.

E. Burke, *A Philosophical Enquiry into the Origin of Our Ideas of the Sublime and the Beautiful* (1757) (Notre Dame, Ind.: University of Notre Dame, 1986), p. 72.

Here is Kant:

> A great height is just as sublime as a great depth, except that the latter is accompanied with the sensation of shuddering [Schauerns], the former with one of wonder [Bewunderung]. Hence the latter feeling can be the terrifying sublime, and the former the noble.

I. Kant, *Observations on the Feeling of the Beautiful and Sublime* (1764) (Berkeley: University of California Press. 1991), pp. 48–49.

16. In the spring of 1993 a large file of these jokes was orbiting my university in electric space. I received my file from Jon Eisenberg on: Wednesday, 5 May 1993, 18:51:32 EDT.

17. This abyss brings the figures of the aesthetic sublime into the positive doctrine of the *Investigations*, but see *PI* par. 209, for a place where Wittgenstein seems to turn away from the aesthetic sublime: "Is it like the case where I interpret what is not limited as a length that reaches beyond every length."

18. N. Malcolm, *Ludwig Wittgenstein: A Memoir* (1958) (New York: Oxford University Press, 1984), pp. 27–28.

19. G. E. M. Anscombe, "Opening Address [of the 6th International Ludwig Wittgenstein Symposium, Kirchberg am Wechsel, August 1981]," in *Language and Ontology*, W. Leinfellner, E. Kraemer, J. Schank, eds. (Vienna: Hoelder-Pichler-Tempsky, 1982), p. 28.

20. I (seem to) remember being drawn to this passage by an essay of Anthony Kenny's,which I have been unable to locate. It figures prominently in Edward H. Minar, *Philosophical Investigations No. 185–202* (New York: Garland Publishing, 1990), p. 43.

21. On the building Wittgenstein designed for his sister during the years 1926–1928, see Bernhard Leitner, *The Architecture of Ludwig Wittgenstein: A Documentation* (New York: New York University Press, 1976).

22. *PI* par. 138 concludes:

> What we grasp in this way is surely something different from the "use" [Gebrauch] which is extended in time! (*PI* par. 138)

PI par. 139 begins:

> When someone says the word "cube" to me, for example, I know what it means. But can the whole *use* [*Verwendung*] of the word come before my mind when I *understood* it in this way?" (*PI* par. 139)

I mention this here only to *enter* the hypothesis that Wittgenstein is making a quasi-technical distinction between Verwendung and Gebrauch.

Here is the distinction I sense in the text: the Verwendung of a word is an empirical concept referring to how, in fact, the word is used by people who speak. Against this empirical notion of the Verwendung of a word, semantic sticklers launch the Gebrauch of a word, which is a normative concept. I am encouraged in this hypothesis by the fact that this distinction recalls the one Ryle claimed to find between the actual *usage* of, for example, tennis rackets (for purposes unrelated to the game of tennis) and the normatively correct *use* of such rackets. I am not now fully confident of this interpretation of Wittgenstein's use of Verwendung and Gebrauch, but the switch to Verwendung in par. 139, the appearance of Gebrauch in par. 1, 43, 198, 199 (but not 197), and even the scare quotes in the last use of *Gebrauch* in par. 138 all seem to confirm this hypothesis. But *PI* par. 116 seems to confute the hypothesis. See G. Ryle, "Ordinary Language" (1953) in V. C. Chappell, ed., *Ordinary Language* (Englewood Cliffs, N.J.: Prentice Hall, 1964), pp. 24–40.

23. "Charm" is discussed in chap. 3, sect. 5.

24. The precise way to understand these considerations is contested. Wright and Kripke are responsible for much of the recent excitement surrounding these passages of Wittgenstein. See:

(a) Crispin Wright, *Wittgenstein on the Foundations of Mathematics* (London: Duckworth, 1980).

(b) Saul Kripke, *Wittgenstein on Rules and Private Language* (Oxford: Blackwell, 1982).

Two explicitly contrasting interpretations of the literature that grew up in this area are:

(c) Crispin Wright, "Critical Notice of Colin McGinn, *Wittgenstein on Meaning*," *Mind* 98 (1989): 289–305.

(d) John McDowell, "Meaning and Intentionality in Wittgenstein's Later Philosophy," *Midwest Studies in Philosophy*, 17 (1992): 40–52.

My interpretation shares McDowell's interest in accepting Wittgenstein's self-interpretation of his project as not producing any substantive philosophical constructions. But I do not share what McDowell shares with Rorty; namely, an interest in removing all the mystery from our linguistic life. Mystery and wonder are rather what I understand Wittgenstein to be restoring, not escaping. Compare the mottos of this chapter with McDowell's flight from mystery in *Mind and World* (Cambridge: Harvard University Press, 1994). The flat world that Rorty and McDowell dream of is explicitly scorned by Wittgenstein at *Z* par. 456.

25. "The Background is the bustle of life [das Getriebe des Lebens]. And our concept points to something within *this* bustle. . . . Not what *one* man is doing *now*, but the whole hurly-burly [das ganze Gewimmel], is the background against which we see an action, and it determines our judgment, our concepts, and our reactions" (*Z* par. 625 and 629).

26. *PI* par. 140 continues "And now it looks as if we knew of two kinds of case" (*PI* par. 140). In the *Remarks on the Foundations of Mathematics*, Wittgenstein raises some considerations to show that we *don't* know these two kinds of case. Even logical compulsion is a characteristic of *our use* of logical rules, not the *rules themselves* (*RFM*3, pp. 82 and 43: 1937–38). See J. Derrida, "Force of Law: The 'Mystical Foundation of Authority,'" in D. Cornell, M. Rosenfeld, and D. G. Carlson, eds., *Deconstruction and the Possibility of Justice* (New York: Routledge, 1992).

27. This (Socratic) feature of the *Investigations* has been a part of Cavell's characterization of that book, at least since "The Availability of Wittgenstein's Later Philosophy" (1962), in G. Pitcher, ed., *Wittgenstein: The "Philosophical Investigations"* (Notre Dame, Ind.: University of Notre Dame Press, 1966, 1968).

28. John Dewey, *The Quest for Certainty* (1929) (New York: G. P. Putnam's Sons, 1929, 1960), p. 3.

29. Wittgenstein's discussion of the rule or law of a series [Gesetz einer Reihe] (*PI* par. 147–51) invites comparison with Derrida's discussion of law in "Before the Law" and "The Law of Genre," in D. Attridge, *Acts of Literature* (New York: Routledge, 1992) and especially "Force of Law: The 'Mystical Foundation of Authority,'" in D. Cornell, M. Rosenfeld, and D. G. Carlson, eds., *Deconstruction and the Possibility of Justice* (New York: Routledge, 1992).

30. The expression "hangs in the air" appears in another discussion of rules in the *Investigations*, *PI* par. 87. At that place, it addresses "explanation" in the terms that *PI* par. 198 addresses "interpretation." Also see the use of Luft in *PI* par. 118. Also see *RFM*3 p. 135: 1938. This semiofficial use of Luft fits Wittgenstein's use of the chemical sense of the verb *sublime*. Anscombe's "houses of cards" have a difficult time being sublime; not so Wittgenstein's Luftgebäude (*PI* par. 118).

31. This is a combination of the translations from the first and third editions.

32. Thus the *Investigations* will not be hospitable to those hermeneuts who espouse the universality of interpretation. Interpretation is not the answer to our prayers. Nothing is. See R. Shusterman, ed., *The Interpretive Turn* (Ithaca, N.Y.: Cornell University Press, 1991).

33. *PI* par. 87, which also uses the expression "hangs in the air," also concludes with a remark about signposts.

34. See P. Winch, "Facts and Superfacts" (1983), in *Trying to Make Sense* (Oxford: Blackwell, 1987), pp. 54–63.

35. I have described this in terms that recall Derrida's criticism of what he calls the "metaphysics of presence." See J. Derrida, *Of Grammatology* (1967) (Baltimore: Johns Hopkins University Press, 1974, 1977). Also see J. Derrida, "The Force of Law: The 'Mystical Foundation of Authority'" (1990), in *Deconstruction and the Possibility of Justice*, D. Cornell, M. Rosenfeld, and D. G. Carlson, eds. (New York: Routledge, 1992), especially pp. 22–29.

36. This example is Stanley Cavell's; see his *The Claim of Reason* (New York: Oxford University Press, 1979), p. 174.

37. This is a Kantian turn. What we are looking for is a criterion which would allow us to distinguish (a) an action that is merely in accord with the law from (b) an action that is, rather, obedient to the law, done for the sake of the law. Although Kant thought that there was a difference between these two, indeed a difference greater than which none could be conceived, Kant did not think there were humanly available criteria for this distinction.

38. See D. Dennett, *The Intentional Stance* (Cambridge: MIT Press, 1987).

39. R. Rhees, "The Philosophy of Wittgenstein" (1966), in *Discussions of Wittgenstein* (London: Routledge and Kegan Paul, 1970), p. 54.

40. See L. Wittgenstein, *Philosophical Remarks* (c. 1930) (Chicago: University of Chicago Press, 1975), I par. 4, page 53:

> If I could describe the point of grammatical conventions by saying they are made necessary by certain properties of the colors (say), then that would make the conventions superfluous, since in that case I would be able to say precisely that which the conventions exclude my saying. Conversely, if the conventions were necessary, i.e., if certain combinations of words had to be excluded as nonsensical, then for that very reason I cannot cite a property of colors that makes the conventions necessary, since it would then be conceivable that the colors should not have this property, and I could only express that by violating the conventions.

41. This sentence echoes paragraphs of Stanley Cavell: one in *Must We Mean What We Say?* (New York: Cambridge University Press, 1969), p. 52; and another from *The Claim of Reason* (New York: Oxford University Press, 1979), p. 178, including the sentence: "We begin to feel, or ought to, terrified that maybe language (and understanding, and knowledge) rests upon very shaky foundations—a thin net over an abyss."

42. Baker and Hacker thank F. Cioffi for locating a possible source for this story in E. von Hartmann, *Philosophy of the Unconscious, Speculative . . .* (London: Kegan Paul, Trench and Trubner, 1931). See Baker and Hacker, *Volume I*, p. 623n25.

43. I will not discuss all the occurrences of "selbstverständlich" and the one of "selbstverständlichkeit," but I list them here in honor of honesty. The form of reference is (paragraph or page).(line): 33.3, 145.10, 146.15, 147.10, 238.2, 238.3, 238.4, 260.4, 352.12, 363.6, 524.1, 524.4, p. 182.12, p. 182.18, p. 190.32, p. 201.23, p. 213.6. I take this data from H. Kaal and A. McKinnon, *Concordance to Wittgenstein's "Philosophische Untersuchungen"* (Leiden: E. J. Brill, 1975), p. 446.

44. See S. Cavell, *This New Yet Unapproachable America* (Albuquerque, N.M.: Living Batch Press, 1989), p. 46, and the back cover:

Wittgenstein's appeal or "approach" to the everyday finds the (actual) everyday to be as pervasive a scene of illusion and trance and artificiality (of need) as Plato or Rousseau or Marx or Thoreau had found. His philosophy of the (eventual) everyday is the proposal of a practice that takes on, takes upon itself, precisely (I do not say exclusively) that scene of illusion and of loss; approaches it, or let me say reproaches it, intimately enough to turn it, or deliver it; as if the actual is the womb, contains the terms, of the eventual. The direction out from illusion is not up, at any rate not up to one fixed morning star; but down, at any rate along each chain of a day's denial. Philosophy (as descent) can thus be said to leave everything as it is because it is a refusal of, say disobedient to (a false) ascent, or transcendence. Philosophy (as ascent) shows the violence that is to be refused (disobeyed), that has left everything not as it is, indifferent to me, as if there are things in themselves. Plato's sun has shown us the fact of our chains; but that sun was produced by those chains.

Cavell takes these themes up again in *Conditions Handsome and Unhandsome: The Constitution of Emersonian Perfectionism* (Chicago: University of Chicago Press, 1990), pp. 1–100.

45. G. E. M. Anscombe, "Opening Address [of the 6th International Ludwig Wittgenstein Symposium, Kirchberg am Wechsel, August 1981]," in *Language and Ontology*, W. Leinfellner, E. Kraemer, and J. Schank, eds. (Vienna: Hoelder-Pichler-Tempsky, 1982), p. 28.

46. The largest single collection of Wittgenstein's letters is: L. Wittgenstein, *Briefe*, B. F. McGuinness and G. H. von Wright, eds. (Frankfurt am Main: Surkamp Verlag, 1980). It reprints (in chronological order) letters to Russell, Moore, Keynes, Ramsey, Eccles, Engelmann, and von Ficker, most (but not all) of which had been published earlier. However this volume includes none of the now (1992) published letters to von Wright, Malcolm, or the Pinsent family.

47. W. Eccles, "Some Letters of Ludwig Wittgenstein," *Hermathena*, v. 97 (1963): 57–65.

48. L. Wittgenstein, "Letters to Ludwig von Ficker," in *Wittgenstein: Sources and Perspectives*, C. G. Luckhardt, ed. (Hassocks, Sussex: Harvester Press, 1979), pp. 82–98.

49. L. Wittgenstein, "Letters to John Maynard Keynes 1913–1939," in L. Wittgenstein, *Letters to Russell, Keynes and Moore* (Oxford: Blackwell, 1977), pp. 107–41.

50. There was probably a fifty-fifth letter. Correspondence between Wittgenstein and Engelmann paused between late 1925 and 1937. It picks up with a letter from Engelmann to Wittgenstein dated June 4, 1937 (par. 240 in L. Wittgenstein, *Briefe*). This letter refers to a confession Engelmann received from Wittgenstein, but the confession appears in none of the published letters. If there were such a letter it would come between letters 53 and 54 in Paul Engelmann, *Letters from Ludwig Wittgenstein with a Memoir* (Oxford: Blackwell, 1967).

51. That figure includes fifty-seven letters and cards to Russell, available in *Letters to Russell Keynes and Moore*, and three more, available in "Unpublished [!] correspondence between Russell and Wittgenstein," by B. F. McGuinness and G. H. von Wright, *Russell* 10.2 (winter 1990–91): 101–24.

52. That number includes the letters to Moore in *Letters to Russell Keynes and Moore*. One curiosity of that book is that the numbering of Moore's letters proceeds from GM.40 to GM.42. The *Briefe* (1980) prints two letters (B.254: 1939; and B.255: 1941) that would fit in the chronological sequence between GM.40 and GM.42, thus bringing the total of published letters to Moore to 58. Letter no. 255 in the *Briefe*, from Mar. 7, 1941, signs itself thus: "I wish you *lots* of good luck. Yours Ludwig Wittgenstein."

Chapter 5. The Wonder of Existential Meaning

1. G. E. Moore, "Wittgenstein's Lectures in 1930–33" (1954 and 1955), now in Moore's *Philosophical Papers* (New York: Collier Books, 1966), p. 317.

2. The history of Wittgenstein's search for a motto is recounted in Baker and Hacker, *Volume I*, pp. 16–18. The passage which—for a time—was to have been the motto of the *Investigations* is italicized in the following quotation:

Our confused wish [to sort out what we know about force and electricity] finds expression in the confused question as to the nature of force and electricity. But the answer which we want is not really an answer to this question. It is not by finding out more and fresh relations and connections that it can be answered; but by removing the contradictions existing between those already known, and thus perhaps by reducing their number. *When these painful contradictions are re~~Copyright Material~~ the nature [of force] will not*

> *have been answered; but our minds, no longer vexed* [gequälte], *will cease to ask illegitimate questions.*

H. Hertz, *Principles of Mechanics* (1894) (New York: Dover, 1956), pp. 7–8. Redpath reports a discussion of this passage conducted by Wittgenstein on February 23, 1939. See T. Redpath, *Ludwig Wittgenstein: A Student's Memoir* (London: Duckworth, 1990), pp. 82–86. Wittgenstein often used this passage to illuminate his conception of philosophy.

3. Johann Nepomuk Nestroy (1801–1862), *Der Schützling* (1847), act 4, scene 10. I have quoted the context of Wittgenstein's motto from Baker and Hacker (*Volume I*, p. 16), but I use von Wright's translation (not Baker and Hacker's) of the motto itself. G. H. von Wright, *Wittgenstein* (Minneapolis: University of Minnesota Press, n.d. [1982?]).

4. Others have felt the same connection between the motto to *PI* and the forewords written in 1930. Two examples:

(1) Baker and Hacker, *Volume I*, p. 16.

(2) B. McGuinness, "Freud and Wittgenstein," in B. McGuinness, ed., *Wittgenstein and His Times* (Chicago: University of Chicago Press, 1982), p. 39.

5. In the version of this foreword (dated November 1930) published with *Philosophical Remarks*, this singular structure becomes plural: "in building ever larger and more complicated structures...." L. Wittgenstein, *Philosophical Remarks* (Chicago: University of Chicago Press, 1975), p. 7.

6. The *Investigations* retains this commitment to the intrinsic value of clarity and perspicuity. The *Investigations* aims at "complete clarity" (*PI* par. 133) and asserts that "the concept of a perspicuous representation is of fundamental significance for us" (*PI* 122). But rather than speaking of Durchsichtigkeit, Wittgenstein settles on the word *Uebersichtlichkeit*. This represents a significant change. The earlier word (*Durchsichtigkeit*) unfortunately suggests that clarity will require looking through the surface of what troubles him. The new word (*Uebersichtlichkeit*) happily suggests that clarity will be found by acquiring an overall familiarity with the language we use to express our troubles.

7. Nestroy, cited in Baker and Hacker, *Volume I*, p. 16.

8. Nietzsche, *The Case of Wagner* (1888), par. 5. I remember this remark because Joseph Volpe recited it for me during a conversation about nihilism.

9. It would be a nice piece of what Austin called "linguistic phenomenology" to determine if there were needs that figured themselves more naturally, as hunger or as thirst. We might try to think of the difference between being hungry for knowledge and being thirsty for knowledge. Does one or the other sound more obsessive? What about sexual desire? Is this a hunger or a thirst? Or can it be on occasion one or the other? See the discussion of hunger and

thirst in *The Philadelphia Story* and *It Happened One Night,* in Stanley Cavell's *Pursuits of Happiness* (Cambridge: Harvard University Press, 1981).

10. I am thinking of a passage from 1931, which reads:

> There are problems I never get anywhere near, which do not lie in my path or are not part of my world. Problems of the intellectual world of the west that Beethoven (and perhaps Goethe to a certain extent) tackled and wrestled with, but which no philosopher has ever confronted (perhaps Nietzsche passed them by). And perhaps they are lost as far as western philosophy is concerned, i.e., no one will be there capable of experiencing, and hence describing, the progress [Fortgang] of this culture as an epic. (*CV* 9e: 1931)

The difficulty with linking this passage to the later one cited in the text (*CV* 62e: 1947) is that the 1931 passage does not seem to yearn for a means of CHANGING our civilization but only of REPRESENTING it as an epic.

In *The Birth of Tragedy,* Nietzsche does indeed lament the supremacy of science:

> Our whole modern world is entangled in the net of Alexandrian culture. It proposes as its ideal the theoretical man equipped with the greatest forces of knowledge, and laboring in the service of science, whose archetype and progenitor is Socrates. All our educational methods originally have this ideal in view: every other form of existence must struggle on laboriously beside it, as something tolerated, but not intended. (*BT* par. 18, p. 110)

Wittgenstein shared this judgment:

> Science: enrichment and impoverishment. *One* particular method elbows all the others aside. They all seem paltry by comparison, preliminary stages at best. (*CV* 60e: 1947)

In spite of these resonances, it would be going too far to suggest that Wittgenstein thought of Nietzsche as possessing "artillery" sufficient to change the Alexandrian spirit of the times we share with them.

11. *The Big Typescript* (TS 213: c. 1933), speaks of a change in attitude, an Umstellung; its sect. 86 is titled:

> DIFFICULTY OF PHILOSOPHY NOT THE INTELLECTUAL DIFFICULTY OF THE SCIENCES, BUT THE DIFFICULTY OF A CHANGE OF ATTITUDE. RESISTANCES OF THE WILL MUST BE OVERCOME.

L. Wittgenstein, "Philosophy," *Synthese* 87 (April 1991): 5; the German text is available in *Revue Internationale de Philosophie* 43.169 (1989): 172–203.

12. Drury reports a related thought expressed by Wittgenstein in conversation with him in 1949.

> My type of thinking is not wanted in this present age, I have to swim so strongly against the tide. Perhaps in a hundred years people will really want what I am writing.   *Copyrighted Material*

M. O'C. Drury, "Conversations with Wittgenstein," in R. Rhees, ed., *Recollections of Wittgenstein* (New York: Oxford University Press, 1984), p. 160.

Here Wittgenstein may be thinking that when the spirit of the present age begins to change then his work may be wanted, but not now. Nietzsche also thought that some authors—including himself—were, as he put it, born posthumously (*Twilight of the Idols* [1888] I.15).

13. See Wittgenstein's letter to von Ficker, F. 23.

14. G. H. von Wright, "Wittgenstein in Relation to His Times" (1977), in *Wittgenstein* (Minneapolis: University of Minnesota Press, n.d.)., esp. pp. 210–15.

15. G. H. von Wright, *Wittgenstein,* pp. 215 and 216.

16. G. H. von Wright, "Wittgenstein in Relation to His Times," p. 216. It remains an open question for von Wright whether the Spenglerian assessment of our culture, which Wittgenstein associated with his philosophical work, is properly construed as logically or only psychologically connected with works such as the *Investigations* (ibid., p. 216).

17. G. H. von Wright, *Wittgenstein,* p. 3. Von Wright cites this expression from Diego Marconi's dismissal of a Anglo-American caricature of Wittgenstein.

18. Heller is earlier but not sympathetic; his line is, more or less, *Wittgenstein is as dangerous as Nietzsche.* This thought still lives on, for example, between the lines of Hampshire's review of Monk's recent biography, *New York Review of Books,* January 31, 1991.

19. O. K. Bouwsma, "The Blue Book" (*Journal of Philosophy,* 1961), now in *Philosophical Essays* (Lincoln: University of Nebraska Press, 1965), pp. 175–201; S. Cavell, "The Availability of Wittgenstein's Later Philosophy," (*Philosophical Review,* 1962), now in *Must We Mean What We Say?* (Cambridge: Cambridge University Press, 1969, 1977).

Both of these essays are the first contributions of these two authors to the question of how to receive the later Wittgenstein. For more explicit comparisons with existentialist thinkers see O. K. Bouwsma, "A New Sensibility" (written 1968), published in *Toward a New Sensibility* (Lincoln: University of Nebraska Press, 1982), pp. 1–5; S. Cavell, "Existentialism and Analytical Philosophy" (*Daedalus* 1964), now in *Themes Out of School* (San Francisco: North Point Press, 1984), pp. 203–34.

I concentrate below on Bouwsma's essays rather than Cavell's, partly because they are less well known, but both of these authors defend a view of Wittgenstein as concerned with the lives of his readers/listeners, not simply or rather than with their philosophical opinions. Cavell's "Availability" ends on this note:

> [Wittgenstein's] writing is deeply practical and negative, the way Freud's is. And like Freud's therapy, it wishes to prevent understanding which is unaccompanied by inner change. Both of them are intent upon unmasking the defeat of our real need in the face of self-impositions that we have not assessed (*PI* par. 108), or fantasies ("pictures") that we cannot escape (par. 115). In both, such misfortune is betrayed in the incongruence between what is said and what is meant or expressed; for both, the self is concealed in assertion and action and revealed in temptation and wish. Both thought of their negative soundings as revolutionary extensions of our knowledge, and both were obsessed by the idea, or fact, that they would be misunderstood—partly, doubtless, because they knew the taste of self-knowledge, that it is bitter. (Cavell, "Availability," p. 72)

20. O. K. Bouwsma, "The Blue Book," (1961), pp. 178–79.

21. Ibid., p. 179.

22. Ibid., p. 183.

23. Ibid.

24. Ibid., pp. 183–86.

25. O. K. Bouwsma, "The Difference Between Ryle and Wittgenstein" (1972), in *Toward a New Sensibility* (Lincoln: University of Nebraska Press, 1982), p. 28.

26. See David A. Weiner, *Genius and Talent* (Rutherford N.J.: Fairleigh Dickinson University Press, 1992).

27. L. Malcolm, *Ludwig Wittgenstein: A Memoir* (Oxford; Oxford University Press, 1958, 2d ed. 1984), p. 58.

28. See Brian McGuinness, *Wittgenstein: A Life* (Berkeley: University of California Press, 1988), pp. 94, 114; Ray Monk, *Ludwig Wittgenstein: The Duty of Genius* (New York: Free Press, 1990), p. 51. The Easter vacation suggestion is made by Monk alone.

29. See Kierkegaard's "Unhappiest One," in *Either/Or*, v. 1, 1843 (Princeton, N.J.: Princeton University Press, 1987), pp. 219–30.

30. From Ricardo Reis's *Odes*, Portuguese with English translation by Edwin Honig, published as Fernando Pessoa, *Selected Poems* (Chicago: Swallow Press, 1971), p. 45. Thanks to Ruth Lorand.

31. The following passage from Emerson defines a still flourishing strain of romanticism. We don't have the courage to accept the simple, right before

our eyes. "Travelling is a fool's paradise." Emerson, "Self-Reliance," 1841, in *Selected Writings of Ralph Waldo Emerson* (New York: Signet Classics, 1965), p. 275.

> Man is timid and apologetic; he is no longer upright; he dares not say "I think," "I am," but quotes some saint or sage. He is ashamed before the blade of grass or the blowing rose. These roses under my window make no reference to former roses or to better ones; they are for what they are; they exist with God today. There is no time to them. There is simply the rose; it is perfect in every moment of its existence. (ibid., p. 268)

The irony of quoting Descartes in this call to avoid quoting, is doubled by the only slightly more veiled citation of Angelus Silesius's poem "Without Why," and redoubled by the citation of this very passage by Emerson's readers, for example, by me. This must be a call no one could answer, and romanticism may name the tendency of those who do not, therefore, give up the attempt. Compare this discussion of quotation to Derrida's in "Signature Event Context," in *Limited Inc.* (Evanston, Ill.: Northwestern University Press, 1988) and in "Envois," in *The Postcard* (Chicago: University of Chicago Press, 1987).

32. Wittgenstein also uses forms of the verb *anerkennen* to write about the origin of meaning. See, in particular, *PI* par. 70, 144, and 607. Forms of *anerkennen* are also used at par. 75, 76, 141, 165, 351, and 402.

33. See S. Kierkegaard, *Either/Or*, 1843, 2 vols. (Princeton, N.J.: Princeton University Press, 1987). I am thinking in particular of Judge William's two long letters published in the second volume. Unsystematic as it is, my own thinking about the meaning of life is indebted both to *Either/Or* and to the classes and conversations around that book that I have had with Nathaniel Lawrence, John Hare, and lately and at length with Melissa Rowell.

34. As in Marianne Moore's "Silence."

35. The figure of the café nihilist entered my reflections on the meaning of life after a long conversation with Joe Volpe in the summer sun of Evanston, Illinois.

36. For opium and dismemberment, see Georges Bataille, *The Tears of Eros*, 1961 (San Francisco: City Lights Books, 1989), pp. 204–7.

37. It might be enlightening to compare the appearance of destruction [zerstörung] in Wittgenstein with the appearance of destruction [Destruktion] in Heidegger's *Being and Time,* paragraph 6, and with deconstruction [déconstruction] in Derrida. See "Letter to a Japanese Friend" (1983), in J. Derrida, ed. P. Kamuf, *A Derrida Reader* (New York: Columbia University Press, 1991).

38. See, for example, "Some Consequences of Four Incapacities," 1868, *Writings of Charles S. Peirce: A Chronological Edition,* vol. II (Bloomington: University of Indiana Press, 1984).

39. Maurice Blanchot, *The Writing of the Disaster*, 1980 (Lincoln: University of Nebraska Press, 1986), p. 12.

40. This is one of the central lessons of Thompson Clarke's densely poetic essay "The Legacy of Skepticism," *Journal of Philosophy* (1972).

41. In the first chapter, I drew attention to Nietzsche's use of lucid dreams in articulating the significance of Apollo (see *BT* par. 1, p. 34–35.)

42. Descartes, *Meditations* (1641), in J. Cottingham, R. Stoothof, and D. Murdoch, eds., *The Philosophical Writings of Descartes*, vol. II (Cambridge: Cambridge University Press, 1984), hereafter "CSM," p. 15.

43. Descartes, *Meditations*, in CSM, p. 16.

44. H. G. Frankfurt makes this observation in *Demons, Dreamers, and Madmen* (Indianapolis: Bobbs-Merrill, 1970), pp. 28–29.

45. Frankfurt, *Demons, Dreamers, and Madmen*: "empty," p. 28; "mindless," p. 174.

46. This point is independently made by Foucault and Frankfurt.

47. Michel Foucault, *Histoire de la folie à l'âge classique*, 2d ed. (Paris: Gallimard, 1972), p. 56 (1st ed., 1961).

48. Michel Foucault, *Histoire*, p. 57.

49. Descartes, *Meditations*, in CSM, p. 13.

50. Ibid.

51. J. Derrida, "Cogito and the History of Madness," 1963, in *Writing and Difference*, 1967 (Chicago: University of Chicago Press, 1978).

52. This is the more striking when one is convinced by M. F. Burnyeat that Descartes's skepticism was itself more radical than that recounted by Sextus Empiricus. See his "Idealism and Greek Philosophy," in G. Vesey, ed., *Idealism: Past and Present* (Cambridge: Cambridge University Press, 1982).

53. M. Foucault, preface to original 1962 edition of *Histoire de la Folie*, cited from *Madness and Civilization* (New York: Vintage, 1965), pp. x–xi.

54. I am here trying to sound like the analysis of anxiety provided in Heidegger's *Being and Time*.

55. S. Cavell, *The Claim of Reason* (New York: Oxford University Press, 1979), pp. 216–17.

56. S. Cavell, *The Claim of Reason*, p. 217.

57. See O. K. Bouwsma, "A Difference Between Ryle and Wittgenstein," 1972, in *Toward a New Sensibility: Essays of O. K. Bouwsma*, J. L. Craft and R.

E. Hustwit, eds. (Lincoln: University of Nebraska Press, 1982). Ryle replied to this paper in *Rice University Studies* 58.3 (summer 1972).

58. Leo Tolstoy, trans., Jane Kentish, trans., *A Confession* (1879) (New York: Penguin Books, 1987), pp. 20–21.

59. For further discussion of this point see my "Wittgenstein and the Uncanny," *Soundings*, 76.1 (spring 1993): 29–58.

60. The fact that these buildings are made of air, together with the chemical sense of the verb *to sublime,* means that these buildings of air are products of the tendency to sublime the logic of our language.

61. Thanks to the *Concordance to Wittgenstein's "Philosophische Untersuchungen"* : forms of hinnehmen appear at *PI* par. 524, and pp. 200, 210, and 226.

62. This method is very similar to the one articulated in *Tractatus* 6.53. Both share the effort to stick to the truth and simply reject the false. The difference is that in the *Investigations*, Wittgenstein no longer thinks that everyday language disguises the sublime logical structure of thought (*TLP* 4.002).

63. The following discussion is borrowed from my "Wittgenstein and the Uncanny" *Soundings* 76.1 (spring 1993).

64. Feminists, among others, have called attention to the historical contingency of what people claim to find "natural," so we should be suspicious of any casual acceptance of the normativity of what we find natural today. But if Wittgenstein is right, it is impossible to off-load the responsibility for our judgments onto any system of imperatives logical, epistemic, or ethical. We hang from our reactions (see *PI* par. 145).

65. *OC* par. 148 recalls the poem of Angelus Silesius (Johann Scheffler: 1624–77) entitled "Without Why," from his *Der Cherubinische Wandersmann* (1657), Book 1, no. 289:

WITHOUT WHY
The rose is without why; it blooms because it blooms.
It cares not for itself, asks not if it's seen.

On December 20, 1919, after meeting Wittgenstein in The Hague, Russell wrote: "I had felt in his book [the *Tractatus*] a flavor of mysticism, but was astonished when I found that he has become a complete mystic. He reads people like Kierkegaard and Angelus Silesius." In L. Wittgenstein, *Letters to Russell, Keynes and Moore* (Oxford: B.Blackwell, 1974), p. 82.

Heidegger provides an interpretation of this poem in *Der Satz Vom Grund.* I learned of the poem from L. Versenyi, *Heidegger Being and Truth*

(New Haven: Yale University Press, 1965), pp. 149ff; also see J. D. Caputo "The Rose Is Without Why," *Philosophy Today* 15 (1971): 3–15.

66. The hope of finding what is enough inspires many of Wallace Stevens poems. I think of "Of Modern Poetry" (1940), which opens:

> The poem of the mind in the act of finding
> What will suffice. It has not always had
> To find: the scene was set; it repeated what
> Was in the script.

and ends with:

> It must
> Be the finding of satisfaction, and may
> Be of a man skating, a woman dancing, a woman
> Combing. The poem of the act of the mind.

Wallace Stevens, *The Palm at the End of the Mind* (New York: Vintage Books, 1972), pp. 174–75.

67. The importance of this slightly more accurate translation is emphasized by S. Cavell in *Claim of Reason* (New York: Oxford University Press, 1979), p. 226.

68. See, for example, R. W. Hepburn, "Wonder" (1980), in *"Wonder" and Other Essays* (Edinburgh: Edinburgh University Press, 1984), pp. 131–54. Hepburn seeks an account of wonder that makes it permanently available. Wittgenstein's wonder is permanently at risk.

69. Thanks to Melissa Rowell for reminding me.

70. Michael Dummett, "Can Analytic Philosophy Be Systematic, and Ought It to Be," in *Truth, and Other Enigmas* (London: Duckworth, 1978), pp. 437–58.

71. I am thinking of the Wittgensteinian sound of such a Heideggerian claim as "But signs, in the first instance, are themselves items of equipment." *Being and Time* (1927) (New York: Harper and Row, 1962), par. 17, p. 108.

72. Perhaps this is what makes Whitehead's mature metaphysics such an unusual product of the twentieth century.

73. N. Malcolm, *Ludwig Wittgenstein: A Memoir*, 2d ed. (Oxford: Oxford University Press, 1984), p. 93.

74. This interpretation of the passion of the *Investigations* follows Stanley Cavell's interpretation of Wittgenstein's fervor:

> It is apt to be controversial to find that his [Wittgenstein's] reception by professional philosophy is insufficient, that the spiritual fervor or seriousness of

his writing is internal to his teaching, say the manner (or method) to the substance, and that something in the very professionalization of philosophy debars professional philosophers from taking his seriousness seriously.

S. Cavell, *This New Yet Unapproachable America* (Albuquerque: Living Batch Press, 1989), p. 30. Cavell's explanation of the fervor of Wittgenstein's writing refers to his attempt to "effect the deliverance from spiritual nausea" (*This New Yet Unapproachable America,* p. 67).

Afterword

1. Stevens's turn from no to yes is clear in "Landscape with a Boat" (1940), in *The Palm at the End of the Mind,* Holly Stevens, ed. (New York: Vintage, 1972), pp. 176–77. It is given a painful twist at the end of "The Well Dressed Man with a Beard," (1941), in *The Palm,* p. 190: "It can never be satisfied, the mind, never."

2. Wallace Stevens, "The Plain Sense of Things" (1952), in *The Palm at the End of the Mind,* pp. 382–83.

Index

Made in the USA
Las Vegas, NV
27 November 2020